CAMBRIDGE SOUTH ASIAN STUDIES

THE DYNAMICS OF
INDIAN POLITICAL FACTIONS

CAMBRIDGE SOUTH ASIAN STUDIES

These monographs are published by the Syndics of Cambridge University Press in association with the Cambridge University Centre for South Asian Studies. The following books have been published in this series:

CE

THE DYNAMICS OF INDIAN POLITICAL FACTIONS

A STUDY OF DISTRICT COUNCILS IN THE STATE OF MAHARASHTRA

BY

MARY C. CARRAS

Acting Chairman of the Political Science Department
Rockford College, Rockford, Illinois

CAMBRIDGE
AT THE UNIVERSITY PRESS

1972

Published by the Syndics of the Cambridge University Press
Bentley House, 200 Euston Road, London NW1 2DB
American Branch: 32 East 57th Street, New York, N.Y.10022

© Cambridge University Press 1972

Library of Congress Catalogue Card Number: 76–186250

ISBN: 0 521 08521 7

Printed in Great Britain
at the University Printing House, Cambridge
(Brooke Crutchley, University Printer)

FOREWORD

This is a remarkable piece of work, a quantum step forward in the political science research of American scholars of South Asia. It combines the best of many strands only now beginning to emerge: a fluent command of a local language, a detailed substantive knowledge of a local situation, the insistence on a set of controlled comparisons beyond the single phenomenon or single time–single place style of analysis, the careful collection of fresh primary data from controlled interviewing and local records, the difficult translation of such data into measurable variables, strengthening the reference point to disciplinary theory, the framing of testable hypotheses, the application of the most sophisticated statistical techniques available to test the hypotheses and the interpretations of the results in tangible, substantive conclusions. This is the mix that promises to enrich our understanding of phenomena in South Asia and to link this understanding to the mainstream of disciplinary advance. Dr Carras has carried them all out well and I can report every one of the skills was acquired from scratch for the project through a mixture of personal perseverance and good taste that is truly remarkable.

The conclusion is a bit too clearcut for my own bias in favor of the impenetrable complexity of human behavior. The fact that this study finds that the prime mover of factional formation lies in the economic sphere makes me even more wary, perhaps because several generations of doctrinaire theoreticians bereft of data have insisted it must be so. Nonetheless, her basic finding is an interesting one that the fundamental political cleavage in India – or in Maharashtra, at any rate – is traceable to competing forms of economic organization represented by private enterprise groups on the one hand, and collective or cooperative economic interests on the other, and that this dichotomy is reflected, in turn, in competing policy orientations within and between party and government. Recent regional and national events could well have been predicted by focussing on this division.

But in all, this is a most worthwhile venture and I commend it to your careful reading.

RICHARD D. LAMBERT

University of Pennsylvania

v

To my Mother, Urania,
and the Memory of my Father, Elias

CONTENTS

vii

TABLES

List of Tables

ix

List of Tables

List of Tables

MAPS

ACKNOWLEDGMENTS

I am thankful for the opportunity to acknowledge even a small part of the debt of gratitude I owe to many people who have contributed to this work in some way – either directly or indirectly.

A principal debt is owed to all those who graciously allowed me to interview them, for without their cooperation this work would not have been possible. Their hospitality added joy to my work. I am equally grateful to those administrative officials of the Government of Maharashtra who greatly facilitated my research, in countless ways. In particular, Mr R. G. Salvi, Secretary, and Mr V. Prabhakar, Deputy Secretary, respectively, of the Rural Development Department, were most cooperative and courteous, as were the administrative officers in each of the districts I visited. Mr V. V. Satav, an elected official of the Poona District Council, and Mr C. S. Natu, Secretary of the Poona City Congress Party, were especially helpful to me during the early phases of my work, giving me freely of their time, knowledge and hospitality. I must, however, reserve a special word of acknowledgment for my friend and colleague, Mr R. P. Nene, who gently, sensitively and intelligently guided me through the barriers of an unknown culture. His assistance and advice in so many aspects of the field surveys proved invaluable.

I also wish to thank all those who contributed in some way toward the final written product. Richard D. Lambert provided guidance throughout the preparation and execution of the study, and I am very grateful to him for his advice, for his suggestions regarding the manuscript, and for his many kindnesses to me. I am also indebted to Norman D. Palmer, not only for reading and commenting on the manuscript but also for his good will toward me. Henry Teune, Paul E. Green and Mark Levine provided much-needed help in the area of statistics and computer analysis, and for this I am very much in their debt.

I have reserved my warmest words of acknowledgment for W. Norman Brown whose generous spirit, kindness and confidence in me these past years have been a source of continual encouragement and comfort to me.

Acknowledgments

Finally, I wish to acknowledge the support of the following institutions: the United States Department of Education for fellowships which helped to sustain me throughout the period of graduate study, including my field work in India; the University of Pennsylvania for a Dissertation Fellowship and for a grant through their Computer Center which allowed me the use of its facilities; and the American Institute of Indian Studies for a travel grant within India and for all other manner of assistance rendered to me.

Only that which is of value in this work may be claimed by my teachers. The responsibility for errors and other inadequacies is mine alone.

There are a few good and loving friends whose names are meaningful only to me and to them. They must know in their hearts how each, in his or her own way, has helped me. Before each of them, I bow my head in love and humility.

Above all else, I am and always will be grateful to all members of my family whose great and abiding love was a source of strength that helped to sustain me during the less joyful hours of my work.

The author and publisher also wish to thank the following for permission to include material previously published elsewhere:

The editor of the *Economic and Political Weekly*, Bombay, for part of Chapter 2, which appeared as an article entitled 'Congress Factionalism at the State and District Level in Maharashtra: Some Theories' in *Economic and Political Weekly*, Vol. VI, Nos. 3, 4 and 5, Annual Number, January 1971.

The University of Chicago Press for part of Chapter 5, which appeared, as an article entitled 'The Economic Determinants of Political Factionalism: A Case Study of an Indian Rural District' in *Economic Development and Cultural Change*, Vol. 21, No. 1, October 1972.

The University of California Press for part of Chapter 7 ('Factionalism in Maharashtra: A Case Study of the Akola Zilla Parishad', © 1970 by The Regents of the University of California. Reprinted from *Asian Survey*, Vol. X, No. 5, May 1970, pp. 410–26, by permission of the Regents).

CHAPTER 1

INTRODUCTION

Factions are the principal structural media through which the political process is modulated in systems of the one-party variety.[1] V. O. Key described factional groupings as 'party systems within the dominant party'.[2] He was referring to factional systems in one-party states in the United States. His observation, however, may be applicable to India, which has often been described as a dominant one-party system. In recent years it has become necessary to modify this characterization: as a result of the 1967 general elections, the dominance of the Congress Party was seriously challenged, both in the parliamentary and in the state assembly elections.[3] The 1971 elections, however, seem to have re-established the dominant one-party model. In any event, the present study does not deal with factions in India as a whole but in one of the more important states of India: Maharashtra. This was one of the few states in which the Congress retained its dominance after the Fourth (1967) General Elections, and its political status has not changed appreciably since then. Hence, Key's description of factional groupings is definitely meaningful for Maharashtra.

What I have attempted is an analysis of factionalism, as a specific facet of political behavior manifested in two rival groups within the dominant political party in Maharashtra, the Indian National Congress. The study was conducted at the district level in the period between September 1964 and May 1966. The groups to which I refer, however, began to take shape in 1962, at about the time when popular elections were held to choose the members of the newly inaugurated bodies of local government in the State.* And it is that division which I investigated, focussing my examination upon the Congress members of the new local bodies. These have been officially termed 'Zilla Parishads' or 'District Councils'

---

* Maharashtra was the eleventh state[6] to accept the recommendation of the Government of India to enact legislation implementing the principle of 'democratic decentralization' or Panchayati Raj, which was embodied in the Report of the Balwantray Mehta Committee on Plan Projects.[7]

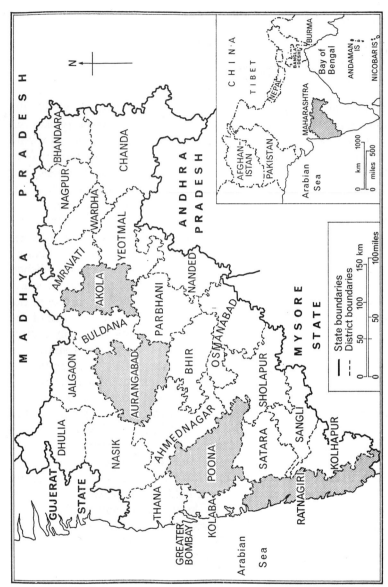

Map 1

2

and both titles will be used interchangeably throughout this study.

I do not mean to imply that these factions emerged suddenly at that particular point in time, or at the district level exclusively. Indeed, I hope to demonstrate later that the conflict which divided these groups had roots in the past, as well as in present conditions, that it had ramifications at higher levels (or rather was itself, possibly, a reflection of higher-level conflicts), and that it may have been inherent in some aspect of the economic philosophy of the Government of India.

As in other states, the functions entrusted to the District Council were entirely of a developmental nature (projects in public works, public health, agriculture, and so on).[4] Economically, the District Councils were and are largely dependent on State Government funds.[5] However, the authority with which they were invested, or which they assumed, to make decisions about the distribution of material benefits in the projects and spheres of activity entrusted to them, gave the Zilla Parishads in Maharashtra considerable political weight as relatively independent dispensers of patronage.

In one of the more radical departures from legislation passed in other states, the Government of Maharashtra introduced the principle of direct popular election of the members of the Councils, on a party basis. It thereby injected, inevitably and explicitly, the element of political competition into the new bodies of local government. From the point of view of an observer of Indian politics, it also provided an opportunity to identify and study the contestants involved in such political competition within a large yet compact political and governmental unit – the district.

The governmental and dominant party organization at the state level wields its authority over approximately 40 million people. The governing elite alone (including ministers as well as members of the legislative assembly) is numbered in the hundreds. There are over two hundred and fifty legislative assembly constituencies in the State, and, unlike most western democracies, the organizational units of the party are not coterminous with the electoral constituencies. Thus, one cannot study the interaction between government and party leaders in any particular *electoral* unit. At the taluka* level, also, one must deal with over two hundred units

---

* The taluka (sometimes also referred to as 'tahsil') is a subdivision of the district in the overall administrative structure of the State of Maharashtra. The

The Dynamics of Indian Political Factions

whose population ranges from 30 thousand to approximately 200 thousand (and even up to 400 thousand in a few cases).[8] What makes this level less useful, however, is the fact that under the Maharashtra version of Panchayati Raj, it is the *district* rather than the *taluka* which is the main executive unit within the three-tier structure of local government.[9] For this reason also, the village is a less useful arena for study; moreover, the large number of villages (almost 36 thousand in the State)[10] detracts from the academic utility of such a unit for the purposes of a study concerned with the dynamics of the party divisions characteristic of the State.

The district, on the other hand, which is the most important executive body of rural local government in the three-tier scheme in Maharashtra, ranges (generally) from about a million to a million and a half in (rural) population size.[11] I have selected for study four out of the twenty-five districts in Maharashtra; and the number of respondents interviewed in connection with this study (one hundred and sixty) constitutes more than a 10% sample of the Councillors in all the Zilla Parishads in the State of Maharashtra, and a 20% sample of Congress Councillors. The population over which these four district councils have jurisdiction constitutes almost 20% of the total rural population of the State. Thus, in terms of the basic characteristic of size, at least, these District Councils are representative of all the Councils in the State.*

The selection of the districts was made with a view to maximizing differences in the broad socio-political environment of the respondents. As the state contains four major administrative divisions which are broadly coterminous with distinct geographical,

collection of revenue and administration of justice have been among the most important functions of administrators in such units. Since the 1961 scheme of local government was introduced in Maharashtra, the taluka has also become in most parts of the state (please see note on p. 149 below for exceptions) one of the units of self-government in the local government structure.

* Excluding Greater Bombay, which is governed by a municipality, there are 25 districts in the State where Zilla Parishads function, extending their jurisdiction mainly over the rural areas.[12]

There was a total of 1,271 elective seats in these 25 Zilla Parishads in 1962.[13] The results immediately following the elections showed that Congressmen had secured 827 of these seats, which would give me nearly a 20% sample of Congress Councillors. However, many of the independents and other-party members crossed the line into the Congress camp after the elections, so that I cannot validly claim that the 160 Congress respondents in this study constitute a 20% sample of Congressmen originally elected; but they are very close to that.

4

Introduction

social, economic and historical units, it was desirable that all these regions be represented in the study. Each of them differs from the others in terms of its experience in local government, levels of literacy, or the degree of economic development or potential there-for[14] –to mention a few features which would be relevant in a political study of this type. To the extent that the variation in regional attributes is maximized, the districts used are a representative sample. It is believed that the observations, hypotheses and conclusions presented here will reflect, as was intended, the major variations in the political setting of the state as a whole.

With regard to the selection of respondents, it should be noted that once the districts had been selected, the choice of respondents was dictated by the focus of my study – namely, the Congress contingent in the Zilla Parishads. All the Congressmen in each Zilla Parishad were interviewed. In other words, the Congress members and officers in these four Zilla Parishads constitute my basic units of analysis.*

The districts are listed below, together with their corresponding administrative divisions and socio-historical areas:

District	Administrative Division	Socio-historical Area
Ratnagiri	Bombay	Konkan
Poona	Poona	Desh (Deccan)
Aurangabad	Aurangabad	Marathwada
Akola	Nagpur	Vidarbha

My analysis focusses on the members of two groups constituting factional alignments within the Congress Party in each Zilla Parishad (hereinafter sometimes referred to as 'Z.P.'). The immediate issue over which these groups developed concerned the nomination of party candidates for the posts of President, Vice President and Committee Chairmen of the Zilla Parishad. Inasmuch as Congressmen had emerged dominant in almost every Zilla Parishad in the May 1962 elections of Z.P. Councillors,[15] it was the nominating procedure within the Congress Party that became critical in the selection of Council officials, rather than the formal

---

* All the officers in each of the Zilla Parishads selected were Congressmen. These officers were elected by the members from amongst themselves, once they had been elected to the local body from their respective constituencies. Nominations for the officers' posts were submitted to the membership by each party represented in the Zilla Parishad.

5

election which was held in the first general meeting of the Zilla Parishad following the election of Councillors (and, of course, following the nomination of candidates by the various parties represented in the District Council).

Although the party leadership (at least at local levels, which I observed at first hand) exercises control in party meetings over members' behavior through the principle of unanimous voting, it appears that on important issues, such as the selection of leaders – as in this instance – majority voting *is* sanctioned by the party. (Even here, however, the unanimous method of voting is preferred.) In these circumstances, dissidents within the party have an opportunity to challenge the established leaders. The Congress Party apparently had to cope with numerous such challenges following the 1962 elections.[16] In many instances, the 'challengers' presented to the Congress members in the Z.P. their own candidates for office, in opposition to those sanctioned by the established party leadership. I have, therefore, termed the two groups 'Rebels' and 'Loyalists', largely on the basis of the Z.P. Congressmen's vote for or against the official Congress Party slate offered for the consideration of members in the Zilla Parishad Congress Party meeting held after the election of Councillors.* The respondents,

* In the case of Ratnagiri, the procedure for identifying factional membership differed somewhat from that followed in the other districts. Here, the Council President and other officials were elected to their respective posts unanimously. Although there had been a latent opposition group at the time, it did not materialize. The reason for this – given by many respondents – was a most interesting one indeed. It appears that the official Congress candidate for the Z.P. Presidency complied with the Congress leadership's request a few months earlier to run – in the face of certain defeat – against a popular incumbent Socialist candidate in the parliamentary elections, held in February 1962. As was expected, the Congressman was defeated. His consolation prize was to be the Presidency of the Zilla Parishad. Most of the Congress Councillors apparently felt it would be lacking in grace to deal another defeat upon one who had 'sacrificed' himself, in a manner of speaking, for the Party. Thus, a compromise was worked out whereby two representatives of the latent Rebel group were given top posts in the Zilla Parishad, one as Vice President, and the other as a Committee Chairman. Within a year, however, the Committee Chairman died, and this top post became vacant once again. The factions which had been muted in 1962 now became manifest. Feelings on the Rebel side were exacerbated when the top district leader decided to give this post – originally held by a 'Rebel' – to a member of the opposing faction. At this point, the Rebel group insisted on a vote within the Party to resolve the conflict. During the election thus held, a Rebel candidate stood in opposition to the one supported by the district leadership. The identification of factional membership in this district, therefore, has been made on the basis of this subsequent vote for a Z.P. official within the Congress Party.

6

then, have been divided into two groups, the criterion for the division being a specific political act.

The model of investigation may be further elucidated if we examine the question underlying the main hypothesis with which my analysis is concerned, namely:

Is the decision taken by a political actor to oppose or to 'rebel' against party authority determined, or could it be predicted, by (a) the characteristics of his socio-economic and political environment; (b) his involvement in the political power structure (another aspect of political behavior); (c) elements of his economic background; (d) the nature of certain emotional commitments and attitudes towards the Congress Party; or, finally, (e) by some particular combination of these factors?*

The answers which are suggested here, and which constitute the essence of this study, are more significant on a practical level than a theoretical one. That is to say, the hypotheses and conclusions developed in the course of this work are directed mainly toward analysis of the political system in an important Indian state. On this level, the significance of the questions raised lies in the implicit challenge which they pose to several hypotheses often advanced or implicitly assumed when Indian politics are discussed or analyzed.

For instance, one of the most frequent, and perhaps least helpful, hypotheses often used to explain Indian politics, is one which implies that the dynamics of political alignments (and almost every other manifestation of political life in India) are to be understood primarily in terms of personal loyalties – sometimes called 'primordial loyalties' – which are guided by feelings of caste solidarity, or community solidarity, or attachments to ascriptive groups, in general. (Such an assertion usually carries with it, explicitly or implicitly, the corollary that such personal loyalties have displaced the commitment to ideology as the basis for action.) This assumption implies that there is a sort of mystical (i.e. irrational) bond between social unit and political action, between leader and follower. Even where the nature of the tie is not so conceived, an explanation of political alignments in terms of personal loyalties is really no explanation at all, but a description at best.

Whether such an assumption about the importance of personal

* The operational definition of categories (a) to (d) will be found in Table C appended to the Note on Methodology (Appendix 1), pp. 215–17. (See also Ch. 3, pp. 47–8, below.)

loyalties in Indian politics is deduced (by methods known or unknown) or empirically arrived at, it is perhaps more relevant to note that observers of Indian politics – whether journalists or scholars (Indian or foreign) – often do not go beyond this type of 'explanation'. When they do, it is more often by way of extrapolation from observation which, while it may or may not be exhaustive, is usually not systematic. One is unable, therefore, to gauge the validity of the sources or methods of investigation or the processes of reasoning.[17] One suspects that, for reasons extraneous to the Indian setting, this type of 'explanation' is particularly appealing to Westerners.

Another 'explanation' of the conflicts besetting the Indian political system suggests that Indian Ministers, whether in the Central Government or in the several state governments, harbor feelings of hostility toward those who hold office in the Congress Party, particularly at higher levels. This animosity is tagged and filed under the 'ministerial versus organizational faction' label. It is not usually made clear *why* a minister should be the enemy of some State Congress Committee President, or whether he is so in all circumstances. If so, why? If not, why not? Why do Ministers and State Party leaders, for example, cooperate in some circumstances (as will be indicated in the course of this study)? And if the main conflict is between the ministerial and organizational wings of the party, why are some of the most bitter political struggles fought between Ministers of the same party in the competition for power? The usual answer may be that they are 'power-hungry'. Again, this explains little, but I will deal with this assertion elsewhere.

Approaches such as these are used to explain Indian politics not only at the national level, but at the state level as well, and in the course of my investigation I often encountered such assumptions in observations made about politics in Maharashtra. It is these with which I attempt to deal.

In addition, more narrowly focussed 'explanations' were attempted at the state level, which may have cultural or historical antecedents. One such hypothesis which has currency is that factions, either at the district or at the state level, may be traced to a long-standing conflict between Patils and Deshmukhs.*[18] One

* These groups have been incorrectly described by some writers as caste groupings. The names 'Patil' and 'Deshmukh' were actually official titles held by families whose heads were appointed by the British (or by the Moghuls before

8

Introduction

reason suggested for the 'bad blood' between them is the fact that the 'taluka' Deshmukhs, who have lost their prestige and power, are resentful of the 'village' Patils, who have usurped this power and displaced them on the status scale. However, my investigations have shown that this hypothesis does not really hold true in most cases, and that even where such rivalries do exist, they are, at most, merely incidental factors which have temporarily coincided with, or have been enhanced by, a congruence of other events and factors.

In a word, it is rather easy to be misled by the existence of feuds between families, castes or personalities, or between some of the more obvious political or social groups, into believing that alignments abound without rhyme or reason, unconnected and unrelated on the landscape of Indian politics. I hope to offer an alternative, and somewhat more inclusive, explanation concerning the factional behavior of political actors – developed, of course, within the limited scope and area of my study – which suggests that this aspect of Indian political behavior is 'rational', not in the sense that it is consciously reasoned out by the politician at all times (although I do not exclude this possibility), but rather in the sense that it is *predictable* to a certain extent, given a certain configuration of environmental and individual factors (and given a reasonable amount of relevant information about them).

The stresses and strains which underlie the factional conflict investigated are numerous and curiously interwoven. My data indicate that the political behavior which I observed has strong economic roots, and further, that the disease of factionalism – if it be such, rather than a corrective mechanism generated by the system itself – is not due, ultimately, to the lack of commitment to party ideology by party functionaries, as is often claimed, but is generated in part by the party ideology itself, and is nurtured by certain conditions in which the relevant political actors function. Among the elements of the official ideology, it is specifically the

them) as head of a village (in the case of the Patil), or of an area roughly equivalent to the taluka (in the case of the Deshmukh), and entrusted either with maintaining law and order or with collecting land revenue, or with both; thus, one may have been a Police Patil or a Revenue Patil or may have combined both functions. In the latter instance, a man might 'bequeath' the 'Patilships' separately to two sons. It is because of this, in part, and also because villages (on which Patils are based) are more numerous than talukas, that Patils today outnumber Deshmukhs. (The generic term for such titles is 'gharana'.)

9

economic philosophy of the 'mixed enterprise' which has produced a mixed or mixed-up political enterprise within the Congress Party organization itself. This ambiguity toward public and private economic activity in the party ideology, reflected in the juxtaposition of incompatible economic practices and interests, is, by extension, carried into the political behavior of Congressmen. The result is factionalism.

It may well be pointed out that this is not a new finding. The fact that there exists a 'right' and a 'left' wing in the Congress organization has been common knowledge for a long time. What is proposed here is the following:

Firstly, that, in the State of Maharashtra at least, this schism underlies some of the other conflict situations which are perceived by so many observers as distinct and isolated phenomena. A hypothesis such as I propose might place in better perspective some of the phenomena which often are seen as the precipitants of political factionalism.

Secondly, and perhaps more importantly, this 'right'/'left' split is observed not only, as is usually assumed, among national and state leaders, the political sophisticates, or the more knowledgeable political actors in the large urban areas. It is also a basic division reaching down to the level of local politics in the rural areas, that is, the district level and perhaps below, precisely the levels often characterized as almost exclusively concerned with personalities, caste, and so forth.

Let me repeat that the rationality of Indian politics is not conceived exclusively in terms of predictability. In other words, I do not wish to imply by my emphasis on 'predictability' that the element of conscious reasoning is entirely lacking in Indian political behavior. What I do wish to suggest is that this element may be more prevalent in one segment of the political elite than in another. It is therefore desirable to distinguish between two levels of political actor and two levels of awareness in analyzing the dynamics of factional alignment.

At one level, there are the political leaders and the protagonists in the factional struggle. At the other level, there are the supporters or followers of political leaders. The relationship between the two is a hierarchical one, as the term 'level' indicates. These two kinds of political actor, then, are motivated by somewhat different ambitions for political office. Two basic kinds of political ambition (often

Introduction

mutually supporting) might be: (1) the ambition for office perceived as an *instrument* to achieve broad ends (that is, relative to one's community or caste, for example) or to achieve personal ends – either political, social, economic or ideological; (2) the ambition for office as *an end in itself*, that is, perceived as something whose possession is in itself gratifying (and by possession I also imply exercise, for to have power means to wield power at some point, as well as to have the potential to exercise it).*

In the case of leaders, either or both types of ambition may motivate the seeking of office.† But in the case of supporters, the office may be perceived largely as an instrument to achieve personal, or perhaps community or village, ends. In other words, its value is chiefly instrumental rather than intrinsic. The prestige attaching to membership of a District Council, for example, is hardly commensurate with that attaching to the office of Minister or State Congress President or – at the district level – Congress Committee or Council President. The benefits accruing to the member of a District Council – and his family or kin – are potentially and actually greater than the prestige deriving therefrom. The average individual who is not a member or associate of this political elite has a very small share, indeed, in the benefits channeled through the District Council.

Although a distinction between levels of political action and motivation has been suggested as desirable in analyzing the dynamics of factional alignments,‡ the data will nonetheless show that, generally, the factional groupings which have developed are identifiable by a more or less distinct policy orientation, among other things. (This is not to say, however, that *all* such distinct sub-sets of the population are either factions or coincide with a particular division on policy orientation – of which there may be more than one.)

---

* In answer to those who assert that politicians are 'power-hungry', it may be useful to note that any goals – whether ideological, social or personal – which require the sanction of political authority can be achieved by most individuals only through political office.

† The term 'office' is used here in a very broad sense. It refers to both members and officials of any elective governmental body. In the analytical chapters which follow, however, the term will refer exclusively to those who hold office, in either the government, the party or cooperative institutions.

‡ Such a distinction will subsequently serve as a partial explanation of some of the apparent anomalies observed in one of the districts (Akola).

The Dynamics of Indian Political Factions

In the following chapter, I will set forth in some detail the outline and substance of the argument which defines the differing policy orientations of each factional group with regard to a particular issue, especially as these find expression in the state political arena. The argument will be introduced in a conceptual framework which will, I trust, allow the reader some measure of comparison, across political systems, of events and phenomena observed in a particular and relatively limited political sphere.

In subsequent chapters, I will describe in general terms the method of analysis employed (Chapter 3), and I will then go on to demonstrate, statistically and otherwise, the validity of this argument in the four differing areas of the State in which the study was conducted (Chapters 4 to 7); these areas will then be examined collectively, in a cross-district comparison (Chapter 8). I will conclude with a few projections regarding the prospects for stability in the political system of Maharashtra.

CHAPTER 2

THE ARGUMENT

The term 'policy orientation' was introduced at the end of the last chapter, and as it is pertinent to the argument which will be developed in this chapter, I will begin by setting down my understanding of this concept with reference to a factional group or group member. I use the term to refer to some attitude, belief or evaluation regarding an issue in a given political context. I am assuming, moreover, that the nature of this orientation has a determining influence on the behavior of a political actor at any given time and that, in fact, such behavior is one of the manifestations of that orientation.

FIRST STATEMENT OF HYPOTHESIS: CONFLICT OF INDIVIDUAL OR GROUP INTERESTS AS SOURCE OF FACTIONALISM

In the context of this study, I am positing a determinative relationship between the specific factional identity of a group or group member, on the one hand, and its or his hypothetical policy orientation regarding something problematical, on the other. This 'something' may be defined in varying terms by a political actor, depending upon, among other things, the level of the political arena.

At the local level – which, in this study, denotes the district – the respondents usually described their political actions as being oriented toward access to material benefits (agricultural loans, seeds, fertilizers, agricultural equipment and so forth).*

The political actors under investigation here apparently weighed the potential effectiveness of differing paths of action in ensuring

* A statement made by one Congress respondent was typical of a sentiment commonly expressed: 'I am against Congress favoritism and other injustices and lack of principle, but I stay in politics because I want to maintain the source of economic benefits which the Party constitutes. If I were not active in politics, if I did not help an M.L.A. in his campaign from time to time, I would be ignored and would not be able to get the seeds, fertilizers, loans, and so forth, as easily. I stay in politics for self-interest, as well as for the interest of my village.'

The Dynamics of Indian Political Factions

access to such benefits. Thus, upon election to the Zilla Parishad, some were predisposed to form or join a group led by leaders in the cooperative organization, while others threw in their lot with a different group. The factional identity of each was linked to a specific policy orientation regarding the form of economic organization and related issues. It was the Rebel group which, according to the findings, was linked with cooperative interests.

At higher levels in the political system, differences in economic attitudes and interests were reflected in the debate over the appropriate balance between public and private activity.* Thus, at the state level, also, the fundamental hypothesis posited is that the interest groups in conflict are again economic. One group represents private business, that is, commercial, financial and trade interests. In terms of social characteristics, this group is urban-based (though its activities also extend to the rural areas). Its members are drawn from certain minority business communities:† Marwaris, Jains, Parsis, Gujeratis.‡ The counterpart of this group

* Technically speaking, cooperatives are a private form of economic organization. That is to say, they are not government-owned or -operated institutions. However, because of the special position which the principle of cooperative economic organization occupies in the official socialist philosophy (*cf.*, below, p. 43, fns. 94 and 95), I have placed cooperatives in the 'public' domain. Equally important is the special relationship of government to cooperatives. Firstly, it may be noted that the State contributes to the share capital of cooperatives. And secondly, the State Governments have the authority to nominate members of the board of management of state cooperative institutions.[1]

For the above reasons, I would classify cooperative activity as 'public'. At the same time, I indicate the special character of cooperatives by enclosing such references to the public domain in quotation marks.

† This is the first of several references to community (or caste) which will be made from time to time in the course of this study. I wish to emphasize at the outset, however, that such references do not negate my earlier assertion that membership in an ascriptive group is not, in and of itself, a determining factor in the facet of political behavior studied here. This assertion will be more concretely demonstrated at a later point. At this time, I wish to make clear that it is the economic attributes of certain communities which are apparently relevant factors in political behavior. Evidently, these attributes are coincidentally associated with such communities in certain areas. Membership in such ascriptive groups, however, did not emerge as an independent determining factor, and I wish to stress this fact in order to forestall charges of inconsistency in the exposition.

‡ According to a study executed by a private institution with the cooperation of the Government of Maharashtra: 'If we look to the social structure of the people of Maharashtra, we shall find that there are very few industrialists and businessmen among those who can be classified as Marathas. Except in Konkan which has some indigenous Vaishyas, there are no trading communities among the Marathas. Even in the days of Maratha rule, commercial classes were imported into Maharashtra from outside....'[2]

14

The Argument

at the district level would be the Loyalists (though their ethnic composition may not necessarily parallel that of the urban-based group at the state level).

The other state-level group also represents certain economic interests. Its members appear to derive their economic strength mainly from landed property rather than commercial capital, although they do also draw some economic and organizational strength from resources harnessed through cooperative ventures. However, since their basic source of wealth is land, we may assume that most of its members are rural-based, either by origin or by political interest. They are drawn largely (but not exclusively) from the Maratha caste, or rather, from a particular segment of the Marathas – and this is an important distinction to note. They are the 'nouveaux riches', the 'upstarts' who entered the political arena after independence was attained and universal suffrage translated numbers into political power.* In terms of district-level factions, this state-level group may be considered as roughly equivalent to the Rebels.

The foregoing constitutes the first statement of the argument which I propose to develop in this chapter. In essence, it suggests that rational interests and considerations are a more or less conscious determinant of political behavior.

* I would not equate this group with Evelyn Wood's 'rural U-sector'[3] nor with Daniel Thorner's affluent society.[4] One reason is that the populations of the Wood and Thorner studies extend largely outside Maharashtra, and their observations are, therefore, not immediately applicable to this political sphere. (The Thorner study does deal with a Maharashtra district – Kolhapur – but the relevant observations in that study are drawn from only one out of a thousand and more villages in the district.) Secondly, they apparently include *all* the rich in their respective groups. I wish to differentiate between segments of the U-sector, and I would justify that differentiation at the very least on the ground of the existence of these two factions, both of which may be considered representative of the U-sector, yet whose economic interests conflict nonetheless. There is still another segment of the U-sector which is not represented at all in the local bodies which I examined, and whose spokesmen are not explicitly identified at either the district or the state level. I am referring to the very big landlord, owning at least 150 to 200 acres or more. An overwhelming majority of the respondents here had holdings which ranged, on the average, considerably below this size of landholding. (See Tables 1 and 2 below, p. 42.) Referring to the landowner as political activist, many respondents said that the very big landlords did not have to and usually did not run for office in a body like the Zilla Parishad since it had little to offer by way of benefits. They were rich and powerful enough to satisfy their needs independently or through other more effective political channels at higher levels.

15

The Dynamics of Indian Political Factions

SECOND STATEMENT OF HYPOTHESIS: CONFLICT OF SYSTEMIC NEEDS AS SOURCE OF FACTIONALISM

What follows is essentially the second and complementary (indeed *integral*) statement of my hypothesis, namely, an exposition of 'impersonal' *systemic* determinants of political behavior.

The political system of Maharashtra is (as any other) differentiated from the larger social system by virtue of the special function it performs for the people of Maharashtra. Its primary task, as part of the larger social system, is the attainment of goals prescribed by the society.* However, in addition to the societal goal, a political system has its own goal, essential to its survival as a political system. That is to say, if a political system is to perform its societal task, it must obviously have the power to sustain itself and to pursue societal goals. Hence, one of the essential prerequisites of the political system *qua* system is the generation of power, or what Talcott Parsons calls a 'generalized something which maximizes the potential of attaining societal goals'[5] (just as the primary goal of the economic system – the production of goods and services – is attained through the 'national income' generated by the economic system).

Included among the elements of power is the legitimacy of societal goals. Attainment of such legitimacy entails a process of accommodation or compromise among possibly conflicting interests, mainly by political party leaders and workers. The success or failure of the politician in executing this function may be reflected in the degree of integration or harmony achieved among the various units comprising the system.

Thus, according to Parsons, *integration* is one of the necessary conditions or 'imperative' needs defining the stability of a system. 'Stability' may be described as a general condition or state of equilibrium of a system at any given time, and, over time, a sustained state of equilibrium characterized by the harmonious interaction between or among its several parts. Thus, he states:

* Although we are dealing here with Maharashtra as a discrete political system, it should be noted that the State Government and the State Congress Party (together with other parts of the political system) are themselves subsystems in the Indian political system taken as a whole. Hence, the societal goals referred to above include among them those goals which have been commonly prescribed for the Indian nation. Having said that, we may go on to deal with Maharashtra's political system (and goals) as, more or less, a self-sustained entity.

16

The Argument

Whatever the units which interact in a system-process, be they the motivational units of personality (need-dispositions) or the roles of individual persons in a social system, or the roles of collectivities in more macroscopic social systems, the actions of the significant units may be such as to be mutually supportive in the functioning of the system, or to some degree mutually obstructive and conflictful. There is, then, the problem of 'maintaining solidarity' in the relations between the units, in the interest of effective functioning. This I call the functional imperative of *system-integration.*[6]

So that (Parsons says), in order that the actions of the various units in a system may not hamper the activities or subvert the aims of one another, a certain level of harmony of action and goals must be maintained among these units if the system is to continue to function without serious disruption.

Another element of power is the accessibility and control of disposable resources. The ability to control or manipulate the varied resources in the human and physical environment toward societal ends involves a process of adaptation by the political system. This entails the definition (or redefinition) and pursuit of societal goals *under conditions or limitations on such resources* imposed ultimately by the general social as well as physical environment. This process of *adaptation* is another imperative function or need of the political system, without which political instability will eventually ensue.

Two of the main structural components of the political system of Maharashtra are the Government of Maharashtra and the Indian National Congress Party of the State. However, since Maharashtra has a dominant one-party system, it is difficult in practice to differentiate between the two. In conceptual terms we may say that the two structures are functionally distinct sub-systems. The main task of the Government of Maharashtra is that of adaptation, i.e., the definition and fulfilment of accepted or legitimate societal goals within given physical and socio-economic limitations. In the performance of this task, it is the authoritative decision-makers who are concerned with the problem of controlling disposable resources in the pursuit of societal goals.

The political party system, on the other hand, is concerned with the problem of rendering legitimate such control by the government, as well as legitimizing government's definition (or redefinition) of societal goals (i.e., of public policy) on a periodic basis. As we have seen, the ability to legitimate societal goals involves the process of integration or accommodation of conflicting interests or

17

values. In a two- or multi-party system, where the opposing party or parties may have the support of important socio-economic interests or sizable segments of the electorate, the agents of competing parties may have to define or redefine their proposed policies in order to accommodate the views or interests of potential opponents. The result may be a compromise acceptable to the broadest possible configuration of interests and views. Such a compromise would then be legitimated through the electoral process. In a dominant one-party system, such as exists in Maharashtra, this function of accommodation and legitimation of conflicting interests and goals is performed largely *within and by* the dominant party, through the medium of factions.

To recapitulate, we are dealing here with two imperative needs or primary functions of the political system in Maharashtra: adaptation (involving control of disposable resources) and integration (involving the legitimation and accommodation of interests and goals). If these needs are met, a greater measure of power should be generated, so that the system may be sustained and societal goals may be pursued by the political system.

However, having assumed that each of these needs is imperative or equally and absolutely compelling, it stands to reason that they 'cannot all be maximized at once, and that, under given conditions and within a limited time span, "pushing" one or two of them will have to occur at the expense of others.'[7] Thus, '...overintegration of the system, in the sense of attempting to avoid all possibilities of internal antagonism or disharmony, may occur at the expense of effective...adaptation.'[8]* Similarly, of course, the function of adaptation may conflict with that of integration, which, as we shall see presently, is the case in Maharashtra. In other words, if the politician attempts to accommodate conflicting economic interests by, let us say, urging a redistribution of capital resources, he may jeopardize the efforts of the authoritative decision-maker to maintain access and/or control over certain necessary resources, disrupting a hitherto cooperative relationship between government and a given economic community which may constitute an access-

---

* A good example of this type of situation in India is the tendency of the central government, from time to time, to locate industrial plants in politically sensitive areas which are unsuitable in terms of production cost factors or overall productivity. Here, the 'integration' imperative seems to be at work. Obviously, extended submission to this compelling need would seriously undermine the societal goal of industrialization.

18

ible source of 'disposable resources'. The situation sketched here constitutes a very simple 'conflict' model and in fact the relationship between government and party is much more complex than this.

Let me amplify this second statement of the hypothesis as it applies to Maharashtra. As is the case in all political systems, we find that in Maharashtra a certain group of individuals is assigned the task of making authoritative decisions about goal priorities and about the manner in which societal goals are to be pursued. Because they function in a democratic system, these decision-makers must derive their authority, periodically, through popular elections. Thus, these political actors have two goal-oriented activities which must command their attention and energies. An initial and necessary goal for aspiring or incumbent decision-makers is to establish their authority as *legitimate* decision-makers, that is, to be elected to public office. The whole electoral process, in fact, is one of societal goal legitimation and accommodation of interests.* This 'electoral' goal of the aspiring decision-maker is an instrumental one, vis-a-vis the primary societal goal.† Once it is attained, the decision-maker presumably goes about the business of organizing the necessary physical and human resources toward societal ends, which is to say, he makes and executes decisions (within his sphere of authority) regarding the production and distribution of these resources.

In the State of Maharashtra (and throughout India, of course), these two sets of activities (adaptive and integrative) are organized around two different structures and two different organizational principles. One is that of functional specialization, and the other is the territorial principle of organization. These two organizations, however, are inter-related and interdependent in a dominant one-party system – particularly in one with a parliamentary form of government. *It is here that the systemic origins of political factionalism may be found.*

* Although we think of the electoral process as one which spans a limited period of time at regular intervals, it should actually be conceived as a continuing process which may change form in the interval, but whose purpose for any given party is the legitimation of its goals (for society) and, toward that end, the accommodation of interests, views or values. As such, it is a process in which the aspiring decision-maker is continuously involved, with greater or lesser intensity over time.

† The fact that a politician may pursue this goal as an end in itself does not alter the fact that, whatever his motivation, he must first attain office in order to function in a capacity as legitimate decision-maker.

19

The Dynamics of Indian Political Factions

The government, which is the structure within which authoritative decision-makers may relate to one another, is organized primarily around specialized social and economic activities, such as education, the welfare of backward classes, industrial production or agricultural development. Through the activities of these specialized ministries and their departments, the government presumably advances toward its societal goals.

The instrumental goal of election to office (and with it, the accommodation of conflicting interests and legitimation of goals) is pursued – by incumbents and aspirants to political office – primarily through territorially organized activities, which usually engage the efforts of the political party system. In Maharashtra this task would fall naturally to the Indian National Congress, which is the dominant party.

THE THEORETICAL RELATIONSHIP
BETWEEN THE FIRST AND SECOND STATEMENTS OF
THE GENERAL HYPOTHESIS

Both of the activities referred to above are energized and sustained by support from 'constituencies' in the political or social system at large. We may call these, for the moment, the 'economic' and 'political' constituencies, respectively, of the Government of Maharashtra and the State Congress Party. This support is contingent on the satisfaction of the 'constituents'' interests through appropriate public policies or actions, and it constitutes a third element of power which a political system needs to have. It should be noted, of course, that, to the extent that the government and the party organization are interrelated, both of these 'constituencies' are of critical importance to the well-being of either organization.

We return to our central question regarding the origins of political conflict. I submit that it arises because, under existing conditions, the 'constituencies' upon whose support the authoritative decision-makers depend to accomplish their twin goals have interests (defined, pragmatically, in economic terms) which are essentially antagonistic. In the pursuit of their divergent interests, these 'constituencies', through a variety of means, make claims or exert pressure on these decision-makers which, implicitly or explicitly, demand of the governing authorities certain courses of action, in return for their support. The decision-maker, aspirant or

The Argument

incumbent, is required, in the process of mobilizing such support, to manipulate 'political' or 'economic' resources in order to achieve either the instrumental (political power) goals or the intrinsic systemic (societal) goals. 'Political' resources may include, among other things, political skills and energies, such as political bargaining, leadership initiative, charismatic qualities, political attitudes or values, and control over decisions regarding the distribution of political favors. These resources may be used in various combinations to generate support – from the political community at large – for various political objects (candidates and their policies, the political party and its platform or philosophy, and so forth). This support may be expressed in the form of votes cast during the periodic elections or through other supportive behavior (e.g., contribution of political funds). In the prevailing political system, the resources to which I have referred have been controlled or heavily influenced by the dominant party organization. In other words, it is through this organization and its members that the aspirant or incumbent decision-maker must attempt to utilize the available political resources toward the achievement of his instrumental goal.

Insofar as the adaptive imperative of the political system is concerned, this need is fulfilled primarily through capital. That is to say, in order for a political system to harness and use the available human and physical energies toward societal ends, it must have access, ultimately, to liquid capital. Of course, other resources – such as intellectual, technical and managerial skills, entrepreneurial skills and natural resources – are also used for this purpose, but their exploitation on a large scale is ultimately dependent upon the availability of liquid capital, particularly within a free democratic system. Immediate control over the production and use of these resources rests largely in the economic system. Nevertheless, it is these resources which the decision-maker must be able to use in order to advance societal goals. Therefore, support from this segment of society – the 'economic constituency' – is essential for the realization of these goals.

The members of the 'political constituency' and its resources are dispersed over the entire area of the State. The broad social and economic features of Maharashtra are such that this 'constituency' may be considered to be largely rural and agricultural in nature.[9]

The critical 'economic constituency', on the other hand, is

21

The Dynamics of Indian Political Factions

highly localized and urban in nature. Except for certain natural sources of wealth, like minerals or agro-industrial products, most of the crucial economic resources – like capital and economic skills – and the leading members of the 'constituency' are concentrated in western Maharashtra, specifically in the Bombay–Poona industrial complex.

Support from the 'political constituency' is needed for the legitimation of societal goals, and support from the 'economic constituency' for ensuring access to resources needed for the attainment of societal goals. When conflicting pressures issuing from these 'constituencies' (manifested by withholding or threatening to withhold support) converge in any particular arena of political or governmental activity, a disturbance may result which disrupts a previously existing state of equilibrium. One such disturbance is the common political phenomenon studied here, namely, factionalism. This may be observed either in the party organization itself, or among Congressmen in any public organization, including the government (at any level) and its various departments.

APPLICATION OF HYPOTHESIS

1. Political Conflict as a Reflection of Conflicting Interests of Socio-economic Groups in Maharashtra

Before the establishment of the Zilla Parishads, the pressures from the largely rural political constituency were relatively diffuse. The channels through which they were directed to higher authorities in the State were Members of the Legislative Assembly (and the Legislative Council, to a lesser extent) and/or politically non-responsive administrative officials, at lower or higher levels. The demands of rural interests found their way to higher levels of government through the auspices of approximately 250 Members of the Legislative Assembly (M.L.A.s) and an incalculable number of administrative officials, from the village accountant, on up to the district revenue officer, and, finally, through other mediating officials, to a departmental secretary; thence, to a Minister. If we contrast this earlier political communications network with that provided by a total of twenty-five Zilla Parishad Presidents, representing a similar number of districts, we can see that the channel available to the rural constituency (or, at any rate, to its most vocal

The Argument

segments) is more streamlined and has a potential for much greater thrust under the present system.

We will return to this rural 'constituency' at a later point. At this time, I would like to focus attention upon the urban economic community with a view to locating the underlying causes of tension with the rural constituency.

Inasmuch as the focus of this study is on conflict observed in the rural areas, I wish to establish the relevance of the rather elaborate discussion of the urban economic community which will follow. In general, of course, I might point out once again that in a political system where the 'adaptive' and the 'integrative' functions merge in interlocking organizations (that is, the government and the party), a conflict ensues as each organization attempts to maximize both functions simultaneously.* In the process, the interests of the respective 'constituencies' are bound to be compromised somehow, in favor of one or the other, or to be otherwise accommodated.

I have indicated that one of these 'constituencies' is urban in nature and I must therefore deal with that 'constituency' and attempt to establish, first of all, that an interest exists which could conceivably come into conflict with that of the 'rural constituency', and, moreover, that this 'urban constituency' is one in which the governmental organization has a vital interest. This is the purpose of the discussion which follows.

The urban economic community, as we have seen, is one which is highly localized. This is a source of strength, and therefore increases the community's importance to the Government of Maharashtra. In order to appreciate the significance of these features for the Government of Maharashtra, it may be useful to set forth some basic information about the degree of economic strength and concentration, as well as of the localization of power, in the private sector.

A commission appointed by the Government of India, which inquired into conditions of monopoly in the industrial field during 1964–5, reported[10] that there was considerable concentration of economic power in the hands of a limited number of business groups, both on an industry-wise basis and in terms of individual

* This may explain in part the 'ministerial versus organizational' feud which is perhaps a reflection of the ministers' attempts to maximize the 'adaptive' function, while the party organization pushes the 'integrative' function.

23

The Dynamics of Indian Political Factions

commodities or services.* Each of the business houses studied had assets of not less than Rs. 5 crores.† The groups, comprising 1,536 companies, totaled 75 in number and had paid-up capital and assets which amounted to 44.1% and 46.9%, respectively, of the total paid-up capital and assets in the entire corporate sector in the country (excluding government and banking companies).[11] Some of the most important had their headquarters or branch offices in Maharashtra, and, more specifically, in the Greater Bombay area.

The localization of this power in Maharashtra is illustrated by the fact that in 1961 Bombay City alone accounted for about 66% of the total industrial employment, 75% of the value of output, and 79% of the value added by manufacture in the State.[16]

Economic power can be exercised through control not only over production and distributive activities, but also over mass media of communication. In a country like India, where mass media such as television or radio are either not at all or poorly developed as effective channels of political or economic communication, the newspaper is an important mass medium – particularly in the urban areas (with which we are here concerned) where it plays a significant role in the political process. Business interests have, to a large extent, pre-empted the publishing field, or at least its most critical sectors.

Such control is evident in Maharashtra if we look at some of the outstanding features of the press in the State.‡ In a country where the English-language newspapers have the largest circulations, Maharashtra had the second highest number of papers in English and they were the most widely read in the State. The *Times of India*

---

* In the Monopolies Report, definitions were given for 'product-wise concentration' and 'country-wise concentration' (i.e., group- or family-wise). Thus, in the former case: 'Where the share of the three top producers is 75% or more, the concentration can reasonably be considered to be high...'[12] And, 'Where 50% or more of the equity capital was found to be owned by an industrialist, or relations like brothers and sons or daughters-in-law individually or jointly we have held that the company is under the control of that industrialist...'[13] Finally, a 'business group' was taken to comprise 'all such concerns which are subject to the ultimate and decisive decision making power of the controlling interest in the group – the group master.'[14]

† This figure, converted to dollars at the current rate of exchange, would be equivalent to about 7 million dollars. Actually, more than half of the business houses included in this study of monopolies had assets upwards of 26 million dollars, and the top groups had more than 500 million dollars worth of assets.[15]

‡ Most of the information regarding the press is drawn from the government publication, *Press In India – 1965*. (*Cf.* p. 272, fn. 10.)

24

had the highest circulation among English-language newspapers. It was owned by a publishing firm which also published several other English-language newspapers in the State, including an economic daily, as well as several Hindi-language papers and one in Marathi.[17] This publishing house was one of 26 companies owned by the fifth largest business house in the country.[18] Its other interests included sugar and edible oil.* One man (Mr Shanti Prasad Jain from an important business community in Bombay)[19] 'and others closely connected with him' controlled all of these publications.[20]

The second largest English-language newspaper in the State (the *Indian Express*) was owned by a firm which also published several other newspapers throughout the country, as well as a number of Bombay papers, both English and Marathi. In fact, the Marathi paper with the highest circulation in the State was owned by this firm, which also published a daily English-language financial sheet. The controlling interest in this publishing company was held by members of the Goenka family, identified with another large business group (by the same name) which controlled a total of 53 concerns, with main interests in jute, cotton and textiles.[21]

2. Political Conflict as a Reflection of a Systemic Conflict between 'Integrative' and 'Adaptive' Needs

The above are only a few of the important features of Maharashtra's economic system which illustrate the strategic position occupied by a small sector of the economic community. Now we may ask what evidence exists that the Government of Maharashtra has a special relationship with this 'economic constituency'.

One study indicates that much of the credit advanced by various public institutions goes to the private sector in industry, and especially the big companies.[22] To give an illustration, out of a total of Rs. 127.7 crores, constituting loans sanctioned by the Industrial Finance Corporation as on 30 June 1963, 71% went to the private sector.[23] It is pertinent to note, in the context of my thesis, that cooperatives received only 29% of IFC credit.[24] These figures, it should be pointed out, are national ones. However, in one of the

---

* I bring attention to the particular business interests controlled by these firms because we shall see that these have some bearing on subsequent observations.

reports (1956) of the Industrial Finance Corporation, it was shown that Bombay State received the largest proportion of loans distributed to the Indian states for most industries.*[25]

A more direct and binding link exists between the Government of Maharashtra and important commercial and industrial interests which function largely in the Bombay metropolitan area, a principal business center in India. In 1961, over half of the registered dealers in the State were from Bombay City, and more than 71% of all sales by these dealers were made in Bombay.[26] The total taxes paid by them in the fiscal year 1960–1 constituted as much as 81% of all such taxes paid in the State. If we combine with this figure the percentage of taxes paid in the Western Maharashtra region, we find that the more industrialized area of the State contributed almost 93% of the total taxes paid during the year by all registered dealers in the State.[27] Further, it may be noted that the revenue from sales taxes, which was the largest of all revenue heads, both in tax and non-tax revenue, constituted more than half of that from all taxes on commodities and services, contributing 46% of the gross receipts. Nearly one-fourth of the total revenue was thus obtained from sales taxes.†[28] In the same vein, it may be noted that the contribution to the State Income of the non-agricultural sector was considerably high. More than 60% of Maharashtra's income in 1962–3 was generated in industry and commerce, with 25% originating in the secondary and 38% in the tertiary sector. Industrial activities in the factory sector alone provided 19% of the State's income, while commercial activities generated nearly 17% during 1962–3.[29]

The commercial and industrial sector is thus a very important source of revenue for the State. As tax-payer, it provides the Government with a substantial part of the money which it needs to execute the tasks entrusted to it. As producer of goods and services, it is the principal contributor to the State's income. Thus, as a member of the Monopolies Commission pointed out, the influence

---

* These figures may be subject to revision given more recent information. At the time of writing, however, no such information was accessible or available as far as I could determine.

† The figures indicating percentages of revenue from sales taxes are for the year 1961–2 and were drawn from the *Budget in Brief* (see p. 273, fn. 28). The percentages indicating the proportion of taxes paid by dealers on a regional basis are for the year 1960–1 and were taken from the *Quarterly Bulletin of Economics and Statistics* (see p. 273, fn. 26).

The Argument

which this 'economic constituency' has on the official decision-makers is probably derived from the control over large resources and areas of production exercised by a relatively small economic community.[30] Inasmuch as a program of industrial expansion (a primary societal goal entrusted to government) depends on the willingness of the corporate sector to invest its savings for such expansion, this sector can influence government policies, regardless of its relationship with any political party or with any individual in authority (through 'contributions' – legitimate or otherwise). The argument, re-phrased within the theoretical framework used in this study, simply states that the support of this 'economic constituency' (in the form of capital investment, technical skills and so forth) is essential for the fulfilment of a critical task 'assigned' to the political system by society. Hence, concentration of economic power, together with the ability of business interests to influence public opinion through the press, provide an effective lever through which this economic community may exert pressure on government to induce it to act in a manner favorable to its interests.*

So far I have tried to give some indication of the extent to which power is concentrated in a particular sector of the economic system, and to establish some basis for the statement that the formal decision-makers and this important economic 'constituency' are bound to each other by compelling ties.

* A graphic illustration of this sort of thing was provided in a recent Indian weekly, under the heading of 'Business'. I quote parts of the item: 'The frequent threats of closing down production held out by all manner of industries when faced with a variety of problems, whether it be shortage of raw materials or credit, are revealing of the character of relations between industry and the government in the country. The threat is most used by industries which are large employers of labour since it is the prospect of labour being laid-off which is expected to bend the government to industry's will....The textile industry ...had threatened a 15-day block closure "as the only solution" to the situation arising out of shortage of cotton. The threat yielded from the government ...the promise of larger cotton imports. The industry is at it again now. This time the provocation is the alleged squeeze on bank credit to textile mills.... The press note issued by the (Indian Cotton Mills' Federation) on Thursday declares that "unless the status quo ante with regard to credit availability is restored immediately, a serious situation would develop, resulting in loss of production and more unemployment". The hint is obvious.' (See *Economic and Political Weekly*, Vol. VI, No. 10, 6 March 1971, p. 555.)

The Dynamics of Indian Political Factions

3. Interrelationship between Statement '1' and Statement '2' of Hypothesis

Now we turn to a consideration of the 'political constituency', whose support, we may recall, is necessary for the legitimation of goals (expressed in the election – direct or indirect – of certain public officials). It should also be recalled that the fulfilment of the 'imperative' integrative need of the political system is dependent ultimately on the relationship of the political party to this political constituency.

The discussion which follows is intended to elucidate the nature of the conflict between integrative and adaptive needs. It should also serve to establish the integral relationship between the first and second statements of my general hypothesis.

I have suggested previously that a conflict of interests exists between an urban economic community (which facilitates the adaptive process) and certain agriculturally-based economic groups in the locus of the 'political constituency' (which plays a critical role in the integrative process). Obviously if a conflict ensues between two individuals or two groups, there must be a common *object* of conflict and a common *arena* where the rival parties engage each other. I will try to identify first the object or objects of conflict and then the arena where the ostensibly distant rivals meet.

The most important item of industrial production in the State is textiles.*[31] This industry had the largest proportion of registered factories, productive capital, employment, output, input and value added, for any single industry in the State.†[32] While jute and woollen textiles, as well as silk and artificial silk, are included in this group, the most important among them is cotton textiles.[33]

If we look at the acreage under different crops in the various regions of Maharashtra, we find that only 5% of the gross cropped area in Western Maharashtra is under cotton.[35] None of this is in

---

* It is important to note that this industry has nation-wide importance as well. Cotton textiles rank third among India's major exports.[34] Hence they are an important source of foreign exchange which replenishes the nation's liquid resources. As such, the industry serves national goals. But, in addition, it aids the State Governments in the execution of their tasks to the extent that such foreign exchange is converted into federal grants to states.

† The figures used in this reference are based on an average for the three years 1959–61, which was the period preceding the year when the conflict studied here evolved.

28

the Konkan area, where Greater Bombay, the principal centre of the cotton textile industry (in the country as well as the State), is located.[36] It appears, then, that this industry must obtain most of its raw material from areas beyond Western Maharashtra. Indeed, we find that the large cotton-growing areas are in the eastern region of the State. Marathwada has 16% of its arable land under cotton, which ranks as the largest single commercial crop in this area.[37] The district studied here (Aurangabad) was the third largest cotton-growing area in the Marathwada region. However, the biggest cotton belt in the State is in Vidarbha, where 29% of the cultivable land supports this commercial crop.[38] Four out of the eight districts of Vidarbha are the principal cotton-growing areas, and Akola (also studied here) is the second largest of the four. The average cotton acreage in these four districts is about 40%.[39] (Akola somewhat exceeds this average.[40]) Thus, in 1960–1, the Vidarbha region accounted for about 55% of all cotton production; another 27% of the cotton produced in the State came from the Marathwada area.[41] Bombay City accounts for 77% of the State's consumption of raw cotton,[42] and much of this apparently comes from Eastern Maharashtra, and particularly from Vidarbha.

We shall see in the analysis of Akola District that the business interests in Vidarbha were led by the Marwari community and that it was this business community (or its spokesmen) which encountered opposition from another economic group in the district.

One long-standing argument in Vidarbha, which may illustrate the nature of the conflict between the rival groups, has been over the price of cotton. In 1961–2, cotton traders were pressing for decontrol of cotton prices.[43] In the prevailing conditions of short supply, the traders, who controlled the rural buyer's market, could have made very large profits by buying from the cotton farmer at low prices and selling in the Bombay market at high prices. Several years later, a Rebel respondent complained that the cotton merchants were doing that even under price controls. Although the Government had fixed ceiling and floor prices, the range was so wide that the cotton traders would all buy at or near the minimum price (of Rs. 125 per quintal) and sell at or near the maximum price (of Rs. 175) in Bombay. The Rebel said he was in favor of raising the ceiling and narrowing the range. The latest news reports indicate that the 'price of cotton' is still very much a live issue.[44]

The Dynamics of Indian Political Factions

Sugar factories and refineries constitute another important and developing industry in the State,[45] and sugarcane production is another object of conflict. While this industry is not as significant as cotton within the State – in terms of its contribution to the State's factory sector – nevertheless, Maharashtra's share in national sugarcane production is considerable and constitutes another source of foreign exchange. The Maharashtra sugar industry ranks first in India in terms of the number of factories, and it is second only to Uttar Pradesh in terms of productive capital, employment and value added.[46] It is also pertinent to note that the growth of this industry in Maharashtra was impressive in the period between 1959 and 1961, immediately preceding the factional dispute with which this study is concerned.[47]

In comparison with other industries in the State, the sugar industry ranked rather low. It accounted for only 6% of the productive capital, 4% of the output and 3% of the total value added by the factory sector in the State.[48] While these proportions are admittedly small, we can appreciate the significance of the industry when we consider that sugarcane was grown on only 1% of the gross cropped area in the State. We may recall that the average acreage for cotton was 29%. Seen in this light, sugarcane appears to be a very profitable crop indeed.

Western Maharashtra is the largest sugarcane area, and Poona is one of the important sugar areas in the region.[49] While most of the other districts in the State also cultivate this lucrative commercial crop, the acreage is negligible as a proportion of the gross cropped area, not exceeding one percent. In terms of the total number of acres under sugarcane, Marathwada ranks second, after the Deccan area. Aurangabad is the top sugarcane producer in Marathwada.[50]

It is no accident, then, that in Poona, as we shall see, it was the sugar interests which were involved in the factional struggle. And in Aurangabad we shall find that one of the rival groups was associated with the cash crop areas of the district, where cotton and sugarcane are among the important crops in the commercial category.

It is worth noting that some of the most important business enterprises have significant interests in this agro-industry.[51] One of these business groups owns the largest sugar factory in Poona.*

* The Walchand group, which ranks eighth in terms of paid-up capital and eleventh in terms of total assets owned, owns Walchandnagar Industries which, in turn, owns the sugar factory in Poona.[54]

The Argument

The remaining two sugar factories (in 1961, prior to the factional struggle) were cooperatives, and their combined crushing and employment capacity equaled or was less than that of the private factory.[52] Among its diverse interests in ten different industrial fields, sugar is the third most important activity for this business house, in terms of aggregate turnover.[53]

In Aurangabad, the only sugar factory is a private one, owned by another of the largest industrial groups in the country.* Yet another – the seventh largest business complex in the country, located in Bombay – was one of many which had an interest in the sugar industry.† This group, moreover, owned a big publishing firm. The *Times of India* and the *Economic Times* (see above) were important Bombay dailies published by this firm.

The sugar industry provides us with a very good illustration of the links between industry and the press, and the manner in which pressure can be exerted on the government by important economic interests. In 1960–1, a bill was pending in the Maharashtra Legislature which proposed to fix limits on very large landholdings. Under the provisions of this Ceilings Act, the private sugar factories in Maharashtra stood to lose 60,000 acres of land,‡[57] more than half of the total surplus land which the Act was expected to yield, according to the Revenue Minister of the Government of Maharashtra.[58] A concerted propaganda campaign was launched by the private sugar interests in an effort to defeat this Bill. Spokesmen for the Maharashtra Chamber of Commerce and other business associations, as well as representatives of the Swatantra Party, spoke in opposition to the Bill, either before Government agencies or in public meetings.

In a typical editorial, the *Times of India* lashed out against the proposal, stating that the sugar interests were 'justifiably' perturbed by the pending measure. It suggested that the forthcoming national Congress Session should urge the state governments to proceed cautiously with 'ceiling and cooperative' measures.[59] In subsequent editorials and articles, it criticised the Bill for not exempting from the ceiling requirement the sugarcane farms owned or managed by sugar factories. When the Government stood firm on the issue, the

---

* Shapoorji Pallonji owns the Gangapur Sugar Mills in Aurangabad.[55]
† This was the Sahu–Jain group.[56]
‡ The cooperative sugar factories' farms were exempted from the application of ceilings provisions.[61]

industry responded by delaying planting of high quality sugarcane, and many plants stopped improvement works in their farms. Mills were closed and sugar stock prices fell as production slowed down.[60] Nevertheless, the Bill was enacted in June 1961, and presumably the private sugar factories did lose a good deal of land. (Of course, there is no easy way of ascertaining whether the provisions of the Act were conscientiously implemented or not.)

For purposes of illustration, I have dealt with only two items which could conceivably be 'objects of conflict', since both agriculturists who cultivate sugar and/or cotton and industrialists who process and sell these products share a common interest in such crops. Other agricultural products which are used in industry and could thus be considered potential 'objects of conflict' are oil seeds, which are produced largely in Western Maharashtra. These are consumed by industries producing not only edible oils but also paints and varnishes. The fruit and vegetable canning industry draws its raw material from the horticultural regions of the State, such as Vidarbha and the Konkan.

The task of identifying the common *arena* of conflict remains. Here I shall discuss the organizational structures in which the rival forces confront each other, as well as the nature of the threat issuing from certain agricultural interests.

The analysis to be undertaken in Chapters 4 to 8 will give ample evidence that cooperative-based agricultural interests, usually with a strong stake in commercial crops, constitute a distinct political group which stands in opposition to those district- or state-based authorities (either in the Congress Party or in the State Government) which are linked to some extent with private economic interests.

In view of the prominent position which large private interests occupy in the economic system, and the considerable power and influence which they command both in the system as a whole and vis-a-vis the Government, one may well ask why such colossi have anything to fear from a fledgling cooperative structure. Yet grounds for such fear exist, and I venture to say that the private economic sector has cause to be reasonably concerned.

Generally speaking, cooperatives must be viewed as actual – and potentially strong – competitors, whether they engage in lending activities, or in the marketing or processing of agricultural products. Secondly (and most importantly, perhaps, in the long run), they

The Argument

are commanding increasing attention from the Government, not only in terms of political favors, but also in terms of funds. Closely related to this is the potential threat which exists of cooperative leaders taking control of the new bodies of local government. As I have indicated, these bodies provide a very effective channel through which the rural interests controlling them can make claims on the State Government. Finally, to the extent that the threat is a real one, it must be increasingly felt because of the growth of the cooperative movement, particularly in recent years. Let us consider this element of growth first.

For various reasons, the development of the movement has been unbalanced, in the sense that growth in cooperative credit has led all other aspects of the movement. Since this is the most important cooperative activity, we shall begin by examining its development.

In the forty-year period between 1912 and 1952, there was a tremendous increase in the credit sector, and loans and advances outstanding in the Maharashtra State Cooperative Bank (the most important cooperative institution in the State) increased more than a hundredfold. In absolute terms, however, the greatest increase took place in the post-independence years. In the four-year period between 1961 and 1965, the increase in credit disbursed was about 70 % of the increase which took place in the first forty years of the Bank's existence, from 1911 to 1951.[62] In the period from 1957 to 1962, with which we are more concerned, there was a more than fourfold increase in the amount of loans and advances extended by the State Cooperative Bank.*

At the local level, the trend has been in the same direction. Between 1955–6 and 1959–60, the number of primary agricultural cooperative societies, which operate at the village level, increased by about 25 %, while the number of members increased by about 43 %.[63] There was also a considerable increase in the membership and capital of cooperative societies of all types between 1961–2 and 1964–5, as well as in the membership and loans advanced by agricultural and non-agricultural credit societies.[64] The advances made by central (district-level) cooperative banks in Maharashtra were higher than in any other state.[65]

* In terms of dollars – at the current rate of exchange – the Bank had increased its credit disbursement from about $74,000 in 1912 to about $9 million in 1952 and $85 million in 1965.

33

Thus, in every respect, there is substantial evidence that the credit cooperative structure has been gaining and continues to gain strength.[66] Moreover, there is probably considerable scope for further expansion of cooperative credit in the rural areas. Several years ago, a study group on cooperatives anticipated that the entire rural population could eventually be covered by cooperatives, and that almost three-quarters of its short-term credit needs could be met by the end of the Third Five Year Plan.[67] A tenfold increase in medium and long-term credit was also considered a feasible goal for the cooperative movement in the State. Another survey of economic conditions in Maharashtra, undertaken about fifteen years ago, while finding such a goal improbable, did express confidence that cooperatives would have become a major source of agricultural finance in the State by the present time.[68]

One may question whether cooperatives are a 'major' source of agricultural finance, but that they are an important one now – and increasingly so – is perhaps less open to question. Indeed, the impression conveyed by most of the cultivators (as well as party and government officials) with whom I spoke was that the moneylender was definitely a vanishing institution in the villages, though not a defunct one by any means. It should be kept in mind, of course, that the farmers with whom I spoke had moderately large landholdings, and they themselves indicated that the very small cultivator still has to depend on the moneylender to meet his agricultural and personal needs.

However, even if we concede that the moneylender's business has been adversely affected, another assertion must be dealt with. In many official and non-official surveys, it has been observed that urban economic power and influence (through the moneylender and/or trader) has infiltrated the directorates and managements of rural institutions such as cooperative societies (as well as village panchayats).[69] To the extent that this is true, it cannot be convincingly argued that the cooperative sector constitutes a real or imagined threat to private interests. However, there is no firm indication that this is the case in Maharashtra. The surveys referred to above offered little evidence that moneylenders or traders dominated – *in any significant degree* – the authority structure in cooperatives at any level in the State of Maharashtra, while several references were made confirming such a phenomenon in other states, like Kerala and Mysore.[70]

34

Although the position of cooperative marketing is better in Maharashtra than in other states, it is still not satisfactory, and certainly not as well developed as cooperative credit. Efforts to link cooperative credit with marketing have not been too successful. Thus, cultivators who receive loans from cooperative institutions – to cultivate their crops or improve their land or for other agricultural purposes – do not sell the crop produced with such aid through cooperative marketing societies.[71] The main reason is that the cooperative marketing societies do not advance enough money to the farmer against the produce accepted by them for sale. At most, they may give a cultivator 60% of the expected proceeds, and he has to wait for the remainder until the sale has been completed. The marketing society does this, of course, because it simply does not have enough money on hand to pay all the farmers who may deposit their produce with it.

The commission agent, on the other hand, who as we have seen is linked with the more affluent private credit structure, can advance the total amount of the agreed sale price to the farmer. He (i.e., the commission agent) has enough capital on hand, and therefore can afford to wait until the price rises. Then he sells the product and can realize a handsome profit. Thus it was reported that the private traders received more than 90% of the cultivators' produce on a nation-wide basis.[72] In Maharashtra the proportion of agricultural produce sold through cooperative marketing unions was a little higher than in other states, constituting about 12.5% of the total marketable surplus.[73]

Another plausible reason for the relative weakness of cooperative marketing (as well as processing), compared to cooperative credit, is that the former activities could probably expand only at the expense of the private sector in the rural areas. It may be expected, then, that opposition from private interests would be stronger and thus more effective in this case. It has, indeed, been reported by various observers that cooperative marketing activities have met with tremendous opposition in the rural areas.[74] This is understandable if we look at the situation in the light of the following facts.

One of the follow-up surveys of rural credit indicated that moneylending had been a complementary activity of the trader, merchant or very big landlord.[75] According to that report, almost two-fifths of the village moneylenders were also traders, as were 83%

of the urban moneylenders (i.e., moneylenders in nearby towns). Among the non-professional moneylenders in the villages 82 % were agriculturists, as were 49 % of the urban moneylenders. Most of the rural credit was provided by the moneylenders. Traders and commission agents also accounted for a small proportion of agricultural credit. This means that the expansion of cooperative credit, while having an adverse effect on the moneylender – e.g. forcing him to reduce his lending rates – would not cause him irreparable economic damage, as he could probably fall back on his trading or other business, or on his farm income. He could, moreover, still count on the small farmer or the landless laborer as a credit customer. The expansion of cooperatives into marketing and processing activities, on the other hand, would directly affect the private entrepreneur and could expand only at his expense (unless agricultural production increased at a much faster rate than cooperative processing and marketing, thus allowing cooperative institutions to absorb the 'new' produce without making inroads into the private sector's supplies). It is therefore interesting to note that, in a survey conducted some years ago (in 1958–9) in a Maharashtra district,[76] Daniel Thorner reported that there was in process a sharp conflict between the district marketing society and the private traders for the control of Kolhapur credit and marketing, especially in jaggery (a sugarcane product). One of Thorner's observations is especially interesting. He states:

In the current conflict, there are many powerful factors in favor of the dalals (traders), and even the officers of the local cooperatives are by no means sure that the Shetkari Sahakari Sangh (Cooperative Marketing Society) and its allies will emerge triumphant. The cultivators say in one breath that the dalals are influential with the Government, and that the Government will give the cooperatives enough backing to ensure their victory.[77]

I have singled out this statement because I believe it illustrates not necessarily confusion on the part of the farmers, but rather the conflict which exists at the State level. Thus, it is likely that the cultivators may have received intimations from elements in the State Government which were favorably inclined towards the cooperatives, thus creating one of the impressions expressed in the above quotation, while at the same time indications may have been given by those state authorities linked with private business interests that the latter would be favored.

36

The Argument

While cooperative activity in the marketing and processing sectors has been rather modest, it should be noted that there has been progress made here and, moreover, that these activities are being actively encouraged by Government.

In the marketing sector, the number of societies established increased by as much as 33% in the period between 1955–6 and 1960–1.[78] They were also beginning to undertake activities other than the marketing of agricultural produce. Some were distributing agricultural items, such as fertilizers, improved implements, seeds and so forth. In all the districts I visited, such societies were functioning and were, in fact, providing these additional services to the cultivators. More significant than the percentage increase in the number of marketing societies, however, was the volume of production marketed on a cooperative basis. Although the absolute volume was modest, nevertheless an upward trend was noted here, too.[79] Agricultural products were also marketed through various cooperative processing societies. Although there were not many such societies in the State, a substantial increase was registered in the period 1959–60 to 1960–1,* when the number of processing societies almost doubled.[80] The various categories into which these cooperative factories fell were sugar, ginning and pressing, rice mills and oil mills.

In a continuing upward trend, marketing societies in 1964–5 sold more than twice the value of goods marketed in 1961–2. A similar upward trend was noted in the volume of cotton ginned as well as in the number of cotton ginning and pressing units.[81] Sugar factories showed an increase of about 38% in the volume of sugarcane crushed, and an increase of about 36% in the volume of sugar produced.[82]

The latter figures give a good indication of the increasingly important role that cooperative sugarcane processing units are playing in the industry. While the cooperative factory sector accounted for only 12% of the country's total sugar production in 1961,[83] in Maharashtra the cooperative factories reportedly accounted for as much as 55% of the total sugarcane production.[84] It is particularly important to note that the cooperative sugar

---

* I wish to add another reminder here that often I cite statistics which may be relevant for the approximate period when the factional conflict under investigation erupted. Where figures for later periods are cited, they are usually intended to illustrate a continuing growth trend.

sector acquired this degree of prominence in the industry very quickly. Of the 13 cooperative sugar factories functioning in 1961, 12 came into existence in the three-year period between 1956–9, and the remaining one had been established in 1950.[85] On the other hand, all but one of the private sugar factories had been established between 1924 and 1942.[86] Within a short span of time, then, the private sugar sector was confronted with a young and very vigorous competitor.

Thus we find that in a few sectors of the economic sphere, such as credit and, to a lesser extent, processing and marketing, private interests were encountering competition. In addition, the private sector apparently faced and is facing competition in the politico-economic sphere, that is to say, in relation to the Government. We have already seen an indication of this in the Government's refusal to exempt the private sugar farms from the provisions of the Ceilings Act, although it exempted cooperative sugar factories from them. The Government also showed an inclination to favor cooperative farming societies by giving them priority in the distribution of the surplus lands acquired as a result of the Act.[87] There were other signs that the Government was committed to assisting the cooperative movement to expand its activities in credit, as well as in marketing and processing.* In addition to contributing to credit cooperatives' share capital, the Government has been allocating plan funds to various cooperative schemes. In the Third Plan, for example, one target was to double the proportion of marketable surplus handled by the cooperative marketing societies.[89] Funds were allocated to supplement the share capital of the marketing structure at all levels, enabling the marketing societies to give bigger advances to cultivators or even to purchase their

* Lest a distorted picture of the relationship between Government and cooperatives be conveyed here, it should be noted that there was also evidence of a competitive strain in this relationship. There was, for example, the matter of Government emphasis on small savings campaigns. At times even cooperative personnel were 'recruited' to work toward the success of such campaigns. In fact, however, the small savings program has been inimical to the cooperative structure's efforts to channel rural savings into cooperative banks for purposes of investing such capital in agricultural improvement. Small savings funds siphon off much of the rural savings. The Government supports this program because about two-thirds of the funds collected in national small savings campaigns come back to the State Governments. Thus, as much as 40% of Maharashtra's financial resources for the Third Plan were to be contributed by small savings.[88]

38

produce outright. To the extent that this becomes possible, the comparative advantage of the private middleman – the commission agent or trader – will be weakened. The Government also planned to assist in the construction of large warehouses at the state and district level, as well as medium-sized and small storage facilities at the taluka and village level.[90] Lack of such facilities has been an important handicap of the cooperative marketing organization.

In addition, Government planned to assist in the establishment of various cooperative factories which would more than double the number of ginning and pressing units, paddy processing societies and storage and preservation facilities. Cooperative sugar factories were to be increased by additional units totaling 60% of the existing number, and these were to receive more finance.[91]

Finally, the threat exists that cooperative leadership may be able eventually to capture the district governing bodies and through them to press their claims on the State Government. (This did, indeed, happen in 1962 in one of the four districts studied and was nearly successful in some of the other districts.) The fact that these local councils function at the district level is advantageous for the cooperatives inasmuch as all (including the two most important) cooperative agencies carry out their executive functions at the district level as well. The district credit cooperative provides a ready means by which cooperative leaders can extend their economic influence into the political sphere.

THE RELEVANCE OF THE ZILLA PARISHAD IN STATE POLITICS

Earlier, I indicated that the principle around which government is organized is functional, while that of the party organization is territorial. In the Zilla Parishad these principles converge. Congressmen, whether or not favored by the district party organization, may occupy positions of authority in this governing body, and 'wheel and deal' in a rich variety of favors and material goods, from appointments to teaching or other posts, to seeds, fertilizers, implements and construction material used for agricultural purposes, such as cement, tin or steel sheets. This gives Z.P. Congressmen a decided edge over non-Z.P. Congress party workers in mobilizing the support of voters for or against a political candidate, whether an incumbent M.L.A. or Minister or an aspirant.

The Dynamics of Indian Political Factions

The possibility exists, then, that the Z.P.s may replace the Congress organization as the agency through which the rural vote is organized.* Indeed many claim that they have already done so. Thus, where aspiring decision-makers have had to depend in the past on the Congress organization to achieve their instrumental goals, now they must curry the favor of the powerful Zilla Parishad leaders. Indeed, the feeling was expressed by many Z.P. officials and members – both Rebel and Loyalist – that Government could not easily or for long ignore the Councils' demands, since it depends on them to carry out many State projects. The Z.P. machinery has, in fact, been entrusted with the implementation of a great variety of projects. Thus, for example, in the fourth year of the Third Plan of Maharashtra, we find that the proportion of Plan funds for major developmental headings allocated to the Zilla Parishads was as much as 43% (see Table 3 below, p. 44). These Councils, therefore, are in a position to aid or obstruct the efforts of aspiring and incumbent authoritative decision-makers in regard to both the instrumental and the societal goals toward which their activities may be directed.

The significance of this, for private economic interests, is that to the extent that the Zilla Parishads can or will be able to exert influence on the Government the influence which can be exerted by the economic community is minimized or challenged (particularly in the event that the Z.P.s are controlled by cooperative-based economic interests). It is highly likely, moreover, that the new rural politicians will not remain satisfied for long with the scope of authority exercised by them in the various subjects entrusted to their care. In their very first term of office, they gave evidence of

* There were many opportunities which Congressmen (especially office-holders) could exploit toward this end. The following provides only one illustration. Members of the opposition in some Zilla Parishads complained that Congressmen would often invite themselves along on tours made by administrative officers in connection with the execution of various projects. In the course of such tours, a Congressman might enter the constituency of an opposition member where he could make contact with the local people and imply or expressly suggest to them that the work being carried out by the Z.P. staff was made possible through Congress initiative. Continuous application of such stimuli could undoubtedly produce over time a favorable attitude toward the Congress Party, or at least persuade or intimidate the local people into thinking that it would be wise to support Congressmen. At the same time, it is the Z.P. Congressman, rather than the non-Z.P. Congress party worker, who can more readily oblige the rural voter and thus rely more confidently on his political support.

40

The Argument

their confidence and ambition to expand their activities. The Poona Zilla Parishad, for example, requested the Government to be allowed to set up a Hume Pipe factory. (These pipes are used in irrigation projects to carry water from canals or rivers to the fields.) The State Government firmly refused to allow the District Council to undertake such an activity.* The highest government authorities indicated to me that they had quashed this project because it would harm important business interests.[92] What were the business interests involved? An examination uncovered the existence of a big Hume Pipe factory in Poona which, interestingly enough, was owned by the same large business group that owned the big private sugar factory in Poona (see above, p. 30). Similar reasons were given by Departmental and Ministry spokesmen for their refusal to sanction a demand made by the Aurangabad Zilla Parishad to be allowed to run a petrol (gas) pump.

It is invariably claimed that rural bodies do not wish to raise land revenues. However, a request to do so was addressed to the Government of Maharashtra by the District Councils. According to Article 156 of the Zilla Parishads Act, these bodies are (or were) empowered to pass a resolution proposing an increase in the rate of land revenue.[93] Apparently 23 out of 25 Zilla Parishads submitted just such a resolution to the State Government, according to some knowledgeable Zilla Parishad officials. In 1964, however, an amendment to the Act was passed by the State Legislature, deleting this provision. Departmental spokesmen said that there would be an uneven distribution of the revenue burden, if some districts demanded (and were allowed) such increases while others did not. Another possible reason (which is mere conjecture) is that such an increase would affect the very large landowners more than any other landowning group. (In this respect, it is worth repeating that the Councillors in the four Zilla Parishads covered in this study fell in a moderate range, as far as landholding size is concerned. (See Table 1.) As much as 9% of the land owned in the four districts studied here was in the hands of 0.3% of the landowning units. More importantly, these units are in the size range of 150 acres and over. The all-state figures are approximately the same.

* It is amusing to note that (according to a Poona Z.P. official), the construction of Hume Pipes was undertaken anyway, but camouflaged in the institutional guise of a Lift Irrigation Society (another type of cooperative) which was organized for that purpose after the Government's rejection of the Council's request.

The Dynamics of Indian Political Factions

TABLE 1. *Average Size of Landholding Owned by Respondents on a District-wise and All-District Basis*

Area	Number of acres owned (Mean)
All Districts	90
Ratnagiri	34
Poona	100
Aurangabad	59
Akola	145

TABLE 2. *Landholding Pattern Comparing Large with Small Landholdings*

Ratnagiri, Poona, Aurangabad and Akola	All Size Ranges	Size Range: 150 Acres or More	Size Range: 1 Acre (or Less) to 7.5 Acres
No. of Holdings	868,035	2,976	509,247
No. of Acres Owned	10,591,614	995,622	1,371,043
% of Holdings	100.0	0.3	59.0
% of Acres Owned	100.0	9.0	13.0
Maharashtra			
No. of Holdings	4,337,903	13,335	2,041,487
No. of Acres Owned	51,828,126	4,071,197	4,270,659
% of Holdings	100.0	0.3	47.0
% of Acres Owned	100.0	8.0	8.0

SOURCES:

For Ratnagiri: *Census of India 1961, District Census Handbook – Ratnagiri* (Compiled by the Maharashtra Census Office), (Bombay: 1964), Table 10, p. 257.

For Poona: *Census of India 1961, District Census Handbook – Poona* (Compiled by the Maharashtra Census Office), (Bombay: 1966), Table 10, p. 264.

For Aurangabad: *Census of India 1961, District Census Handbook – Aurangabad* (Compiled by the Maharashtra Census Office), (Bombay: 1964), Table 10, p. 251.

For Akola: *Census of India 1961, District Census Handbook – Akola* (Compiled by the Maharashtra Census Office), (Bombay: 1964), Table 10, p. 207.

The Argument

By contrast, it may be noted that just about the same amount of land (8%) is owned by 47% of all landholders in Maharashtra, and that these plots range in size from an acre (or less) to 7.5 acres. (See Table 2.) Thus, an increase in land revenue would place much of the burden on very large landowners, who are probably politically influential people whom the Government may not wish to antagonize.

SOME OBSERVATIONS

The Government of Maharashtra is committed to a socialist pattern of society[94] which assigns a central position to the cooperative principle of economic organization.[95] Because of this ideological commitment, and its apparent appeal among increasingly important elements of the population, official references to the cooperative movement are always positively weighted. This may explain Government's efforts to assist in the development of the movement. At the same time, however, it is committed to the goal of economic development and industrialization and therefore has to seek the assistance and support of the private economic community, which controls an important part of the resources required to achieve the societal goal of industrial development. Beyond a certain point, the expansion of cooperative economic activity is bound to encroach upon the sphere of private economic interests. In such circumstances, it will become increasingly difficult to accommodate the conflicting demands of these two 'constituencies'. One may speculate that recognition of this possibility may have prompted the vacillating or contradictory actions which the Government of Maharashtra has taken from time to time. For example, it has on the one hand offered incentives to private sugar interests* and on the other attempted to aid cooperative sugar factories, imposing ceilings on private sugarcane holdings while exempting cooperative factories' farms from the application of such provisions; imposing a tax on the production of private sugar factories but not on the cooperative units.[96]

* Between 1958 and 1960, the price per weight unit paid to growers was increased, and a 50% rebate in basic excise duties was granted to the industry on production exceeding the average of the past two seasons.[97] Technically, this incentive was enjoyed by both the private and the cooperative sugar factories. However, with regard to the latter incentive in particular, the benefit would likely accrue to the private factories which had been in production for some years, while the cooperative factories had only just started production and would not get much of a rebate.

43

TABLE 3. *Revised Budget Estimates, 1965-6, of Expenditure for Schemes in the State Five-Year Plan and Similar Revised Estimates for the Same Year, on Schemes Transferred to Zilla Parishads and Panchayat Samitis*

Major Head of Expenditure	Estimated Expenditure on Schemes in the State Five-Year Plan	Estimated Expenditure on Schemes Transferred to Zilla Parishads and Panchayat Samitis
	(Amounts in Rupees)	
Education	150,588,060	98,628,500
Public Health	37,799,000	1,758,000
Agriculture	160,898,700	68,185,300
Animal Husbandry	15,079,000	1,164,000
Cooperation	24,209,900	398,800
Community Development Projects, N.E.S. and Local Development Works	96,181,000	75,627,000
Irrigation	38,107,000	25,800,000
Public Works	35,777,500	7,149,400
State Road Fund	92,608,000	41,069,700
	651,248,100	279,773,700

Percentage of Total Estimated Expenditure on Schemes in the State Five-Year Plan on the Above Subjects Transferred to Zilla Parishads and Panchayat Samitis, 42.9

SOURCE: *Government of Maharashtra, Detailed Estimates of the State Five-Year Plan Schemes For The Year 1966-67.*

It was intriguing to find that this ambivalence with regard to socialist principles is also reflected in some of the attitudes of the respondents analyzed in this study. As many as 49%, for example, ranked 'private property' last among the individual rights guaranteed by the Indian Constitution. Another 17% ranked it next to last. Thus, a total of 66% of the respondents ostensibly viewed the right to private property as one of the least important of all the rights guaranteed by the Constitution (see Table 4). Yet most of them were fairly well-to-do farmers, with considerable private property in the form of land, houses or agricultural equipment. One of the few Congressmen who ranked private property first said, almost apologetically, that he knew this was against the

44

principles of the Party, but that, nevertheless, he placed a high value on the right to own private property.

TABLE 4. *Ranking of the Constitutional Right to Private Property According to Respondents' Perceived Order of Importance*

Rank Sample size:	All Districts 171 (%)		Ratnagiri 51 (%)		Poona 36 (%)		Aurangabad 41 (%)		Akola 43 (%)	
First	4	2	—	—	3	8	—	—	1	2
Second	10	6	3	5	2	6	4	10	1	2
Third	8	5	3	5	—	0	2	5	3	7
Fourth	23	13	5	10	5	14	6	14	7	17
Fifth	13	8	4	8	4	11	3	7	2	5
Sixth	29	17	6	12	3	8	11	27	9	20
Seventh	84	49	30	60	19	53	15	37	20	47

The expansion of credit may not create much of a disturbance, but as cooperative activities begin to expand into marketing and processing, we may expect political conflict to become much sharper in Maharashtra than it has been thus far.

After a discussion of empirical analytical concepts and methods used here, the validity of the argument expounded in this chapter will be examined in each of the districts studied (individually and collectively) with a view to determining its applicability at the district level.

CHAPTER 3

POLITICAL INTEGRATION: EMPIRICAL CONCEPTION AND METHOD OF ANALYSIS

In the previous chapter, I suggested that political factionalism defines a condition lacking integration. Political integration has been described as a 'relationship of community among people within the same political entity' who are held together by 'mutual ties...which give the group a feeling of identity and awareness.'[*1]

Although the Congress government and party organization in Maharashtra have been generally considered among the few in the Indian states which enjoy a satisfactory degree of political integration, this study will demonstrate that latent conflicts exist within the Maharashtrian polity which may, within the next five or ten years, threaten the stability of the political system, at least insofar as that stability has been ensured by a heretofore unified Congress Party. I propose to establish that these underlying tensions were manifested in the factional formations observed in the course of this study, and that these factions were developing their own 'feelings of identity and self-awareness', centered around conflicting interests.

In order to substantiate these claims, it is necessary to establish initially that each of the groups to which I refer does, in fact, have some (significant) degree of cohesion which distinguishes it from the other. This directs me toward a search for visible attributes of cohesion which could conceivably generate divisive feelings between the groups.

Toward this purpose, I have examined a limited number of factors which may suggest the sources of disruptive influences on

---

* Note that Parsons (see Ch. 2) has defined integration as, essentially, a *process* of interaction among the parts of a system, while Jacob's definition speaks of a *relationship...among people*. Both, of course, are talking about the same phenomenon, each examining it from a different perspective. Parsons is viewing impersonal units in relation to one another, while Jacob focusses on personal units.

46

the political system under examination, or which may at least establish useful guidelines for future studies of this kind.

Several factors have been suggested as empirical measures of political integration.[2] Among them are the following which I consider relevant to this study: (1) homogeneity; (2) mutuality of interests; (3) shared functional interests; and (4) the 'motive' pattern of a group. Actually, the last three may also be regarded as measures of homogeneity, broadly speaking. In that sense, we may look upon all of them as cognate factors.

Social, economic and political characteristics of the political actor's environment have been included among the indicators of *homogeneity*. The assumption is that common distinctive features of the social environment within which particular groups function tend to create manifest or latent feelings of group identity, which may provide a basis for common political action. (Or, conversely, socio-economic heterogeneity among two or more groups could provide the setting for political conflict.) These features have been categorized as *environmental* variables. They may include such characteristics as the relative level of urbanization in the respondent's taluka; or the proximity of respondent's village to certain political or communication centers; or they may describe political or economic characteristics of the respondent's taluka, such as the potential level of opposition to the Congress Party, or the average size of landholdings.*

Secondly, it is assumed that a *mutuality of interests*, as suggested by, among other things, common economic attributes of individuals, may be seen as an index of political integration by virtue of the fact that these attributes define 'mutual ties' which may give a particular group a 'feeling of identity and awareness'. (Such a feeling would, by implication, posit a polarized relationship with those who do not share similar interests – or at least would suggest that possibility.) These attributes are hereafter referred to as the respondent's *economic background*. Here we would find indicators of the respondent's personal economic status, such as the size and value of his farm, the extent of irrigation on his landholding, the extent of cash crop cultivation, or the value of various assets.

* For a precise enumeration of the *environmental* characteristics, as well as the remaining categories of variables referred to above and on the following pages, please see the *Note on Methodology*, pp. 215–17, below.

The Dynamics of Indian Political Factions

Recognition of such a mutuality of interests, moreover, may be reflected in the undertaking of similar activities designed to further such interests. Activities of this type may be considered indices of common *functional interests*. Membership or, more importantly, office in credit cooperative institutions could be an indicator of shared functional interests. Political party or government office may also be interpreted as a potential vehicle for the promotion of functional interests. As we are dealing here with an individual's *activities* (undertaken in various official roles), the indices of functional interests included are described as *behavioral* variables.*

Finally, it is suggested that factional behavior may be explained by examining a group's 'motive' pattern, its shared or common attitudes which (together with its values) are described as energizers of political action. Indices of the selected political predispositions, feelings and views of an individual are here grouped together under the term *attitudes*. We are concerned here mainly with identifying positive or negative postures toward political or governmental authority.

In the chapters which follow I have tried to isolate and identify among a set of hypothetical influences one or more which apparently determine membership in one observed political group as against another, in each of the districts studied. The empirical identification was made on the basis of data gathered through a uniformly structured interview (see Appendix 1, *A Note on Methodology*), and on the basis of information compiled from printed primary sources.† All of the *environmental* variables were drawn from official sources. The items included in the last three categories above (*economic background, behavioral* and *attitudinal* variables) were derived from the interview data. These were subjected to discriminant analysis (see *Note on Methodology*), as were

* It may be noted that the first category of variables described above deals with *environmental* stimulants of a sense of identity more remote from the political actor than those of the second and third categories; that is, particular economic attributes, or politico-economic roles which are assumed in order to pursue functional interests, are part of the more immediate 'environment' of political actors. In Parsons' action theory, such characteristics – of the immediate or more remote environment – may be said to define the 'situation' of action, and they are distinguishable from the energizers of action which are subjective feelings, beliefs or values.[3]

† This material was supplemented by background information obtained through unstructured interviews with respondents and others (journalists or civil servants, for example) regarding the intricate details of local politics.

48

Political Integration

constituency and village measures of 'homogeneity'.* Other *environmental* characteristics which refer to the *taluka* unit, however, were first subjected to factor analysis; thereafter, composite factor scores were computed (for each respondent) which were subsequently used in the major analysis.

The statistical techniques employed served two purposes: (1) to reduce the large number of variables yielded by the sources noted above to more manageable proportions; and (2) to analyze selected variables in order to determine whether they could be considered reliable discriminators between members of the two factional groups. Factor analysis and cross-tabulation were used primarily for the former purpose, and discriminant analysis for the latter. The substantive aspects of these methods are briefly described below.†

Factor analysis[4] is a procedure (or rather a series of procedures) used to analyze the intercorrelations within a set of variables. The application of this technique may vary, depending on the user's needs.[5] Here, it was used in order to determine whether there might be a small number of 'factors' underlying the forty-two measures of social and economic attributes‡ characteristic of the respondents' areas of origin.§ Once these variables were reduced to fewer dimensions, it was possible to use these 'factors' for purposes of discriminant analysis in the same way as individual variables are used.¶

The cross-tabulating technique used was a correlating procedure suitable for qualitative data.[6] It measures the degree of association between two (or more) variables, and provides a test of significance

* A village-level measure may refer to the distance from various focal points, such as Zilla Parishad or Panchayat Samiti headquarters. The latter is the middle level of the three-tiered structure of local government. In Maharashtra, this is usually coterminous with the taluka (or revenue) unit, except in the eight districts of Vidarbha (the Nagpur Division) where the relatively oversized talukas were divided into two or three units, each of which was assigned to the jurisdiction of one Panchayat Samiti. Other focal points from which respondents' villages may be more or less isolated would be railway or bus stations.

† For a more detailed exposition of the various methods of analysis used, please see *Note on Methodology*.

‡ Please see Table A in Appendix 1 (*Note on Methodology*) for a listing of these variables (pp. 209–10).

§ The taluka is the unit described by all of these measures. The respondents, collectively, represented all 46 of the taluka units in the four districts studied.

¶ See *Note on Methodology*, p. 194, for a description of the factor scoring method used.

by which that association may be evaluated.* Thus, the relative strength of the association between factional alignment and any number of other variables could be tested. Where the association appeared to be very weak, a decision was made to eliminate the variable or variables involved.

All the variables thus selected were submitted to discriminant analysis. Essentially, what this technique does is to 'predict' or to identify an individual's membership in one of two (or more) groups. This identification is based on a composite score assigned to the individual which reflects a whole set of attributes, examined simultaneously. To put it in another way, this technique enables us to know whether the groups we have observed are from a single (homogeneous) population rather than two (or more). The (independent) 'predictor' measures for each individual are reduced to a single discriminant score that can be located along a single discriminant line for members of both groups. *Each* group's (derived) profile can then be described in terms of a single 'canonical variate' instead of 47 variables. Thus, each respondent's group membership has been 'predicted' on the basis of 47† individual and broad ecological features shared in common – to a greater or lesser degree – with other group members. It is on the basis of such findings that interpretive statements have been made in the area analyses regarding the bases, as well as the strength or weakness, of factional alignments.

A few observations are in order here regarding the strength, predictive scope and stability of each variable cluster, and the relative predictability of each factional group. The commentary which follows is intended to provide the reader with some useful yardsticks for evaluating the district analyses of factional formations which follow this chapter.

* Table B in the *Note on Methodology* lists all the variables which were tested for association with factional membership, and the level of significance is shown for those variables which did correlate highly with factional alignment.

† Actually, all 47 variables were not used simultaneously at any one time. As indicated earlier, they were grouped into four categories, and the discriminant analysis test was executed first for each of the variable clusters separately. Then, those indices within a cluster which were found to discriminate 'significantly' between factions were grouped with similarly 'significant' variables from each of the other clusters. (See footnote on page 199, below, for interpretation of 'significance' in this context.) A final test was executed wherein the 'predictor' cluster consisted of 'significant' variables from each of the four variable categories. Thus, we have, in effect, a total of five tests or variable clusters which were used to determine or 'predict' factional alignments.

Political Integration

The 'strength' of a variable cluster refers to its capacity to explain variance between groups, that is, to discriminate between Rebels and Loyalists. It is interpreted on the basis of the canonical correlation coefficient. The higher the canonical correlation, the greater the variance accounted for (see *Note on Methodology*). This also means that the features which distinguish one group from the other are more pronounced than if a lower value had been registered for the canonical correlation.

The relative strength of a variable cluster is reflected also in its 'predictive scope'. This refers to the ability of that cluster to classify correctly a certain proportion of the *total* sample of respondents in both groups. Generally, when the 'strength' of a variable cluster is high, we find that the proportion of respondents accurately classified is also quite high.

The 'predictability' of each group refers to the percentage of correct classifications of Rebels and Loyalists. This may be interpreted as a measure of the homogeneity within each group. Obviously, if large numbers in a given collection of individuals share certain characteristics (and this is what a group classification tells us), we are dealing, by definition, with a homogeneous group (in terms of these characteristics, at least).

The 'stability' of a variable cluster refers, on the other hand, to the evenness with which the group classifications are made. It is inferred from the range between percentages of correct classifications for each group. Thus, if a given cluster of variables is able to accurately classify, let us say, 80% of the Loyalists and only 10% of the Rebels, we may conclude that this cluster does not have a very even predictive capacity. If, on the other hand, we find that it classifies all the Rebels and all the Loyalists correctly (or half of both, or none of either group), we may reasonably conclude that this cluster of variables is an extremely stable (*though not necessarily effective*) predictor of factional alignments.

In addition to the canonical correlation coefficient and the percentage of correct classifications for each group, two other statistics are relevant in interpreting the nature of political alignments. One is the 'coefficient for the canonical variable' and the other the absolute group mean.

The canonical variable is a composite derived from certain correlation procedures which test, in a step-wise fashion, the relationship between independent predictor measures (of the analytically

51

derived groups) and dependent test measures (of the observed groups). The step-wise procedure ultimately reduces the variable measures in each group to a single measure. A set of 'coefficients for the canonical variable' is then computed for each of the significant variables in a given cluster. Each of these 'coefficients' serves as a weight for the individual respondent's variable scores. Through these, an individual's discriminant score can be computed, which tells us whether he is a member of one or the other group. The higher the value of this coefficient (which is somewhat akin to a regression coefficient), the more effective it will be in discriminating between groups. Hence, we can make inferences about the relative predictive strength of individual variables by ranking their coefficients for the canonical variable.*

Having determined that a variable has a relatively high discriminating capacity, we check the absolute (observed) group mean value to see which group has the higher average score on that variable. Thus, for example, while the 'coefficient for the canonical variable' may indicate that the 'number of acres owned' by an individual in a given area will help us to differentiate sharply between Rebels and Loyalists, the absolute group mean on that variable (for each of the two groups) will tell us which of the two factional groups contains on the average the bigger landowners, thereby suggesting a possible base for group identification, or conversely, a possible source of conflict between groups.

Finally, the 'within-group correlations' statistic† gives us some information which may corroborate, clarify and, in general, add dimension to the basic findings regarding discriminants of factional groups. Very roughly speaking, this statistic, computed from group means and deviations, tells us about the correlation between variances within groups, on any two variables.‡

Now, I wish to comment briefly upon the precise standing and strength of my findings about the four districts surveyed, in the context of some of the terms discussed above. The commentary

---

* See page 199 below.

† For a more elaborate explanation of this statistic, see William W. Cooley and Paul R. Lohnes, *Multivariate Procedures for the Behavioral Sciences*. (New York, John Wiley & Sons, Inc., 1962), Chapter 4.

‡ Please note that the tables showing 'within-group correlations', as well as those indicating the absolute group means mentioned above, appear in two separate appendices at the end of Chapter 9. Each appendix contains all of the relevant information for each of the districts individually and for all districts combined.

Political Integration

TABLE A. *Strength, Predictive Scope, Predictability and Stability of Variable Clusters on a District-wise and All-District Basis**

Sample

	Rebels	Loyalists
Ratnagiri	16	17
Poona	10	30
Aurangabad	12	31
Akola	35	9
All Districts	73	87

	Ratnagiri	Poona	Aurangabad	Akola	All Districts
Combined Variables					
Strength	70	69	72	52	25
Predictive	96	97.5	95	90	76
scope (no. identified out of total sample)	(32/33)	(39/40)	(41/43)	(40/44)	(121/160)
Predictability	100/94	90/100	91/98	94/77	73/78
Stability	6	10	7	17	5
Environment					
Strength	50	44	44	22	17
Predictive scope	79	88	84	80	73
(no. identified out of total sample)	(26/33)	(35/40)	(36/43)	(35/44)	(117/160)
Predictability	81/76	70/93	75/87	77/88	67/78
Stability	5	23	12	11	11
Behavior					
Strength	38	49	61	26	10
Predictive scope	82	88	90	79	60
(no. identified out of total sample)	(27/33)	(35/40)	(39/43)	(35/44)	(96/160)
Predictability	75/88	80/90	75/98	88/44	57/62
Stability	13	10	23	44	5
Economic Background					
Strength	25	50	13	14	13
Predictive scope	64	90	65	64	69
(no. identified out of total sample)	(21/33)	(36/40)	(28/43)	(28/44)	(110/160)
Predictability	50/76	70/97	50/70	68/44	60/77
Stability	26	27	20	24	17
Attitudes					
Strength	37	25	10	36	12
Predictive scope	76	72	70	84	65
(no. identified out of total sample)	(25/33)	(29/40)	(30/43)	(37/44)	(104/160)
Predictability	75/76	100/63	75/68	83/88	68/62
Stability	1	37	7	5	6

* Description of terms used:
Strength: % of variance accounted for.
Predictive scope: % of accurate classifications (and number of respondents accurately identified out of total sample).
Predictability: % of Rebels and % of Loyalists accurately predicted, respectively.
Stability: Range between % of Rebels and % of Loyalists predicted.

The Dynamics of Indian Political Factions

which follows will only highlight the strengths and weaknesses of particular clusters in general and with reference to particular districts. For a more thorough examination of the relevant statistics, please see Table A.

STRENGTH

For each of the districts investigated, the *combined variables* cluster* was generally found to be the strongest discriminant of factional alignments, explaining more of the variance between groups than any other single category of variables. It was uniformly high in all of the districts. (The lowest score was registered in Akola, where only a little over 50% of the variance was accounted for, in contrast to approximately 70% in each of the remaining three districts.)

Environmental, behavioral and *attitudinal* variables accounted, individually, for at least 35% or more of the variance in at least two of the four districts. In Ratnagiri, Poona and Aurangabad, *environment* could explain 50% (in the first district) and 44% (in the remaining two), respectively, of the variance among respondents. The *behavioral* variables accounted for 38%, 49% and 61%, respectively, of the variance among respondents in these three districts, while *attitudes* could explain 37% and 36% of the variance in Ratnagiri and Akola, respectively.

In all but one of the districts, the *economic background* cluster of variables registered a low discriminating capacity, explaining only 13–25% of the variance. In Poona, however, the economic attributes of respondents accounted for 50% of the variance among them.

It is significant to note that at the all-district level,† none of the variable clusters displayed any discriminating capacity above 25%. This is merely noted at this stage, and some of the possible reasons will be explored in Chapter 8 when cross-district comparisons and broad interpretations of the findings are undertaken.

With regard to the individual districts also, few tests were able to reach the strength, predictive scope, predictability or stability of

---

* This is the fifth cluster (mentioned above) comprising variables found to be significant discriminators of factional alignment (by reference to the coefficient for the canonical variable) when each of the *environmental, behavioral, economic background*, and *attitudinal* variable clusters were tested.

† This refers to the analyses computed on Rebels and Loyalists from all districts combined.

the *combined variables* cluster. The closest any one cluster came to the 70% discriminating strength of the *combined variables* (attained in 3 out of 4 districts) was 61%; this percentage of variance was explained by the *behavioral* cluster in Aurangabad. The lowest discriminating capacity for any one category of variables was registered at 10% – also in Aurangabad – by the *attitudinal* cluster, and at the all-district level, by the *behavioral* cluster.

PREDICTIVE SCOPE, PREDICTABILITY AND STABILITY

The predictive scope, which tells us the proportion of accurate 'predictions' or classifications as a percentage of the *total* sample (i.e., of both Rebels and Loyalists), generally reflects the strength of a particular variable cluster. Thus, the *combined variables* cluster, which accounted for approximately 70% of the variance in three out of four districts (see above), was also responsible for classifying correctly over 95% of the respondents in each of those districts. This proportion, however, does not differentiate between the percentage of respondents accurately classified in one group as against the other. Thus, we cannot compare the accuracy of classifications in one factional group as against the other within a given district, or of the same factional grouping across all districts. The predictability of each group allows us to do that and also to make some rough estimate of the stability or evenness with which a variable cluster accurately classifies respondents into their respective (observed) groupings.

For example, we can say that the *combined variables* cluster is a very accurate classifier of respondents: 90% to 100% of Rebels and Loyalists were accurately identified in all districts, with the single exception of Akola Loyalists (and, in general, of respondents at the all district level). Moreover, unlike their counterparts in the other districts, respondents in Akola were unevenly predicted, proportionately speaking: 94% of the Rebels were properly classified by the *combined variables* cluster, as against 77% for the Loyalists.

As far as the remaining variable clusters are concerned, their ability to predict accurately the proportion of respondents in each of their respective groups, and to do so evenly across both groups in each district, varied considerably from cluster to cluster and from district to district. The *attitudinal* variables, for example, together with the *economic background* cluster, were not only poor discriminators of factional alignments, but also poor, as well as uneven, classifiers of respondents into their respective groups.

It would appear, then, that, next to the *combined variables* cluster, the strongest discriminators of factional alignments, as well as the most accurate and stable classifiers of respondents, were the *environmental* and *behavioral* variables in the individual district analyses, and more particularly in Ratnagiri, Poona and Aurangabad.

Having commented upon the strength and standing of my findings in terms of variable clusters, I feel it might be useful for the reader to bear in mind similar guideposts about the strength of findings, organized along district lines.

The most sharply outlined and most homogeneous factional groups in terms of all or most variable clusters were those in Poona and Ratnagiri. In Poona, particularly, the amount of variance accounted for by each of the variable clusters was generally high, as was the percentage of accurate classifications in one or both of the factional groupings. This was also true, though slightly less so, in Ratnagiri, which was further distinguished by the general evenness of factional identifications. In general, then, we may say that both Rebels and Loyalists in Poona and Ratnagiri were highly predictable and homogeneous groups, and appeared to be in the process of crystallizing into distinctive and stable factions.

The Aurangabad factions, on the other hand, while very sharply outlined in terms of *environmental* and *behavioral* characteristics, were not easily distinguishable by *attitudinal* and *economic background* traits. All in all, both Rebels and Loyalists in Aurangabad were rather unstable in the broad range of characteristics defining their respective groups, though highly homogeneous and sharply defined if we consider only the *behavioral* and *environmental* traits of respondents.

The weakest findings yielded by this analysis were those for Akola District. The discriminating capacity of the various tests was relatively poor, as compared to other districts. Within the district, however, we find that it was the Loyalists who, on the whole, were the less stable and less homogeneous group. The Rebels were more readily identified by most categories of attributes and were particularly well-predicted by the *combined variables* cluster. Compared to the other districts, however, the tests used here to measure differences between the two groups were not quite as effective, which suggests that the differences between the average Rebel and Loyalist were not as sharp here as in some of the other districts. (Or perhaps this suggests that other measures might be more effective in differentiating between the two groups.) In other words, the outlines of these groups had not hardened to the extent that they had in some of the other districts (at least not in terms of the characteristics examined here).

As indicated earlier, at the all-district level the tests proved most deficient in discriminating between factional alliances and in adequately identifying respondents as members of their observed groupings. This suggests that the Rebels and Loyalists were not as homogeneous at the all-district level as they appeared in their respective districts, nor as sharply defined. That is to say, not as many Rebels, for example, shared as many common characteristics when pooled together from all areas as when examined in their individual districts. This was also true – though to a somewhat lesser extent – of Loyalists. In addition, the characteristics which were shared by members of one group or the other, on this inclusive level, did not differ quite sufficiently to distinguish each group sharply from the other. However, identifications of factional membership were evenly, if not effectively, made by each of the variable clusters. Thus, approximately the same proportions of Rebels and Loyalists shared a given set of characteristics.

By way of introducing the reader to the analyses which follow, I would like to conclude this chapter with some final observations regarding the substantive findings.

While the factions in each district differ demonstrably from their counterparts in other districts, it will yet be found that in terms of one basic dimension they are the same or similar. In particular, it will be seen that the Rebel group in each district is distinguishable from the Loyalist group by its ties to cooperative institutions – whether such ties are evidenced in the group at large or among the leaders of the group. An individual district analysis, therefore, will provide the foundation upon which a meaningful comparison may be made among districts, allowing us to discern both the unique features of each district and those characteristics shared by two or more districts.

The ensuing analyses, then, provide the empirical underpinning of the argument expounded in the two opening chapters of this work. Hence, we shall be concerned hereafter with demonstrating

The Dynamics of Indian Political Factions

the proposition that the political divisions observed are ultimately based on economic factors, which are often related to other factors in some particular configuration peculiar to some area. It is not claimed that all elements of the pattern will remain the same in all areas. The fact is, as we shall see, that the precise configuration of auxiliary factors may differ from district to district. However, the common element in all districts will be of an economic nature, and it will be manifested in terms of involvement, by respondents or their leaders, in cooperative institutions.

We may now proceed to examine the factional groups within each district, beginning with Ratnagiri.

CHAPTER 4

RATNAGIRI DISTRICT: FACTIONAL ALIGNMENTS IN CONDITIONS OF POVERTY

THE SETTING: A TANGLED PATTERN OF POLITICAL AND ECONOMIC RELATIONS

In order to obtain an adequate perspective of the political situation within which factions evolved in Ratnagiri, I shall begin my discussion by sketching in some of its broad dimensions. More specifically, I shall attempt to analyze the pattern of political and economic relations which exist both horizontally, at the district level, and vertically, between the district and the State political arena. I hope subsequently to demonstrate that the pattern in these relationships complements or corresponds to that revealed by the findings of the more systematic, close-range analysis of ecological and individual characteristics. That is to say, the observations and 'hearsay' evidence introduced in this first section will, I trust, be largely substantiated or elucidated by the 'hard' analysis which will follow.

If I had relied only upon the 'inside' information or the suppositions of the leading figures in the district (and some of the lesser lights) regarding the bases of the factional alignment, I would have been confounded by the breadth and variety of divisions to which the factional dispute was traced. More than half a dozen rivalries were mentioned which, on first glance, seemed to have little or no relation to each other. A knowledge of the district, however, suggested a connection among some of these splits, and a further examination of these divisions, in themselves and in relation to each other, as well as in the light of the statistical findings, indicated that ultimately they could all be reduced to the terms which I have suggested in my main hypotheses.

Some of the usual reasons (which I mentioned in the introduction) were suggested as the cause of the factions; for example, the

59

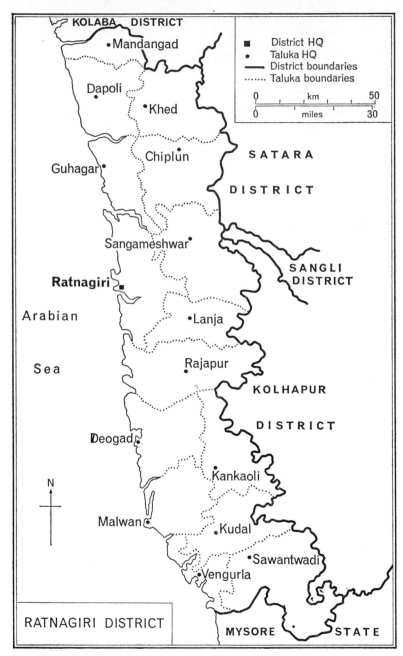

Map 2

caste factor, which pitted the Marathas against the minority non-Maratha communities. Then there was the perennial factional divide between the ministerial and the organizational wing of the party, which was incarnated in the Minister of Agriculture of the Government of Maharashtra, who was from Ratnagiri District, and the President of the Ratnagiri District Congress Committee. Some local issues were also mentioned. There was said to be a feud between the northern and southern talukas of the district (a long, narrow strip of land on the western coast of Maharashtra). Others interpreted the factional rivalry as essentially one between urban and rural talukas. Still others were certain that this was an instance of personal animosities – between members of two clans (the Sawants and the Bhosles), or within the same clan (Bhosle versus Bhosle); or that it was most decidedly a feud between Ministers: the Deputy Home Minister (D. S. (Balasaheb) Desai) and the Agriculture Minister (P. K. Sawant). What was most intriguing was the fact that there was some truth in all of these contentions. In other words, the respondents saw certain surface phenomena and reported them more or less accurately.

However, the links which joined all these apparently disparate phenomena were not immediately obvious. Indicative of this was the fact that two other issues mentioned by some respondents were not at all linked to the factional dispute; yet at least one of them was probably central to the factional struggle, and the other certainly had bearing on it. The latter concerned Ratnagiri before the Zilla Parishad was established, and had to do with the linguistic issue which agitated Maharashtrians around 1957. The political actors who had participated in the Samyukta Maharashtra movement, or against it, did not vanish from the scene, nor can we assume that the interests which motivated them to act for or against Samyukta Maharashtra dissolved upon the attainment of the movement's goal of a united Maharashtra, minus Gujerat.

The issue current at the time of the study which most effectively illustrates the nature of the interests with which each group is possibly aligned is the abolition of the octroi,* which will be discussed below.

If my hypotheses are valid, we should be able to discern an economic dimension in each of these issues, and, more importantly, to

* A tax on commodities which are being brought into or pass through a town.

The Dynamics of Indian Political Factions

associate the Loyalists and/or the Rebels* with the relevant sides of each issue.

'SAMYUKTA MAHARASHTRA' ISSUE AS SOURCE OF CONFLICT

The Samyukta Maharashtra issue contributes rather scanty information in support of our hypothesis (in part because it was not directly broached in the course of the interview but emerged in rather peripheral comments). It does, however, provide some insight regarding the economic groups with which the Loyalists might be linked. We find, for example, that a few leading Loyalist figures had supported the Government's policy, which favored merger of Maharashtra (or rather the old Bombay State) with Gujerat. This position was also supported by the major business interests of Bombay City which, as I have already indicated, are composed of important business communities, like the Marwaris, Parsis, Gujeratis and Jains.

The man who was president of the Zilla Parishad at the time this study was conducted was one of the main leaders of the Loyalist group, and he had stood in the Assembly elections of 1957 on a Congress ticket, but was defeated, as were many other Congressmen who stood against the Samyukta Maharashtra Samiti (S.M.S.).

One of the two men reportedly involved in the intra-clan feud, which was mentioned by some of the respondents as the basis of the factions among Z.P. Congressmen, also ran on a Congress ticket in 1957, and he was defeated by his clansman who contested as an independent, supported by the S.M.S. This defeated Congressman was eventually elected to the Legislative Assembly (in 1962) from a constituency in the Z.P. President's taluka. According to some of the more knowledgeable respondents, this

---

* I refer here to the leading Rebels and Loyalists in each group. They are my major source of information on the various issues mentioned, although information from a few knowledgeable rank-and-file members is also drawn upon. For the most part, however, I am dealing here with that level of political actor which I have termed the 'leader', who is so identified in this instance on the basis of his office, personal observation and the assessment of other Z.P. members, officers and administrative officials. I would maintain that it is these 'leaders' who are most likely to approach the political arena with some sort of policy orientation. Hence, if any further clues about the nature of the factional alignments are to be found, they can be sought most fruitfully in the statements or actions and interactions of such leaders.

M.L.A. was a strong supporter of the Z.P. President in the current factional dispute.

On the other hand, the opponent of this 'Loyalist-supporter', who in 1957 was backed by the S.M.S., subsequently supported the Rebel group in the factional struggle which developed in the Zilla Parishad. Thus, the division between Rebel and Loyalist leaders in 1963 seems to have developed along the lines of the Samyukta Maharashtra issue, which itself possibly had an economic as well as a cultural dimension. The central role of the language issue in the 1957 dispute is generally acknowledged. So far as I know, however, no systematic examination has been made of the economic factors underlying that dispute. Hence, such a basis can neither be confirmed nor validly denied.

A CASTE CONFLICT?

Although the political struggle was also described as one waged between Marathas and non-Marathas, the primary contestants were, in fact, both Marathas, but from different clans. However, they did represent constituencies in the major geographical regions of the district, namely North and South Ratnagiri. This territorial division is, in fact, broadly coterminous with certain economic and social characteristics of the district which were also suggested as indices of the factional alignment. Thus, the Maratha versus non-Maratha and urban versus rural issues, and perhaps even the debate over the octroi (which may otherwise be defined as the 'industrial versus agricultural development' issue) may all be subsumed under the North versus South dispute, which has persisted for a long time, and certainly since the days of the District Local Board in the 1950s.

There is, therefore, a possibility that this dispute basically engaged Marathas against the minority, non-Maratha castes and communities. Although the two official rivals were both Marathas, nevertheless the Loyalist candidate's taluka was in South Ratnagiri, and he was supported by the President, who was also a Maratha from South Ratnagiri. The caste composition of this region, which is reportedly dominated by the Maratha caste, is believed to be more homogeneous than that of the North. The northern talukas are said to be as a whole more heterogeneous, caste- and community-wise, with a very strong contingent of low-caste Tillori

Kunbis, as well as Brahmins, Muslims and Vaishyas. Indeed, it is estimated that the Kunbis constitute about one-third of the whole population of Ratnagiri, and the local residents indicated that most of these are concentrated in the northern talukas. Among the respondents, all those who were Kunbis were from the northern part of the district. Moreover, the alleged leader of the Rebels was an educated Kunbi from North Ratnagiri.

However, the 'caste' argument collapses when we consider that more than half of the Loyalists were non-Marathas (even as we concede that a still larger proportion of the Rebels were also non-Marathas).

A CONFLICT BETWEEN ECONOMIC REGIONS CONSIDERED

The argument that the factions have a territorial basis appears on the face of it to have more merit, and must be examined very carefully. One weakness which may be immediately admitted is that both the foremost leader of the Loyalists (the Agriculture Minister) and most of the important leaders of the Rebels came from Northern talukas, while another Rebel leader came from the (Loyalist) President's own taluka in the south. Nevertheless, the outlines of the factional split become more intelligible in regional terms when we consider some of the major economic (and related) features of the two regions in question which set them apart.

Although Ratnagiri is part of an area which is considered one of the most economically backward in the state, namely the Konkan, nevertheless within the district itself there are variations in the degree and nature of economic development between its two major regions. The southern talukas are decidedly more advanced economically, in terms of road mileage, the number of industries functioning there, irrigation, and other indices.*

* For a discussion of the two major regions of Ratnagiri District, see a report issued by the Government of Maharashtra discussing the development potential of the district.[1] A point of clarification is in order here. The reader may be puzzled by the statistics cited in Table A, App. 2, pp. 220–2, showing group means on variables with reference to each factional group. Here, the Rebels, who have been identified with the northern talukas, appear to register higher scores on some of the economic indicators, which seems to contradict the reference above to the poverty-stricken north. It should be noted, however, that in the text I refer to the regions themselves while the statistics appearing in Table A with reference to Variable Nos. 14 to 21 describe the personal economic background of each factional group. Within each district, the Councillors tended to come

All the main cash crops grown in the district – mangoes, cashewnut, coconut and san-hemp – are concentrated largely in southern talukas, as are the main processing industries for these products. These constitute the main agricultural resources which lend themselves to industrial utilization. The forest resources which similarly have industrial possibilities are also found in southern talukas, as are the existing mineral resources, such as iron ore, silica, clay, ochre and mica. So far, the exploitation of all these resources has been in the hands of private entrepreneurs for the most part. Thus, for example, in a report sponsored by the Department of Industries and Labour of the Government of Maharashtra, it was suggested that some of the fruit and cashewnut growers concentrated in certain southern talukas should be encouraged to form cooperative societies for processing their produce.[1] The southern talukas also have an advantage in their existing and potential port facilities. In an economic survey of the Konkan conducted by the Indian Merchants' Chamber of Commerce, the development of Ratnagiri as an all-weather port was favorably considered. According to this report, Ratnagiri, together with the other two Konkan districts, has tremendous potential for industrial development. It has mineral, forest and horticultural resources, as well as hydroelectric and deep sea fishing potential.[2]

With less than 30% of its land under cultivation and little possibility of extending that, Ratnagiri can hardly expect to rise far above its present low economic level through agricultural development. Its best hope for economic progress seems to be in industrial development.

The next logical question to ask is: Who is going to undertake to develop this potential? The investment required is, in terms of funds, skills and personnel, of staggering proportions. The Government of Maharashtra can at best provide a small supplement. A realistic assessment of the situation compels one to accept the only available alternative. The big capital is in the hands of the large private industrial and commercial interests of Bombay, who apparently have some interest in undertaking the task. Few persons

from the higher economic strata of the population and therefore would not be likely to mirror in every detail the broad economic profile of their respective regions. Moreover, it may be noted that this particular set of figures is highly unreliable for some variables, owing to inadequate sampling. Because of this, two variables (value of landholding and value of houses) were omitted from the discriminant analysis in this district.

in positions of authority would want to alienate such groups, even in a small way. Thus, the various policy stands on the octroi issue (among others) become more understandable. We find, for example, that the President of the Zilla Parishad and a few other Loyalist leaders have been exerting themselves to abolish the octroi. As indicated earlier, this is a tax on commodities and raw materials brought into or through towns from rural areas or other towns, which is borne largely by the business classes in the district. The President said he wanted to abolish this tax in order to encourage the entry of industry into the district.

Both on the basis of observation and discussions with the Z.P. President and the Minister of Agriculture, and on the basis of comments made by other respondents, it would appear that the Minister of Agriculture was the real leader of the district; the President was more or less his deputy. Hence, we may assume that this Minister was also in favor of abolishing the octroi, and that, in general, he may have tended to favor the business interests. In any case, it may be relevant to note at this point that he has had no connection with the cooperative movement during any period of his career.[3]

The President of the District Congress Committee, on the other hand, who was one of the leaders of the Rebel group, had been Vice President of the District Central Cooperative Bank since 1958 and became Chairman in 1965, shortly before he was interviewed. One of his more trusted lieutenants became Vice President of the District Central Cooperative Bank and President of a newly formed (1965) District Industrial Cooperative Association. Another Rebel leader, who was Vice President of the Zilla Parishad, was at the same time Vice President of the Land Development Bank, and had long-standing links with the cooperative movement through his father.

At least two of the four top Rebel leaders mentioned the octroi and indicated that they were in favor of continuing it. It is the main source of the Zilla Parishad's own funds (that is, apart from the funds received from the Government of Maharashtra, which constitute about 90% of the Z.P.'s Budget).[4]

Ratnagiri District

THE WEAKNESS OF COOPERATIVES

When we consider that the Rebel leadership controlled certain key positions in the local power structure, such as the presidency of the District Central Cooperative Bank and the District Congress Committee, the question arises why this group was unable to capture control of the Zilla Parishad. I would suggest several possibilities.

The main reason, in my view, is that the cooperative movement was extremely weak in this district, and that the office of the cooperative bank president therefore had no real sinews of power. A simple reason for the weakness of the cooperative structure can be traced to the fact that this has always been an agriculturally backward region. Moreover, relatively few cash crops have been cultivated here. This means that those cultivators who could potentially benefit from and give substantial financial support to the development of cooperative institutions are few in number. As we have seen, the larger group of cash crop growers is to be found in South Ratnagiri and seems to have developed strong links with private credit sources.

Another major source of weakness is the competition which the Bank faces from joint stock companies in attracting deposits. It cannot compete with the higher rates of interest which the joint stock companies have begun to offer.[5]

LEADERSHIP CHARACTERISTICS

In addition, the leadership qualities of the top Rebel leader were so inadequate that it was sometimes difficult to determine whose side he was on. As one Rebel leader said, it was not so much that this man, who was District Congress Committee and Cooperative Bank President, led his group against the Agriculture Minister; in fact, he was often loyal to him. Rather, there were certain people who supported and promoted him. It appears, then, that he was a leader almost in spite of himself. His uncertain command is said to have cost the Rebels control of the very important Works Committee which they attempted to capture.*

The Minister of Agriculture, who had been in the public eye for a long period of time in his capacity as M.L.A., past District

* See Ch. 5, pp. 85–6, for a discussion regarding the importance of the Works Committee.

3-2

Congress President, and in various other offices, had therefore been able to exert far greater control over the affairs of the district, because his potential opponent was a diffident and vacillating leader. Incidentally, a good illustration of the Rebel leader's weakness (and the Minister's corresponding strength) may be seen in the finding mentioned below (see p. 75) that Loyalists, more than Rebels, are identified with the power structure of the party. It would seem that, even though the Rebel leader was President of the District Congress Committee, control of the organization really rested with the Minister and his supporters who were thus able to place their followers in more positions of authority in the Congress organization.

A WEAK PARTY ORGANIZATION

Finally, the weakness of the party organization itself worked against the Rebels. This weakness can be traced not only to the President of the organization, but also perhaps to the land settlement pattern in the district which, because of a highly uneven terrain and small, fragmented landholdings, results in small and widely scattered nuclear settlements. The harsh terrain also impedes transport. This means, in effect, that anyone trying to organize the people in meetings or activities of any kind must have a difficult time of it; at best, he can work only with small groups which have little contact with one another. These, then, are some of the features of the political scene in Ratnagiri as viewed from a broader perspective.

THE BASES OF POLITICAL FACTIONS: A STATISTICAL ANALYSIS

We may now consider specific factors found to be important in determining the nature of political alignments here. We begin with the attitudinal variables which define the common 'motive' pattern of the respective groups.

One indicator from this set made the highest contribution to the discriminating power of both the *combined variables* cluster and the *attitudinal* one. This was the respondent's predisposition to resign from Congress under hypothetical circumstances (Table 1.1 and 1.5).* The Rebel group expressed a stronger inclination

* All tables will be found in the text of their respective chapters unless otherwise indicated.

to resign from the Party if it did not live up to the principles which purportedly had attracted the respondent to Congress (Table A, p. 220 below).* The correlations (in the *combined variables* factor) revealed that such people (i.e., those predisposed to resign) were likely to be found within the party officialdom of the village.†

Moreover, it could be inferred from the *attitudinal* correlations that the Rebel might be generally dissatisfied both with the Z.P. leadership and with the Congress organization. Thus, respondents who tended to evaluate the Z.P. leadership rather negatively were likely also to express a willingness to resign from Congress. Such potential party 'drop-outs' (who have been identified as Rebels above) tended to disapprove of the process of selecting Congress candidates.

Turning to the *environmental* dimension, we find that there were three socio-economic characteristics of the respondent's area which contributed considerably to the discriminating strength of the *combined variables* cluster. Two of these might be interpreted as 'isolation' factors (Table 1.1).‡ In terms of both, it was found that Rebels were more deficient than Loyalists (Table A, p. 220, below). That is to say, they came from areas which were relatively isolated geographically, economically and socially.

Correlations of these two variables with others (in the *combined variables* cluster) revealed that, in general, the greater the isolation, the larger the number of people who took part in the elections to the Zilla Parishad. And, as we will see, the Rebels' more isolated constituences were distinguished by greater public electoral participation in this district (Table 1.2 and Table A, p. 220, below). Projecting ahead for a moment, we find that on an all-district basis also Rebels came from constituencies where the voter turnout was greater (see Ch. 8, Table 1.2 and Table E, p. 232). However, unlike Ratnagiri, public electoral participation on an all-district basis was poorly correlated with isolation factors (Table I–I. E., pp. 237, 242). This suggests that, regardless of relative isolation, Rebels are likely to come from areas where possible opposition to Congress is

* This table contains the absolute group means for each variable. It and similar tables in other chapters will be found in Appendix 2 at the end of this book.

† All of the correlation tables, for this and subsequent chapters will be found in Appendix 3 at the end of the book.

‡ Distance from railway and communications potential.

greater than in Loyalists' constituencies,* and that therefore opposition to the Congress Party is not necessarily a function of communications. That is to say, such opposition does not always 'ferment' and spread by exposure or contact with other opposition 'carriers'. At most, then, we may consider communications a contributing factor in political dissidence, but not sufficient, in and of itself, to generate such dissidence.

Another interesting correlation with the communications variable which was noted serves, indirectly, to underline the economic and regional nature of the conflict. It appears that those who lived in areas where the potential for communications was low – where there were fewer fairs or weekly markets and the literacy level was low† – tended to have less highly valued agricultural equipment. Now, with regard to the 'communications potential', it may be noted that this variable was a significant discriminant of factional alignment (see Table 1.1), and that the Rebels had a rather low group mean on the 'communications potential' scale (see Table A, p. 220). Secondly, with regard to agricultural machinery, as only the Loyalists owned such machinery, and since two-thirds of them came from southern talukas (while their opponents were predominantly from the north), this correlation simply reflects the fact that the Rebels, who were indeed more isolated, had no valuable agricultural equipment. In this instance, the economic discrepancy between northern and southern regions is reflected in the factional groups themselves.

The third *environmental* variable which contributed significantly to the discriminating power of 'combined variables' was the percentage of cultivators serviced by village agricultural credit cooperatives (Table 1.1). The findings here indicate that Rebels came from talukas where the percentage of cultivators so serviced was higher than in Loyalists' talukas. (See Var. No. 13, Table A, App. 2, p. 221.) This confirms a similar link established between Rebels and cooperatives on an all-district basis.

---

* The 'possible opposition to Congress' is inferred from the high correlation (0.8) registered between the proportion of voters (in all four of the districts) who participated in the Z.P. elections, and the proportion of those among the participants who voted for non-Congress candidates (see Variables 5 and 12, Tables I–I.A. to I.E in App. 3, pp. 237–42).

† For the list of indicators defining 'communications potential', please see Table E in App. 1, p. 219.

Ratnagiri District

TABLE 1.1. *Discriminant Analysis Findings: Coefficients for Canonical Variable Ranked in Order of Importance*

Combined Variables Cluster Variable	Coefficient
Predisposition to resign	0.90
Distance – Railway	0.82
% cultivators serviced by cooperatives	0.64
Involved in Cooperatives – District	0.57
Simultaneous Office – Cooperatives	0.57
Communications Potential	*0.52*★
Value of machinery owned	0.48
Number of acres under cash crops	0.47
Number of offices – Party	0.39
Agricultural prosperity	0.34
Public electoral participation	0.32
Involved in Party – District	0.26
Voting preference (majority v. unanimous)	0.22
Caste role in distribution decisions	0.09

TABLE 1.2. *Environment*

Variable	Coefficient
Communications potential	1.08
Agricultural prosperity	0.65
Public electoral participation	0.61
Distance – Railway	0.52
% cultivators serviced by cooperatives	*0.50*
Agricultural Cooperative Activity	0.33
Average landholding in taluka	0.17
Distance – Bus	0.15
Distance – Panchayat Samiti	0.10

Variables Not Entered
Distance – Z.P.
Urbanization
Eligible Votes Polled by non-Congress candidates
Total Votes Polled by non-Congress candidates

★ Italics here and in all tables of *Coefficients for Canonical Variable* indicate a cut-off point of significance for the coefficient. See note below on p. 199 for explanation of significance.

71

The Dynamics of Indian Political Factions

TABLE 1.3. *Behavior*

Variable	Coefficient
Simultaneous Office – Cooperatives	1.46
Involved in Cooperatives – District	1.26
Number of Offices – Party	1.12
Involved in Party – Village	*0.93*
Involved in Cooperatives – Taluka	0.49
Involved in Party – District	0.29
Involved in Government – Taluka	0.28
Number of Spheres – Over Time	0.26
Number of Offices – Government	0.26
Involved in Government – Village	0.12
Variables Not Entered	
Simultaneous Office – All Spheres	
Simultaneous Office – Party	
Simultaneous Office – Government	
Number of Offices – Cooperatives	
Involved in Party – Taluka	
Involved in Cooperatives – Village	
Involved in Government – District	

TABLE 1.4. *Economic background*

Variable	Coefficient
Value of machinery owned	0.83
Number of acres under cash crops	0.80
% of acres under cash crops	*0.78*
Value of landholding	0.31
Size of landholding	0.30
Value of loans (from cooperatives)	0.22
Variable Not Entered	
Value of shares (in cooperatives)	

The correlations of this with other variables (in the 'combined variables' cluster) provide interesting insights into the operations of these village agricultural credit societies (see Tables V.A. 1 and 2, pp. 260–1). We find, for example, that within both the area of the Rebels and that of the Loyalists these societies provide their services in talukas which are relatively more prosperous agri-

Ratnagiri District

TABLE 1.5. *Attitudes*

Variable	Coefficient
Predisposition to resign	0.73
Voting preference (majority v. unanimous)	0.73
Caste role in distribution decisions	*0.52*
Comments about leadership of Z.P.	0.41
Selection of candidates	0.37
Loan distribution machinery	0.36
Variables Not Entered	
Evaluation of M.L.A. vis-a-vis Z.P. official	
Economic role in distribution decisions	

culturally; that where the cash crop cultivation of respondents is more extensive one is also likely to find more cultivators serviced by village cooperatives. Finally, we find that the respondents who have expensive agricultural machinery are likely to live in areas where a larger proportion of cultivators may be serviced by these village credit cooperatives. With regard to this last observation some clarification is in order. We have noted that Rebels owned absolutely *no* agricultural machinery of high value. Hence, the correlation here noted can apply only to the Loyalists. Keeping this in mind, we may re-phrase our observation to indicate that Loyalists who *have* more expensive agricultural equipment tend to live in talukas which are more widely serviced by village agricultural credit cooperatives. It must be further noted, however, that this correlation does not – or rather *cannot* – suggest that these cultivators financed their purchase of agricultural equipment with help from the village cooperatives. The funds that would be provided by a cooperative institution for purchase of expensive equipment would be classified as long-term loans, and they would normally be advanced by banks set up specially for the purpose (i.e., the land mortgage or, as they are now called, land development banks).* There was no district land development bank in Ratnagiri until 1964–5.[6] The State Land Development Bank – which did maintain an office in the town of Ratnagiri – was therefore the only cooperative institution from which such long-term loans could be obtained. However, the procedure involved in obtaining a loan

* I might add, incidentally, that formal establishment of such institutions does not mean immediate operation.

73

under such circumstances was rather tedious, in terms of travel to district headquarters alone.

The inference to be drawn is that Loyalists, who, as we have seen, are distinguished from Rebels by their more highly valued machinery, would alternatively have *had* to finance such purchases either from their own resources or from the private credit structure. Although the reasoning here is rather circuitous and perhaps cumbersome, nevertheless it does point to a possible relationship between Loyalists and the private economic community in their region. This proposition is complementary to the central one which links Rebels with cooperative institutions.

The correlations among *environmental* variables (as distinct from those among the *combined* cluster) serve to further reinforce the impressions gleaned from the earlier analysis. The *environmental* test (Table 1.2) tells us that 'communications potential' and 'distance from railway communication' are significant discriminators. An examination of the group means on these variables (Table A, p. 220, Var. Nos. 3 and 7) confirms the relative isolation of Rebels. The dissidents were likely to live in areas where communications were poor and in talukas which were not highly urbanized (compared with those of Loyalists). Moreover, both these isolation measures were positively correlated with measures of the opposition vote to Congress. In other words, in such relatively isolated areas more centers of electoral opposition to Congress were encountered. We may recall that Rebels seem to abound in such areas in Ratnagiri.

Two of the most significant discriminators among the *environmental* variables were (1) public electoral participation and (2) agricultural prosperity (Table 1.2). An examination of the group means for these variables (Table A, p. 220) tells us that the Rebels, on the average, lived in areas which were relatively poor (even though the dissidents themselves may not have been) and where the voter turnout was relatively high. These findings conclusively confirm the associations suggested by the above correlations.

The link between Rebels and cooperative institutions, which was only suggested by the within-group correlations, was definitely established as a predictive factor in Ratnagiri in the computations on both the *behavioral* cluster (Table 1.3) and the variables drawn from all the individual clusters (Table 1.1). (See also Table A, p. 222.)

74

Two indicators describing involvement in cooperative institutions contributed to the discriminating power of *combined variables* and were the most important discriminators in the *behavioral* cluster (Tables 1.1 and 1.3, respectively). With regard to both, Rebels registered a high score: there were more Rebels holding office in cooperative institutions, and they often held two or more such offices at a time (Table A, p. 222).* However, they were not extensively† involved in the Congress Party. This suggests that they were relative newcomers to the organization. Although Ratnagiri had the largest proportion of Congressmen who had entered the Party after 1957, nevertheless, in the absence of a significant correlation between the incidence of Rebels and the later entrants to the Congress, a different and more plausible link may be suggested between being a Rebel and not holding party office. It may be, for example, that many of these Congressmen, having been denied access to party office above the village level, resented the district leadership. In this connection, we must remember that the effective leader of the district (*and of the Loyalists*) was not the District Congress Committee President but the Minister of Agriculture, whose home district was Ratnagiri.

The correlations in the *combined variables* cluster indicated that there was a strong association between holding office in a district cooperative and holding two or more offices simultaneously at any one or more of the various levels of the cooperative structure (Table V.A.1 and V.A.2, pp. 260–1). This finding was generally confirmed by the correlations in the *behavioral* cluster, where it was found that those respondents who were intensively involved in the cooperative organization were also extensively involved in it, and that the level of organization at which these people were usually found was the district (Table II–II.A., pp. 243–4). As we have seen, the group which was thus involved was the Rebel group. The Loyalist group, on the other hand, was identified more closely with the party power structure. That is to say, Loyalists were distinguished from Rebels by the fact that they held more offices in the party organization. The correlations among *behavioral* variables indicate further that those (like the Loyalists) who had held several

---

* Of course, given the weakness of cooperative institutions in Ratnagiri (see above, p. 67), such office ought not to be considered a significant index of power.

† This term refers to the number of offices held *over time* (as opposed to simultaneously) in any of the levels of the organization.

offices in the party tended to be active at all levels of the organization, but particularly at the taluka level.

The economic background of respondents, while not distinguishing between Rebels and Loyalists in the *combined variables* analysis, did contribute some significant discriminators in the separate analysis of the *economic background* cluster (Table 1.4). This confirmed some of the findings from the other analyses: Loyalists, compared with Rebels, had more highly valued machinery, and larger plots of land under cash crops. In other words, the Rebels not only came from poorer areas (see page 74, above) but were themselves, *relatively speaking*, a 'have-not' group, having no modern agricultural machinery of any value, and less land under the more profitable cash crops (see Table A, Var. Nos. 17 and 20, p. 221).

The only other point I wish to note here is that the value of machinery owned was significantly and positively correlated with the size of respondent's landholding. The latter variable might have emerged as a significant discriminator in this district, identifying the Loyalists as the larger landowners. For technical reasons, which account for other similar results, it did not. The reason 'size of landholding' did not appear as an independent discriminator is that it was rather highly correlated with the 'value of machinery'. (See Table III–III.A., pp. 249–50.) The latter variable, which was entered before the 'size of landholding' in the step-wise discriminant analysis, reduced the discriminating power of the 'landholding size' variable, and its strength was, so to speak, absorbed and reflected by the variable with which it was so highly correlated, namely, the 'value of machinery owned'. To all intents and purposes, however, it may be considered significant within this cluster. We then find that the Rebels were the smaller landowners of the two groups, thus deviating from the all-district norm. A discussion of such deviations will be reserved for the eighth (comparative) chapter so that we may keep the outline of the individual analyses as simple and concise as possible.

SUMMARY

Reconstructing the major findings of this chapter, I have sketched a profile of the average Ratnagiri Rebel which largely substantiates one of the main assertions made regarding the nature of factional alignments. The Rebel of Ratnagiri can be positively identified through his association with cooperative institutions, an activity posited as an effective discriminant of factional groupings. He holds or has held more than one office simultaneously (or possibly over time) in cooperative institutions at some level; the level with which he is most conclusively identified is that of the district.

Some of the other significant characteristics suggest that the dissident Congressman of the Ratnagiri Zilla Parishad is a relatively strong-willed independent individual who does not submit to authority as readily as do the Loyalists. In addition, he is likely to live in an area which is not agriculturally prosperous and which, in general, discourages extensive contacts of an economic or social nature. Although more farmers in his area have access to village agricultural credit cooperatives than do cultivators in a Loyalists' taluka, it would appear that the possibility of such access is greater if the area is relatively urbanized, agriculturally prosperous, populated by relatively larger landowners and more extensively serviced by district-level cooperative institutions.

Finally, the Rebel is probably a relatively small landowner, and owns no expensive agricultural machinery of any kind. Although the *proportion* of land which he cultivates under cash crops is higher than that of the Loyalist, in absolute terms it is a smaller plot of land than that of the Loyalist – as is his total holding – and therefore possibly less profitable. Hence, one may assume that the risk he takes in setting aside land for cash crop cultivation is greater, as would be the need to get a successful crop. Such a risk can be minimized if a farmer can assure the proper cultivation of his crop through timely and reasonable financing. For this reason, the services of cooperative institutions which provide short-term credit must be more highly valued than would be the case for the relatively more prosperous Loyalist. The institution to which I refer is the District Central Cooperative Bank which finances the village credit cooperatives. It may be recalled that the President of this institution was the foremost Rebel leader in the district and that other Rebel leaders also had strong links with cooperative institutions.

The characteristics which most strikingly distinguish the Rebel from the Loyalist, however, are his predisposition to resign from Congress, together with his greater involvement in the cooperative power structure, the fact that most farmers in his area are serviced

TABLE 2. *Discriminant Analysis Findings: Canonical Correlation –*
Ranked in Order of Importance

Variable Cluster	Canonical Correlation	% of Variance Accounted For
Combined Variables	0.84	0.70
Environment	0.71	0.50
Behavior	0.62	0.38
Attitudes	0.61	0.37
Economic Background	0.50	0.25

TABLE 3. *Discriminant Analysis Findings: Accuracy of Prediction of Factional Alignment Achieved by Each Variable Cluster (% of Correct Classifications)*

Factional Groupings	Environment			Behavior			Economic background			Attitudes			Combined variables		
	L	R	T	L	R	T	L	R	T	L	R	T	L	R	T
Actual Membership	17	16	33	17	16	33	17	16	33	17	16	33	17	16	33
Discriminant Analysis Classification	13	13	26	15	12	27	13	8	21	13	12	25	16	16	32
% of Correct Classifications	76	81	79	88	75	82	76	50	64	76	75	76	94	100	97

* The letter headings under each variable cluster represent the following: L, Loyalist; R, Rebel; T, Total (both Rebels and Loyalists).

by village agricultural cooperatives, and, finally, his relative economic and social isolation. These variables, examined as components of the *combined variables* cluster, appear to have been extremely effective indicators of factional alignments in Ratnagiri when we consider the fact that this cluster accounted for 70% of the variance between the two rival groups (see Table 2). These are the variables which largely account for the highly accurate classification of 94% of the Loyalists and 100% of the Rebels (i.e., 16 out of 17 Loyalists and all 16 of the Rebels) (see Table 3). This means, in effect, that if I had conducted this study when I did without knowing who the Rebels or Loyalists were, I could have accurately identified all of the Rebels, on the basis of the variables mentioned above, and as many as 16 out of 17 Loyalists.

POSTSCRIPT

An item which appeared in a Bombay newspaper shortly after the 1967 elections provides a significant footnote to the analysis set forth in this chapter. It confirms that the factions which I observed at the time of the study in 1965–6 were not merely momentary eruptions. The Rebels who had tried – unsuccessfully – to capture the Works Committee in 1963 succeeded in 1967 in capturing the Presidency of the Zilla Parishad.* The 1963 Rebel candidate for the Works Committee Chairmanship was the successful Presidential candidate in the Zilla Parishad in 1967. It was reported in the newspaper, however, that he and seven other supporters were expelled from the Congress Party for six years in this connection. According to the news item, 'action was taken against the dissidents for being instrumental in the defeat of the official Congress nominees for the posts of president and vice president of the Zilla Parishad, a statement by the Maharashtra Pradesh Congress Committee...stated.'[7] Apparently, the M.P.C.C. President suggested that the Z.P. Presidency should be rotated between a member from the southern and northern parts of the district, each holding the post for two and a half years of the five-year term. When the Rebel President-elect was accordingly requested to resign and make way for the official nominee, he refused and was expelled. Five of the remaining seven who had been expelled were identifiable from their names as members of the Rebel group under study. The other two are apparently new members of this group.†

* See note on p. 6, above.
† The next scheduled elections for the Z.P. had not been held at the time of writing (March 1971).

CHAPTER 5

POONA DISTRICT:
THE POLITICS OF SUGAR

As we move northeast from the coastal plain in the Konkan to the Deccan plateau we come upon Poona District, whose population of two and a half million (approximately) exceeds that of Ratnagiri by about 700,000.[1] Nevertheless, in terms of the number of citizens who come under the jurisdiction of the Zilla Parishad, the Poona Council is slightly smaller. The reason for this is that Poona is more highly urbanized than Ratnagiri. In fact, the densely populated City of Poona accounts for much of the urban population of the district. Because municipalities have their own local governing bodies, the population in such urban areas does not fall within the purview of the Zilla Parishad, which is a rural body. Hence, the constituency of the Poona Council is smaller.

THE IMPORTANCE OF SUGARCANE IN THE RURAL ECONOMY

This district is of particular significance in the context of this study because of the important position that a cash crop, namely sugarcane, occupies in the rural economy. Poona produces more low-energy and lower-valued crops (like millets) than the State as a whole, while production of more highly-valued (and higher-energy) staples, like rice and wheat, is lower than the State average. However, as one official publication points out, the 'relieving factors are the higher proportions of area under the commercial crop "sugarcane"' and larger irrigated areas, which raise the gross value of output per acre of cultivated area very near to the State average.[2]

The cane-growing area of the district is concentrated in two or three talukas and it is pertinent to note, as I begin the analysis of Poona District, that the top-level Rebel leadership* was centered

* I stress the fact that I am referring here to 'leaders', as the factional alignment of respondents from these talukas does not reflect the Rebel strength there. One reason is that I was unable to interview many of the Councillors from these

in two out of these three talukas. The reasons for the absence of Rebel leaders in the third will be discussed below.

ECONOMIC POWER BASES: THE LOYALISTS AND PRIVATE BUSINESS INTERESTS

In the statistical analysis – which will be set forth at a later point – I have been able to locate a distinct base of operations for the Rebel group, namely the cooperative organization. The Rebels may be properly considered an institutional interest group for whom the Zilla Parishad provides the major vehicle for promoting cooperatively organized economic interests. Thus, cooperatives constitute for them both a political base of operations and a means of promoting economic interests.

As far as the Loyalists are concerned, however, such identification with a distinct economic power base could not be statistically validated. There is substantive ground for this, which is also reflected in a technical reason. The research design is deficient in that it does not include indicators of involvement in the private economic structure (such as 'cooperative office' provides in the 'public' domain) with which to link Loyalists in a rural milieu. Private banks, of course, are one type of organization which could have been included to correct this deficiency, but banks are sparse in the rural areas. While one may find a cooperative in practically every village, and in each taluka and district headquarters, private banks operate only at the district level as a rule, and are less common at the taluka level. In a village, banks are a rare sight indeed.

At these lower levels, then, where most Councillors function (in their political and economic roles), it is the private moneylender and trader who 'represents' (to some extent) the private economic sphere. Private commission agents, merchants, contractors – all of these may be considered representative of private economic interests. Such individuals, however, do not function in a visible economic structure such as the cooperatives constitute, for example. It is difficult to trace any kind of formal association between

areas. In fact, the response in this district was generally deficient. I was able to interview only 65 % of the Z.P. members. However, I did interview most of the Congressmen on this body (80 %). More than half of those whose interview I was unable to obtain, however, were from the 'Rebel' talukas. Nevertheless, even with a small Rebel sample, I was able to confirm my hypotheses, as we shall see.

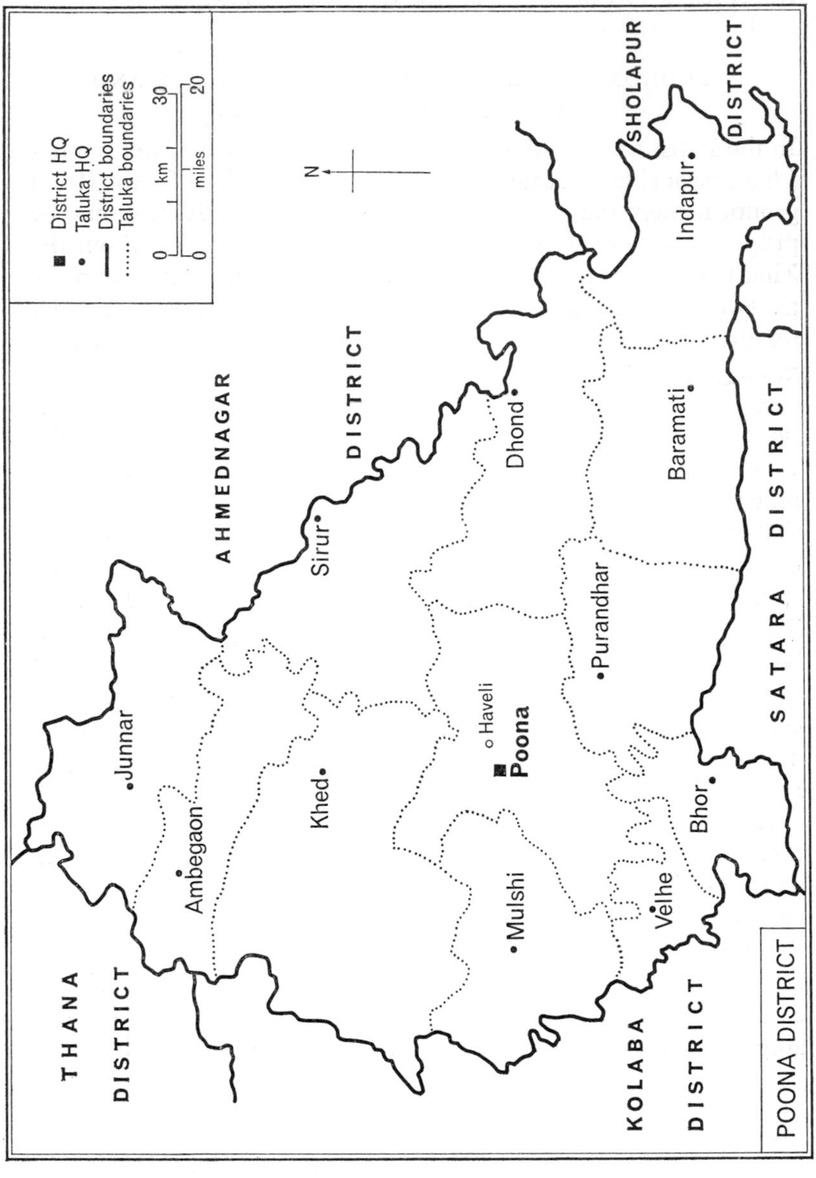
POONA DISTRICT
District HQ
Taluka HQ
District boundaries
Taluka boundaries
0
km
30
0
miles
20
N
AHMEDNAGAR
DISTRICT
THANA
DISTRICT
KOLABA
DISTRICT
SATARA
DISTRICT
SHOLAPUR
DISTRICT
Junnar
Ambegaon
Khed
Sirur
Dhond
Indapur
Baramati
Purandhar
Haveli
Poona
Mulshi
Velhe
Bhor

Map 3

Councillors and individuals engaged in private economic activities such as those enumerated above. Cooperatives, on the other hand, are visible in terms of their physical plant as well as in terms of their staff. The existence of a formal association can be established merely by asking whether an individual is a member or officer of a cooperative organization at the village, taluka or district level. It is, moreover, an organization which was officially associated with the Zilla Parishad through a provision of the legislation creating these governing bodies. According to the Zilla Parishads Act, representatives from each of the major cooperative institutions in the district are associate members of the Zilla Parishad.[3]

It is perhaps best, therefore, for us to examine the leaders of the Loyalists in order to determine the nature of the group's economic interests; we may learn something by examining the economic interests and associations of these leaders and/or their policy orientations on relevant local issues.

TABLE 1. *Frequencies Indicating Respondents' Views Regarding District's Leader (Sample: 40)*

Variable Title	Code No.	Variable Category	Frequency
Name of district leader	1	Past District Congress Committee President	29
	2	Z.P. President	1
	3	Not ascertained	10*

* In the case of five respondents, the question was inadvertently omitted from the interview. One of these five was President of the Zilla Parishad who, as indicated in Chapter 5, above, was the choice of the leader identified as the district's most powerful political figure.

In the case of the five remaining respondents, the question was incorrectly phrased by the interviewer. Of these five, one was the district leader's first lieutenant.

Thus, it may be safely stated that at least 31 (or approximately 80%) of the 40 Congressmen constituting the Poona sample identified the same individual as district leader.

The man who was undisputed leader of the district – according to the almost unanimous view of respondents (see Table 1) was also leader of the Loyalists at the time of the Z.P. elections and thereafter. It is significant to note that this man had had no connection

83

with the district cooperative organization until 1963, one year after the Presidential elections were held among the Congress members of the Zilla Parishad. He was, however, at the time of the Z.P. elections President of the District Congress Committee and a (if not *the*) leading member of the Poona District Parliamentary Board, which nominates candidates for all district elections. This body was composed of five members, of whom three at least (including this D.C.C. President), were responsible for drafting what was, in effect, the 'Loyalist' slate. Only one member of this body was a Rebel leader, and I was not able to determine the inclinations of the remaining member.

As I have indicated, the top Loyalist leader had no significant discernible association with the rural cooperative structure at the time of the nominations. On the other hand, we do find evidence of a different association when we examine his personal economic interests. He was a very wealthy man indeed, and by his own admission had made all his money in business. Starting out in life as a poor, uneducated village boy, he had become the owner of a chain of movie houses which he still owned at the time he was interviewed. What can one deduce from this? Obviously, one does not finance such costly business ventures through rural cooperative banks. It seems equally obvious that, unless one has large private resources, it is not possible to remain solvent and functioning for long in such a capital-intensive enterprise without becoming enmeshed in a whole network of business contacts, characterized by relationships of dependence and interdependence. Although such contacts brought him into the urban sphere, this man had nevertheless managed to maintain his links with the rural areas of which he was himself a product. Moreover, he seemingly had the confidence, respect and affection of most of the rural people with whom I spoke. It was curious that in spite of his urban connections he identified himself, as others did, with his rural origins.

While in social demeanor and costume he favored rural styles, his political tastes betrayed an urban bias. This was evident from his choice for the important office of president of the district council. The official Congress candidate for this post, whom he reportedly handpicked, was a man of definitely urban origins. He had lived all his life in Poona City and had completed his college education there. And what was the economic background of this candidate? It is significant to note, once again, that the main source of income for this Loyalist leader was from a business venture. He was a wholesale fruit dealer, in a business which he was taking over from his father.

Another Loyalist candidate for office on the Zilla Parishad (as Chairman of one of the Committees) had also been in business, as a potato dealer. The top leader's first lieutenant, who became Chairman of the Land Development Bank at the same time as the leader assumed the presidency of the District Central Cooperative Bank (one year after the nominations), had been a roads-and-buildings contractor. Thus, it would seem that almost all the Loyalist leaders for whom information was available had had some association with the private economic sector.

Their positions in, or links with, the Zilla Parishad provided good opportunities to build on and expand such connections. It is important to establish at this point why control of the Works (Building & Communications) Committee of the Zilla Parishad is so important.* Under the Act establishing the District Councils, these bodies are empowered, through their working bodies (i.e., committees and the general meeting) to decide, among other things, where certain development works will be located and how much of the money allotted under a particular head (say, buildings and communications) will go towards building or repairing village roads or bridges or canals, and so forth.[4] Once it is decided that a certain number of primary school buildings are to be built, for example, or that so many irrigation channels are to be repaired, the Zilla Parishad, through its Works Committee, invites contractors to bid for the construction job. The invitation would normally be issued through printed Tender Notices, published in the local newspapers. However, either because the rules about this procedure are vague, or because the administrative officers are lax in ensuring that procedures are followed, it is possible for a contract to be negotiated without benefit of a printed Tender Notice. As one Committee Chairman said, 'If it is known that a contractor does good work, then no bids are invited.'

For works that range between Rs. 10,000 to Rs. 30,000,† the Chairman of the Committee has the authority to accept a contractor's bid.[5] For more costly undertakings, the contractors to be

---

* We may recall that the factional struggle in the Ratnagiri Zilla Parishad centered about control of this Committee Chair.

† Roughly $1,500 to $5,000.

used are decided by the Committee. (Here, of course, if a Chairman is strong, he can push through what he wishes.) The possibilities for favoring one contractor over another, and for even less delicate operations, are legion.

Hence we find that the key committee posts were filled by the Loyalist candidates, who had opportunities not only to develop such business contacts for personal economic gain, but also to exploit them for political purposes.*

The foregoing discussion has demonstrated that the Loyalist leaders at least have a strong interest in the private economy; by contrast, only limited or very recent connections with the co-operative structure are in evidence.

CONFLICT BETWEEN PRIVATELY AND COOPERATIVELY
ORGANIZED ECONOMIC INTERESTS: AN ILLUSTRATION

The question may remain why any rivalry should exist between the two groups under study here. In the second chapter some of the basic reasons were examined. There and elsewhere we have traced such rivalry to a conflict of economic interests, which is exacerbated by conflicting values embraced in the dominant economic philosophy of the party and government. In Poona, the possible source of animosity between the groups of opposing interests is simply and graphically illustrated by the following account of a dispute dominating local politics in one of the Poona talukas at the time I traveled through it. The taluka of which I speak had been the home area of a man who was, together with the D.C.C. President, a very important leader at the time of the Z.P. Presidential nominations; he was also a staunch supporter of the Loyalist slate, as a member of the District Parliamentary Board to which I referred earlier. This man died less than a year after the Z.P. elections were held, but at the time of his death the dispute to which I refer had already begun to assume serious proportions.

* The following account was given in one district of the manner in which contractors may be manipulated by candidates (and vice versa) for election purposes. If bids are invited for some projects the contractor will submit an inflated estimate. Let us say that the work involves building a road. It may actually cost Rs. 60,000 but an estimate of Rs. 100,000 will be given. The contractor thus will get a clear profit of Rs. 40,000. At the time of elections, he will spend Rs. 5,000 to Rs. 10,000 to help his candidate get elected.

The argument was about whether to locate a cooperative leather dye factory in the taluka. One of the main commercial products in this area is a dye extracted from the flower of the 'hirda' tree. This tree is grown by the poorer tribal peoples of the region, and the dye-producing flower of the tree is sold by them at Rs. 6 to Rs. 7 per bag to the Marwari and Gujerati merchants at the taluka headquarters. (One of these merchants, incidentally, was President of the Taluka Congress Committee at the time of my visit.) The merchants, in turn, sell it at about Rs. 20 to Rs. 25 per bag. The taluka produces about 60,000 bags. The returns to the merchants at these rates would be well over a million rupees, or about four or five times what the tribal cultivators get for their product.

The local Block Development Officer (hereinafter, the 'B.D.O.') said he had suggested that the Taluka Sales Purchase Union (that is, the cooperative marketing society) should handle this trade, giving advances to producers on the basis of the expected crop, in the same way that the merchants had been doing. Shortly after his appointment to the Block,* the B.D.O. had submitted such a proposal to the State Government, and he informed me that this proposal had been pending at the State level for the previous year and a half, since he had arrived there. The State Government had not yet authorized the taluka cooperative marketing society to use its funds for such advances.

The local merchants bitterly opposed this plan, and they refused to back the formation of a cooperative factory to produce the dye. The reason for this is obvious. If a cooperative factory were to be located there, they would stand to lose much or at least some of their business; the flower from which the dye is extracted could be sold and marketed through the cooperative factory instead of through the merchants. The B.D.O. felt that there was tremendous pressure being exerted on the State Government by these wealthy merchants against sanctioning this scheme.

* Prior to the introduction of Panchayati Raj, the Community Development Block was the administrative unit which was responsible for the execution of various developmental projects. When the new scheme of local government was implemented, these projects were transferred to the Zilla Parishad, or more specifically to the Panchayat Samitis, whose area of jurisdiction is coterminous with that of the Block and the taluka in most districts of the State. The B.D.O., who had been administrative head of the Block, became the chief administrative officer of the Panchayat Samiti. In effect, he was the appointed counterpart of the Samiti Chairman, an elected representative.

The Dynamics of Indian Political Factions

I would venture to add that the Loyalist leader who was elected to the Legislative Assembly from this taluka in 1962 probably had the support of these powerful economic groups in his area and, presumably, reciprocated in kind. It is also reasonable to assume from the foregoing that there is a group in the State Government which affords protection and sustenance to such private business interests.

PRIVATE VERSUS COOPERATIVE SUGAR FACTORIES

The incident I have related above was not, however, directly linked by any of the respondents with the factional groupings then in existence in the Poona Z.P. Indeed, there was only one explicit reference made to cooperatives as the basis of the factions during the 1962 elections. One respondent indicated that the dispute had developed over a policy issue regarding permission to open more cooperative sugar factories in Poona District. Unfortunately, he could elucidate the issue no further than this. However, we may assume, temporarily, that Rebels would be in favor of establishing another cooperative sugar factory in Poona, while Loyalists might oppose it. The credibility of this assumption may be enhanced if we consider the following information about the Rebel leaders and about the state of affairs in the sugar industry in Poona at about the time that the factional dispute evolved.

One taluka in Poona has (or had, at the time of this study) both the largest proportion of arable land under sugarcane and the biggest irrigated tract, both proportionally and in absolute terms, of all the talukas in Poona. The leader of the sugar interests in this taluka was, significantly, the Vice Presidential candidate on the Rebel slate.* At the same time, he was Chairman of the District Cooperative Sales and Purchase Union (i.e., the district marketing society). His brother was Chairman of the District Central Cooperative Bank at the time that the Congress fight was being waged. (It was this important position that the top Loyalist leader took over after his group won control of the Zilla Parishad.) Another relative was Chairman of the Poona District Cooperative Industrial Association.

Let us see now what links cooperatives and sugar interests. Cooperative institutions provide a critical source of credit for

* When the Rebel group lost their bid for control of the Zilla Parishad, he resigned his seat. Thus I was unable to include him among respondents.

88

Poona District

TABLE 2. *Average Loan Per Acre (Net) Sown, Distributed Taluka-wise by Agricultural Primary (Village) Credit Cooperative Societies**

Name of Taluka	Loan Per Acre (Rs.)
Ambegaon	7.40
Baramati	28.39
Bhor	2.77
Dhond	5.70
Haveli	4.06
Indapur	19.60
Junnar	8.58
Khed	8.46
Mawal	2.43
Mulshi	2.21
Purandhar	4.39
Sirur	3.09
Velhe	1.61

* The amount of loans distributed in each taluka was averaged over a two-year period: 1961–2 and 1962–3. The net area sown in each taluka was averaged over the same period.

The figures under the column entitled 'Loan Per Acre' constitute a ratio of loans (distributed in the taluka over a two-year period) to the average number of acres (net) sown in each taluka (over the same two-year period).

SOURCE: Bureau of Economics and Statistics, Government of Maharashtra, Bombay. *Socio-Economic Review and District Statistical Abstract of Poona District – 1962–63 and 1963–64*: Table 20, pp. 67 and 69 (for average loans); Table 3, p. 26 (for average net area sown).

many sugar cultivators. I was informed by a very knowledgeable Rebel leader that it costs Rs. 2,400 per acre to cultivate sugarcane. The District Central Cooperative Bank, either directly or through its agents, advances loans of Rs. 800 per acre to sugar cultivators in general and Rs. 1,000 per acre to those cultivators who are members of a cooperative sugar factory.[6] The average loan per acre and per member distributed by village credit cooperatives in this taluka (Baramati) over a two-year period (around the time of the factional dispute) was far higher than in any other taluka in the district (see Tables 2 and 3).

Thus, while a sugar cultivator or other agriculturist may not sell his product through a cooperative marketing society (and many

The Dynamics of Indian Political Factions

TABLE 3. *Average Loan Per Member Distributed Taluka-wise by Agricultural Primary (Village) Credit Cooperative Societies**

Name of Taluka	Loan Per Member (Rs.)
Ambegaon	125.50
Baramati	634.63
Bhor	51.44
Dhond	164.75
Haveli	90.97
Indapur	424.00
Junnar	156.34
Khed	167.37
Mawal	56.64
Mulshi	39.58
Purandhar	61.76
Sirur	91.40
Velhe	42.88

* The amount of loans distributed in each taluka was averaged over a two-year period: 1961–2 and 1962–3. Similarly, the number of members in these village societies was averaged over the same two-year period.

The figures under the column 'Loan Per Member' constitute a ratio of loans (over two years) to the number of members (over the same period).

SOURCE: Bureau of Economics and Statistics, Government of Maharashtra, Bombay. *Socio-Economic Review and District Statistical Abstract of Poona District – 1962–63 and 1963–64*, Table 20, pp. 67 and 69.

said they did not), he is very likely to turn to credit cooperatives for loans to finance cultivation, particularly of the commercial crops. One Rebel respondent from the sugar taluka said, for example, that he needs at least Rs. 1,000 to Rs. 1,200 *per acre* for fertilizer.* Therefore sugar cultivators in particular need sizable loans each year in order to cultivate even a small plot of land. The profit is considerable, however, and this lures to the sugarcane enterprise more and more of those who are able to grow this product (given the right soil, irrigation facilities and financial ability).

* Most food crops, on the other hand, are cheaper to cultivate, and so the cooperative bank gives only a 50-rupee loan per acre to grow millet, for example. The effect of the cooperatives' loan policy is, of course, to encourage the cultivation of the more profitable cash crops, and to discourage the cultivation of staple food crops.

Let us now examine the history and characteristics of the sugar industry in Poona District, to see whether they can give us some clues about the factions under study.

The first sugar factory was established in Poona sometime between 1933 and 1936.[7] It was and remains the only private sugar factory in the district. This factory operated for well over twenty years without any competition in Poona and at about the time of the Z.P. elections was the biggest employer in the private sugar sector in the State.*

It was not until 1956 or so that the first cooperative sugar factory was established in Poona. In fact between 1956 and 1959 two cooperative processing plants were set up.[8] The bigger of the two is in the largest sugarcane taluka of the district, to which I have referred earlier (Baramati). The second was established in the taluka where the private factory was functioning (Indapur). The combined crushing capacity of these two factories is about the same as that of the private plant. It also appears that the cooperative processing plants are slightly more efficient than the privately-owned factory, in terms of the average percentage of recovery of sugar pulp.[10] All three factories are located in neighboring talukas. Therefore they service the same areas, that is to say the same sugarcane cultivators. The newer, cooperative enterprises have thus provided stiff competition for the old, well-established private sugar industry in the area.

The private sugar factories usually have their own farms which are worked by tenant farmers. The cane produced is then sold to and crushed by the factories.[11] In cooperative factories the cane is supplied by the landowner members of the cooperative society, who join simply by purchasing shares in the factory. Their produce is then turned over to the sugar factory for processing. The question of a cooperative factory *purchasing* sugarcane does not arise, as it does with the private sector. The cooperative is expected, however, to market the cane after it has been processed into gur or sugar.[12] The sugarcane growers, whether tenants or landowners, are thus vitally concerned with the manufacture of sugarcane products. And the private processors are equally concerned with maintaining access to a supply of their raw material.

I have said that one of the cooperative factories in Poona was situated in the taluka where the private concern was operating.

* There are eight sugarcane-growing districts in Maharashtra.[9]

A few words must be said about this private factory. I have already indicated that it is a much larger processing plant than either of the cooperatives. Moreover, it is common knowledge that this business enterprise is only one of many in a very large industrial complex in Maharashtra.*

We may note further that the Chairman of the Taluka Panchayat Samiti and one other member from this taluka were both Loyalists. (These were the only two Congressmen interviewed here.) More significantly, the M.L.A. elected from this taluka was also a supporter of the Loyalist group. This man was more than a mere Member of the Legislative Assembly, however. He had been Deputy Minister of Agriculture until 1962 when, as a result of the Kamaraj Plan, he returned to his home district. After the Z.P. nominations were over, he was picked by the then D.C.C. President (and strongman of the district) to succeed the latter in the D.C.C. Presidency.

The district leader is said to have favored this man over another who wanted the position. The latter was perhaps the most important Rebel leader in Poona. Within two years, the district leader again bypassed this rival leader by recommending to the State leadership the ex-Deputy Minister of Agriculture for the post of Deputy Revenue Minister (which had just become vacant). We may recall, once again, that the man who had been Deputy Minister of Agriculture, who then became President of the District Congress Committee and who finally was given another important post in the Ministry – all through the support of the top Loyalist leader – was an M.L.A. from the taluka which was host to the biggest sugar factory in Poona and perhaps in the entire sugar-growing area of the State; a concern which, moreover, was associated with one of the largest private industrial enterprises in the State.

The foregoing discussion serves to confirm the hypotheses which are central to this study. However, it was intended also to throw some light on another secondary hypothesis suggested above. I indicated earlier that only one respondent had connected the cooperatives with the factional dispute, but that he had not provided much information about the specific nature of this policy issue, except that it revolved about the question of opening more sugar factories in Poona District. The tentative assumption that

* Reference here is to the Walchandnagar Industries (see above, Chapter 2, p. 30).

Rebels might be in favor of establishing another cooperative sugar factory, while Loyalists might oppose it, is perhaps more credible now. However, it needs some modification.

The respondent's observation regarding a possible policy dispute did indeed have some basis in fact. It would appear that in 1960 or 1961 a committee was appointed by the State Government to select suitable sites for five additional cooperative sugar factories in the State, one of which was to be located in Poona District.[13] The dispute may have developed over *whether* to accept another cooperative sugar factory. However, since the government offer would have the effect of promoting economic progress in the district – however one might regard the nature of the establishment – it is more likely that the dispute revolved around the question of *where* to locate it. Apparently the dilemma was resolved in the Loyalists' favor. A new cooperative sugar factory began operating in the taluka of the newly-elected (Loyalist) President of the Zilla Parishad in 1962–3.[14]

The District Council is – or undoubtedly can be, under the proper leadership – a strong power centre, particularly in its capacity as a patronage-distributing agency *and* as an organizational instrument. It would seem, then, that control of the Council became the issue which divided the cooperative-based interests from the district's established leaders, whose *organizational* base was the district Congress organization and whose *economic power* base was largely in the private economic sector.

THE BASES OF POLITICAL FACTIONS:
A STATISTICAL ANALYSIS

Office in cooperatives, local government and Congress Party

In the context of the above discussion, it is important to note that the variable which was most effective in discriminating between Rebels and Loyalists in Poona had reference to the cooperative organization (Table 4.1). It showed that there were characteristically more Rebels than Loyalists in cooperative offices at the taluka level. (Table B, p. 225.) Another variable from the *behavioral* cluster which emerged as an important discriminator of factional alignment indicated that Rebels were more intensively involved in local government than were Loyalists, and that this involvement was generally at the village level. (Tables 4.1 and 4.3, and Table B, p. 225).

The Dynamics of Indian Political Factions

TABLE 4.1. *Discriminant Analysis Findings: Coefficient for Canonical Variable Ranked in Order of Importance*

Combined Variables Cluster Variable	Coefficient
Involved in Cooperatives – Taluka	0.72
Evaluation of M.L.A.	0.69
Irrigated landholding size	0.62
Simultaneous Office – Government	*0.53*
Value of shares owned in cooperatives	0.44
Landholding size	0.42
Involved in Cooperatives – Village	0.35
% Cultivators serviced by cooperatives	0.34
Involved in Party – Taluka	0.32
Distance – Railway	0.30
Urbanization	0.18

Variables Not Entered
   Number of Spheres – Over Time
   Average landholding in taluka
   Communications Potential
   Involved in Government – Village	

TABLE 4.2. *Environment*

Variable	Coefficient
Communications potential	1.17
% cultivators serviced by cooperatives	0.74
Distance – Railway	0.70
Average landholding in taluka	0.63
Urbanization	*0.61*
Total votes polled by non-Congress candidates	0.39
Agricultural prosperity	0.35
Public electoral participation	0.32
Distance – Bus	0.22
Distance – Panchayat Samiti	0.16

Variables Not Entered
   Distance – Z.P.
   Agricultural Cooperative Activity
   Eligible Votes Polled by non-Congress Candidates	

TABLE 4.3. *Behavior*

Variable	Coefficient
Simultaneous Office – Government	2.51
Number of Spheres – Over Time	1.42
Involved in Cooperatives – Village	0.70
Involved in Government – Village	0.63
Involved in Party – Taluka	0.57
Involved in Cooperatives – Taluka	*0.56*
Involved in Government – Taluka	0.36
Involved in Party – Village	0.33
Simultaneous Office – Party	0.23
Involved in Government – District	0.16
Variables Not Entered	
Simultaneous Office – All Spheres	
Simultaneous Office – Cooperatives	
Number of Offices – Cooperatives	
Number of Offices – Party	
Number of Offices – Government	
Involved in Cooperatives – District	

TABLE 4.4. *Economic Background*

Variable	Coefficient
Landholding size	1.06
Value of shares owned in cooperatives	0.91
Irrigated landholding size	*0.90*
Value of machinery owned	0.38
Number of acres under cash crops	0.36
Value of loans (from cooperatives)	0.27
Value of houses owned	0.09
Variables Not Entered	
Value of landholding	
% under cash crops	

95

The Dynamics of Indian Political Factions

TABLE 4.5. *Attitudes*

Variable	Coefficient
Evaluation of M.L.A.	*1.09*
Loan distribution machinery	0.28
Selection of candidates	0.25
Voting preference (majority v. unanimous)	0.21
Comments about Z.P. leadership	0.18
Variables Not Entered	
Predisposition to resign	
Caste role in distribution decisions	
Economic role in distribution decisions	

These two activities suggest something of the nature of the political struggle in the Poona Zilla Parishad. They, of course, confirm the Rebel link with cooperatives (at the taluka level). Probing further into the nature of this involvement, we find that those holding office in taluka cooperatives also tend to be officers in their village cooperative societies. The Rebels' link with the cooperative power structure is thus further strengthened. (Table II–II.B., pp. 243, 245.)

In addition, these two types of activity are interrelated: those involved in taluka cooperatives also tend to hold or to have held more than one office at a time in local government (*ibid.*). The Rebel is most visible, in fact, in leading positions of the village panchayat (Table 4.3 and Table B, p. 225).

We find, then, a relative concentration of Rebel Congressmen at the taluka and village levels, while an insignificant number are evident in district offices of the party and cooperative organizations. This suggests that the struggle here is, among other things, a vertical one, between higher and lower levels of the power structure. The Rebels are stronger at the lower levels, and particularly in taluka cooperatives. Even though the statistical analysis does not establish the dominance of Loyalists at the district level in any of the spheres of power, we know from our earlier discussion that this group's strength definitely resides in this higher level and specifically in the party organization. We need only recall that the undisputed leader of the district and of the Loyalists at the time of the election fight was President of the District Congress Commit-

96

tee and a recently elected Member of the Legislative Assembly. He himself selected his successor to the post of D.C.C. President and, as we have seen, the latter was also a Loyalist supporter.

The rivalry between groups can thus be identified at least in terms of different structural levels. The forces of the dissident group, at the village and taluka levels, apparently were not strong enough to counter the very strong party-based leadership of the Loyalists who combined, among them, several key positions in the district and State power structure. Most of the local M.L.A.s were on their side, as was a Deputy Minister, a past president of the District Local Board and the District Congress Committee President.

All of this confirms what had been suggested earlier: that the main political power bases appear to have been the cooperative structure and the party organization. The Zilla Parishad was merely an instrument in the struggle between two differently-based factions. The capture of the key Z.P. positions by Loyalists meant, in effect, that the district party organization had captured the Zilla Parishad in a struggle with the cooperative leadership. (It was not until *after* these posts were won by the Loyalists that their top leader became President of the District Central Cooperative Bank, displacing a man who had been one of the foremost Rebel leaders.)

AGRICULTURAL ASSETS AND COOPERATIVE ACTIVITY

There is further evidence to support some of the assertions made in the first part of this chapter. The measures of respondents' economic assets distinguish the Rebels as the wealthier of the two groups (Table 4.4 and Table B, p. 224). They also establish the existence of a very strong agricultural base for Rebel wealth, evidenced, among other things, by the larger plots of land owned by Rebels. This land was much more valuable than that owned by Loyalists, probably because more of it was irrigated. Sugarcane is a wet crop, so that the incidence of larger irrigated plots among Rebels serves to confirm the assumption that they were largely sugarcane cultivators. So does the high positive correlation between the size of irrigated landholding and both the number of acres under cash crops and the value of agricultural machinery owned (Tables III–III.B., pp. 249, 251). (The latter correlation, of course, reflects the fact that expensive pumps and engines are needed for purposes of irrigation.)

The earlier observations are even more conclusively confirmed by the finding that Rebels tended to have made a heavier financial investment in cooperative institutions (Table 4.4 and Table B, p. 224). In fact the Rebels' shares were valued at a ratio of about 9 to 1 in comparison with those of Loyalists. Clearly the Rebels had a greater interest in cooperatives than the Loyalists. This proposition is supported by the positive correlation between land-holding size, on the one hand, and the value of machinery owned and of loans secured from cooperative sources, on the other (Tables III–III.B., pp. 249, 251). We also find a tendency for the value of shares owned to increase in direct proportion with the number of acres cultivated under cash crops. It is reasonable to conclude that the larger shareholders among Rebels were also the larger cash crop cultivators.

It is relevant to note, at this point, that Rebels *were* by far the bigger cash crop cultivators (see Var. No. 20, Table B, p. 224). They had about 18 acres of land, on the average, under cash crops, while Loyalists had less than half that amount. The same is true of the value of machinery owned. Rebels, a smaller group by far (in the sample) owned equipment which was valued, on the average, at around Rs. 21,000, while the larger Loyalist group had among them, on the average, only Rs. 6,000 worth of machinery.

We have here indisputable evidence of the Rebels' vested interest in cash crop cultivation and cooperative institutions.

OTHER CHARACTERISTICS OF FACTIONAL GROUPS

Rebels were also distinguishable – in terms of attitudinal indicators – by their negative evaluation of the M.L.A.s political stature vis-a-vis that of Z.P. office-holders. This point of view was particularly effective in distinguishing Poona Rebels from Loyalists (Table 4.3 and Table B, p. 225); I discuss below some of the reasons for the groups' respective attitudes.

The only other finding of relevance here is the strong positive correlation between the attitude mentioned above and the Rebels' view that the selection of candidates by Congress was generally improper (Table IV–IV.B., pp. 255, 256). This finding confirms the Rebels' discontent with the party which is more vividly shown, of course, by their Rebel status and does not need to be further documented.

'ENVIRONMENT' AND POLITICAL CONFLICT

The analysis of ecological variables revealed some interesting and, in some respects, surprising aspects of the factional groups, which we have not touched upon as yet.

The most puzzling finding was that Rebels were distinguishable from Loyalists by the fact that they lived in talukas where the percentage of cultivators serviced by village cooperatives was smaller (Table 4.2 above and Table B, p. 224). In interpreting this characteristic with reference to Rebels, certain other considerations must also be taken into account, which suggest a possible reason for the Rebels' defeat in the Congress nomination struggle.

I have indicated elsewhere that sugarcane production was a somewhat localized affair in Poona. The bulk of it was cultivated in three neighboring talukas. As already noted, the size of loan per acre and per cultivator distributed by village cooperatives was largest in the leading cane-producing taluka (Baramati – which was also the center of Rebel opposition and site of the largest cooperative factory in Poona). The average size of loan also fell considerably as one moved into other talukas. Thus, while the proportion of cultivators serviced in the latter talukas may have been large (and we have found, indeed, that Loyalist talukas' cultivators were more widely serviced), the average loan was probably quite small.*

The localization of cooperatives' economic power in the sugarcane growing talukas proved to be politically disadvantageous. The Rebels, in order to attain district-wide political goals, needed to translate economic power into political power in the context of a widely dispersed 'political constituency'. This could not be done, because their base of operations limited their effectiveness to a relatively small area.

Another facet of this finding is revealed by one of the correlations which indicates that, within each factional group, the proportion of

* Note, for example, that the amount of loan per member in the big sugar (Rebel) taluka – Baramati – was Rs. 634.63, while the equivalent amount in a rice-growing taluka (controlled by the Loyalists) – Velhe – was only Rs. 42.88 In the same two talukas, the average loans per acre were Rs. 28.93 and Rs. 1.61, respectively (see Tables 2 and 3 above).

99

4-2

farmers having access to agricultural credit societies in their villages increases with the size of respondent's irrigated landholding (Tables V. B.1 and V. B.2, pp. 262, 263). This suggests that the larger landowners among both Rebels and Loyalists live in talukas whose farmers are more widely serviced by village cooperatives. This association is supported by certain other findings, discussed immediately below.

Dissident Congressmen in the Poona Zilla Parishad were identifiable by the fact that they lived in areas where the average landholding was higher than that in Loyalists' talukas (Table 4.2 and Table B, p. 223). It was found, moreover, that as the average size of landholding increased in the various talukas, so did the amount of loans disbursed by district-level credit banks (see Var. Nos. 6 and 8, Tables I–I.B., pp. 237, 239). This confirms the association discussed in the preceding paragraph. The inference to be drawn from these findings is that the agents of cooperative institutions, whether located in Rebels' or in Loyalists' areas, either were most generous with the larger landowners, or were most visible in talukas dominated by larger landowners.

In terms of other ecological indicators, it was found that Poona Rebels were favored by an environment characterized by a higher degree of socio-economic exchange (Table 4.2 and Table B, Var. Nos. 3 and 9, p. 223). For example, they generally lived closer to railway transportation than Loyalists, and in talukas which were more highly urbanized. This means, in effect, that Poona Rebels functioned in areas where a larger proportion of the population was engaged in non-agricultural activities. And they lived in or close to towns with banking and other urban facilities.

In addition, the dissident Congressmen in the Poona Z.P. may be characteristically found in talukas where the 'communications potential' on a social and economic level is greater. (See Table 4.2 and Table B, Var. No. 7, p. 223.) That is to say, they live in areas where the literacy level, not only of the rural male population in general but of their fellow cultivators as well, is higher. This means that the Rebel and some of his neighbors, friends, relatives and acquaintances may be able to read a newspaper, or keep accounts (if they are inclined to – though many respondents said they never did), or write letters and the like. They are also likely to live in areas where a larger proportion of villagers are perhaps stimulated by activities such as fairs (economic or religious) and weekly markets.

Inasmuch as there are more roads linking one village to another or to main roads in such areas, such a Rebel respondent might also be able to visit some of the fairs in his general area, or to purchase (or even sell) agricultural or other goods in an outdoor market held weekly in some nearby village, or perhaps even in his own village. Such facilities, of course, provide a very good vehicle for the exchange of information of all kinds, political, social, economic or cultural. More significantly in the context of this type of study, they make organization of a political group on more sophisticated and efficient lines easier.

All these communication variables, it may be noted, are inter-correlated in such a way as to indicate that the more distant a village from railway transportation or from district or taluka head-quarters, the less urbanized it will be (Table I–I.B., pp. 237, 239). This would constitute a more useful characterization of the Loyalists' talukas.

SUMMARY

It would appear, then, that the socio-economic environment of the Rebels has acted as a stimulus to their political behavior.* Reviewing the major findings of this chapter, we may conclude that the Rebels' image has been rather sharply defined, at least in respect of some features.

One outstanding characteristic of the dissident Congressman in this district is his greater wealth, as evidenced particularly by his more extensive irrigated landholdings and larger landed property. His wealth is obviously based on agricultural activities. And it is apparently quite closely related to his more intimate involvement in the cooperative structure, in terms both of financial investment and of 'power' assets (manifested in offices held in village and taluka-level cooperative institutions).

The Rebels' involvement in the total power structure is in fact quite extensive, although it is generally focussed at lower levels, such as the village and taluka. Whatever his activity in the party or in local government may be, however, he is most readily identifiable by cooperative office at either or both of these levels. On the other hand, he seems to have been excluded (it is unlikely that he

* In Chapter 8 we shall look into some of the reasons why the opportunities for greater economic and social exchange induced greater Rebel incidence in Poona, while in Ratnagiri such an environment was found to be more characteristic of the Loyalists.

excluded himself) from the district level. In the light of the discussion just concluded, the reasons for this may be evident.

Rebels, who generally function in an environment providing economic and social stimulation, expressed a certain degree of animosity, or at least a negative attitude, toward legislators elected from the Poona area. This was coupled with an expression of dissatisfaction with the Congress Party. Their view of legislators is understandable, for almost all the important M.L.A.s whose names were mentioned in the course of the interviews and informal discussions were Loyalists. This, in turn, suggests that the district-level party leadership, which is in effect the Loyalist leadership, may share certain common interests with local M.L.A.s. In many other states M.L.A.s are seated on the Zilla Parishad. In Maharashtra, however, they are not and they waged a fierce struggle at the time the Act was being drafted for inclusion of the M.L.A.s in the membership of the Zilla Parishads. Most of the Ministers were against this proposal, however, and the M.L.A.s lost their case. Since these bodies began to function, M.L.A.s have felt increasingly that their power and status is threatened within their constituencies (which are almost coterminous with the Taluka Panchayat Samiti) by the new popularly elected officials.

The District Congress Committee, on the other hand, which had been the most important political center at the district level, now has a potential rival in the Zilla Parishad, unless it can control it. The Z.P. could thus be considered a common threat to both the Congress organization and the local M.L.A.s.

The cooperatives, a fast-developing political power center, also have an interest in controlling the Zilla Parishad, since that control would invest their economic power with legitimate political authority. The power potential of such a structural combination would be formidable.*

* For information regarding the relative ability of variable clusters to discriminate between groups in Poona (shown in terms of the variance accounted for by each test cluster), see Table 5. In addition, Table 6 indicates the proportion of accurate classifications made by each set of test variables.

TABLE 5. *Discriminant Analysis Findings: Canonical Correlation – Ranked in Order of Importance*

Variable Cluster	Canonical Correlation	% of Variance Accounted For
Combined Variables	0.83	0.69
Economic Background	0.71	0.50
Behavior	0.70	0.49
Environment	0.66	0.44
Attitudes	0.50	0.25

TABLE 6. *Discriminant Analysis Findings: Accuracy of Prediction of Factional Alignment Achieved by Each Variable Cluster (% of Correct Classifications)*

	Variable Cluster*														
	Environ-ment			Behavior			Economic background			Attitudes			Combined variables		
Factional Groupings	L	R	T	L	R	T	L	R	T	L	R	T	L	R	T
Actual Membership	30	10	40	30	10	40	30	10	40	30	10	40	30	10	40
Discriminant Analysis Classification	28	7	35	27	8	35	29	7	36	19	10	29	30	9	39
% of Correct Classifications	93	70	88	90	80	87	97	70	90	63	100	72	100	90	98

* The letter headings under each variable cluster represent the following: L, Loyalist; R, Rebel; T, Total (both Rebels and Loyalists).

CHAPTER 6

AURANGABAD DISTRICT:
STATE VERSUS DISTRICT LEADERS

SOCIAL AND ECONOMIC BACKGROUND OF
POLITICAL CONFLICT

This district became a part of Maharashtra in 1956, with the enactment of the States Reorganization Act. Previously, it had been part of the State of Hyderabad which, until 1948, was under the rule of a prince descended from the Moghuls, the Nizam of Hyderabad.[1] Its social and economic backwardness testify to the general neglect of public welfare by the prince. Thus, of the four districts studied, the Aurangabad Zilla Parishad was the only one whose president had completed only the fourth grade in primary school. Most of the other Presidents and Committee Chairmen had a college education, and quite a few held law degrees. In Aurangabad, only the Vice President had completed his college education; the educational level of the two remaining officeholders was similar to that of the President. The consequences of this often became painfully obvious during the meetings of the general body and the various committees, when none of the top elected officials (except the Vice President) could deal with any of the questions raised by members. The appointed administrative officers usually, in effect, conducted the meetings, rather than the elected representatives of the people. It was a situation which the opposition, both within and outside the Congress Party, could and did exploit to embarrass the ruling group within the Zilla Parishad.

While the district is socially backward (in terms of education, for example), it has considerable potential for economic development, particularly in agriculture and agro-industry.[2] It has good soils which can support such crops as cotton and oil seeds which, together with sugarcane, constitute the chief commercial crops of the region. Indeed, about one-third of the cultivable area is under commercial (food or non-food) crops, and in some areas this proportion approaches or exceeds 40% of the total area sown (see

Aurangabad District

Table 1). Given the reliance of the cash crop cultivator on agricultural financiers, one might expect that a cooperative credit agency, if one existed here, would assume not only economic but also political importance. It does, in fact, exist, and it *has* played a major role in the political sphere, as we shall see presently.

Ample evidence exists linking the Rebel group with the cooperative structure and agricultural economic interests (in commercial crops, for example), which will be discussed in this chapter. There is also information available pointing to the private economic sector (non-agricultural or agro-industrial) as the source of wealth among prominent Loyalist leaders.

What is perhaps most surprising about the Rebel group in Aurangabad is that, in spite of their control over the most important political and economic spheres of the rural power structure, they failed to capture the Zilla Parishad. Possible reasons for this failure will also be discussed here.

Finally, I shall introduce some evidence of a possible link between the economic interests identified with the Rebel group and the ideological inclinations of this faction.

FACTIONAL LEADERS: THEIR POWER BASES

The leaders of the Rebel group all came from areas where cash crop cultivation was considerable (from 25% to almost 50% of the cultivable area).* The two most important cooperative banks in the district† were headed by the two top leaders of the Rebel group. They held these positions at the time of the Zilla Parishad Congress Party presidential nominations (in 1962) and thereafter (at least until 1965, when they were interviewed). Some of the Loyalist respondents claimed, in fact, that the Rebel votes had been bought with oil engines, pumps and crop loans.‡

* I am referring to the talukas of Kannad and Soegaon. For the crop pattern of this district, see Table 1 below.

† The District Central Cooperative Bank, which provides short-term loans (for the purchase of seeds and fertilizers, for example, or so-called 'crop loans') and medium-term loans (e.g., for the purchase of bullocks), is perhaps the most important cooperative agency in the district. The other important credit organization is the District Land Development Bank, which provides long-term loans (e.g., for the purchase of engines, pumps, or for land improvement, such as bunding or leveling, or the building of wells).[3]

‡ Apart from the obvious dependence which the cultivator and would-be borrower may have on the cooperative lending institution (and hence the benefit

105

TABLE 1. *Crop Pattern Indicating Incidence of Cash Crop Cultivation on a Taluka-wise Basis in the District of Aurangabad*

Details of Cropped Area	% of Gross Cropped Area in:						
	Aurangabad	Kannad	Sillod	Soegaon	Bhokardan	Jafferabad	Khuldabad
Area under cereals, pulses and other food crops	68.77	76.26	74.03	53.42	61.93	60.19	78.16
Area under sugarcane, oil seeds, cotton and tobacco	30.22	22.69	24.95	46.03	37.56	38.60	20.16
Other crops (non-food, including fodder crops)	1.01	1.05	1.02	0.55	0.51	1.21	1.68

	Vaijapur	Gangapur	Aurangabad	Jalna	Paithan	Ambad
Area under cereals, pulses and other food crops	77.71	73.39	76.47	62.01	66.78	61.10
Area under sugarcane, oil seeds, cotton and tobacco	21.59	25.66	22.47	35.85	32.39	37.78
Other crops (non-food, including fodder crops)	0.70	0.95	1.06	1.14	0.83	1.12

SOURCE: *Census of India 1961, District Census Handbook, Aurangabad,* compiled by The Maharashtra Census Office, Bombay, p. 35.

106

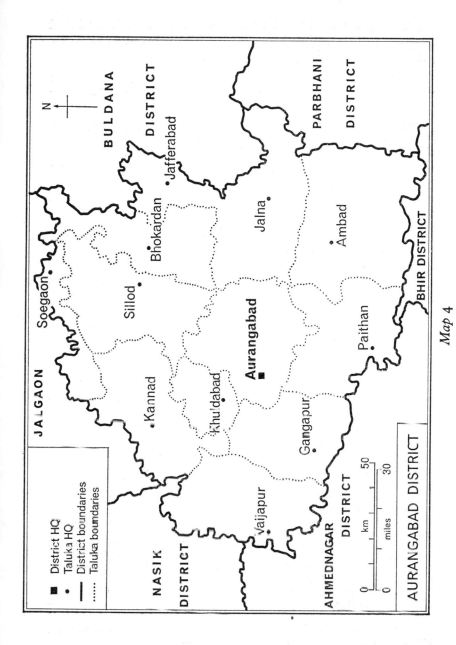

Map 4

AURANGABAD DISTRICT

Sufficient evidence will be presented later on (in the statistical analysis) to substantiate these associations between Rebels as a group and cooperatives, the cultivation of commercial crops and other related features and activities. Here I would like to dwell for a moment on the economic interests and associations – political and economic – of the Loyalist leaders.

The successful Loyalist candidate for the Z.P. Presidency, a very large landowner,* lived in the most highly industrialized taluka in the district. The town nearest his village, wherein he maintained another residence, was the largest urban center and headquarters of the district. In addition to owning very expensive agricultural equipment (which he had financed independently), he was a shareholder in one of the industrial concerns in Aurangabad. By contrast, he had no significant investment in any cooperative institution nor any position of authority in such an institution (except in his village, where he controlled all activities).

This Loyalist leader appeared to be a very powerful man, at least in his own area. A suit was pending against him in court regarding the allegedly improper division of his land among family members, but he was confident that he was going to win.†

The Vice President of the Zilla Parishad and Chairman of the important Works Committee, another prominent Loyalist leader, was entirely the product of an urban environment and had had no

---

he may derive by supporting it), there is also the possibility that the unsophisticated farmer is susceptible to pressure from the bank (or its agents) in order to ensure support. Control over the farmer can be exerted, for example, through the lending institution's inspecting staff. The inspector visiting an applicant's farm advises the bank whether that farmer is eligible for a loan, and it is on the basis of the inspector's report that the loan is approved. The inspector may say, either on his own initiative or at the instruction of superiors, that the farmer is in arrears or that, for other reasons, he is not eligible for a loan. There are other ways in which such support may be exacted. In Poona, one respondent claimed that a would-be Loyalist had been 'persuaded' to give his vote to the opposing group upon being assured that his large arrears on loans incurred to irrigate his land would be forgotten.

   * He owned 200 acres of very good land which he valued at one million rupees.

   † The details of his lawsuit are not known, nor was it clear whether this was to be a test case of some sort. The question of partition of jointly held land had come before the courts in a number of cases, and different benches of the Bombay High Court had given conflicting interpretations of the concept of partition. However, in 1963, a full bench of the Maharashtra High Court held that partition of land owned and possessed by a joint Hindu family did not come within the meaning of the Bombay Tenancy and Agricultural Lands Act of 1958, inasmuch as 'partition' did not constitute a transfer of land.[4]

agricultural links until he became involved in the politics which preceded the establishment of the Zilla Parishad.* His main source of income was real estate. He owned ten houses, valued at Rs. 200,000, the rents from which constituted his main livelihood. He was also a shareholder in two private manufacturing companies situated in the City of Aurangabad, where he lived and where his real estate was located. His own constituency in the taluka of Aurangabad was in an industrial area where several manufacturing industries were operating.[5]

Finally, one of the strongholds of the Loyalists was a taluka where the only sugar mill in the district was located. This was a *private* rather than a cooperative factory.[6] It was a significant business enterprise, which had assets valued at almost two crores rupees[7] (or almost three million dollars). Moreover, it was one of many ventures in a larger industrial complex which owned other sugar and cotton processing firms, as well as being involved in steel, chemicals, building construction and publishing enterprises.[8] The complex was one of the twenty largest private corporate groups *in India.*[9]

There was not a single Rebel among the four respondents from this taluka. The same was true of Aurangabad taluka, which was the main industrial center to which I have referred.

THE ROLE OF STATE LEADERS IN DISTRICT POLITICS

We now have some idea of the economic power base of some of the most important Loyalist leaders of this district. I have already indicated that the Rebels' base of operations was in the district's cooperative banks. I might add here that they also controlled the district's party organization at the time of the nominations fight among Z.P. Congressmen. The concentration in the hands of the Rebel leaders of key political and economic positions in the district raises the question why they lost the struggle for dominance in the local government sphere of the district power structure.

The principal reason appears to be that powerful state-level leaders intervened in the dispute, tipping the balance in the Loyalists' favor. It happened that the then President of the Maharashtra Pradesh Congress Committee (now deceased) was

---

* According to the Zilla Parishads Act, a Councillor must be a rural resident.[10] One way of establishing residence is to purchase land, as this respondent did.

from Aurangabad District, and his home taluka was adjacent to that in which the big sugar mill was located. By coincidence or design, he became President of the M.P.C.C. only a few months before the Z.P. Presidential nominations were to be held in the party, at a time when the two groups had already begun to take shape – during the state elections.* The new State Congress President reportedly sent a 'mandate' to all the Congress members elected to the new District Council, directing them to vote for the big landlord and the rentier to whom I have referred above. Some members of the Ministry were said to be backing the M.P.C.C. President and the Loyalist. In fact the newly appointed Deputy Minister of Agriculture was from this district and was, moreover, a close relative of the Presidential candidate on the Loyalist slate. He too was a supporter of the Loyalist group.

Thus there were powerful forces pitted against each other in this struggle, and their strength was reflected in the tied vote at the first party meeting held to select the Congress nominees for President and Vice President of the Zilla Parishad. When the first ballot produced a tie, the Loyalist candidate for the Presidency reportedly visited another Congressman who apparently had neglected to attend this important meeting, and commandeered him into breaking the tie in the Loyalists' favor by promising him a committee post. Within forty-eight hours, a vote was taken again, and the Loyalist group was in. The man who is supposed to have broken the tie was subsequently elected chairman of one of the district-level committees.†

The Rebel group refused to accept their defeat in the party, and openly contested the official Congress slate in the formal elections which followed at the first general meeting of the Zilla Parishad. They were defeated there also, again by a fairly close margin. This was the only district of the four studied where the Rebel group did not abide by the majority decision in the party and chose, instead, to challenge publicly the authority of the party. The struggle must have been very bitter. It was reported in a Bombay paper that 200 Congressmen from this area, including 24 Zilla Parishad members,

---

* These elections were held in February 1962, and the new M.P.C.C. President was elected at the end of March. The nominations fight in the Z.P. Congress Meeting took place in August 1962.

† According to the procedure followed, the party nominates the Presidential and Vice Presidential candidates first, and then chooses two more candidates for the post of Chairman of several district-level committees at a subsequent date.

had submitted their resignations to the District Congress President (one of the top Rebel leaders), complaining of 'unconstitutional pressure' brought on them by the M.P.C.C. President to vote for a particular candidate during these elections.[11] There was no subsequent reference in the press to this particular incident, however, and I assume that most of the Z.P. members eventually returned to the party, since I subsequently interviewed many of them.* The Rebel Presidential candidate, however, did not return to the party so far as I was able to determine.

Thus intervention by State leaders appears to have been largely responsible for the defeat of the Rebel group. The previous experience of this district with an authoritarian style of rule provides some insight into the effectiveness of State intervention in this instance.

There is one other consideration which must be kept in mind when interpreting this defeat, and that is the potential political strength of a cooperative-based group like the Rebels. We must remember that the institutional credit structure is not confined to the cooperative sector. The Office of the Collector, which is a part of the Revenue Department, is also authorized to sanction certain types of agricultural loans. In addition, certain loans which at one time were distributed through the Department of Agriculture are now channeled through the Zilla Parishads. These bodies have been given responsibility over various agricultural projects, such as the horticultural loan scheme, which is particularly relevant in this context. If we assume that economic blandishments were a factor in attracting Congressmen to one faction rather than another, then it appears feasible that a Loyalist leader could lure undecided Congressmen with promises of horticultural loans. It is also relevant to note that these loans are ultimately allocated to the district by the Department of Agriculture, whose Deputy Minister was from Aurangabad and was a supporter of the Loyalists.

* It was curious that not one of the respondents interviewed referred to this development. It was apparently a very sensitive political incident. Out of the forty-three Congressmen interviewed, however, 20 did indicate a willingness to resign from the party under hypothetical circumstances. This number corresponds fairly closely to the number of Z.P. Congressmen (24) who reportedly did resign after the nominations fight.[12] Of the 24 said to have cast their vote against the official slate in the party meeting, only 12 appeared as Rebels in my sample. And although only about 25 Z.P. Congressmen sided with the Loyalists in the Party elections according to Congress Councillors, 31 appeared on my sample as Loyalists. The discrepancy may be due to the fact that some of the Councilmen originally elected subsequently died or resigned, and to the possible reluctance of timid Congressmen to admit their Rebel status.

The Dynamics of Indian Political Factions

In the circumstances outlined above, the success of the Loyalist group over apparently overwhelming odds may appear more understandable. The organizational base of the Rebel group at the district level could not withstand the evidently strong pressures exerted by the State Congress organization and probably by certain influential ministers.

AN OLD POLITICAL CONFLICT RE-ENACTED?

I indicated at the beginning of this section that I intended to discuss the relative ideological orientations of the political dissidents. Some general information about the Congressmen in this District Council may provide a perspective in this respect. Of 48 Congressmen interviewed,* about 25% (13) had at some time belonged to or sympathized with another party. Of these as many as 9 had belonged to leftist parties, such as the Praja Socialist Party (5), the Peasants and Workers Party (1) and the Communist Party of India (3). It may be noted that this was the only one of the four districts studied where Congressmen had ever been C.P.I. members. (See Table 2.)

Although there was no direct relationship established between former membership in another party and factional alignment, nor

TABLE 2. *Frequencies Indicating Past Membership by Congressmen in Parties Other Than the Indian National Congress*

Parties Other Than Congress In Which Respondents Had Held Membership	Ratnagiri	Frequencies in:		
		Akola	Poona	Aurangabad
Praja Socialist Party	4	1	2	5
Peasants and Workers Party	4	1	–	1
Republican Party of India	–	4	–	1
Jana Sangh and Hindu Mahasabha	2	–	–	–
Communist Party of India	–	–	–	3
Other	1	–	2	3
Total	11	6	4	13

* Only 43 of these were used in the sample for discriminant analysis. The remaining five were eliminated largely because their factional membership could not be ascertained or because they were not party or Z.P. members at the time of the nominations fight.

TABLE 3. *Cross-Classification of Predisposition to Resign from Congress Party by Attitude to non-Congress Movement (Samyukta Maharashtra Samiti or Others)*

Frequencies: Past Sympathies with non-Congress Movement:		Percentage Distribution Predisposition to Resign:	
		Would Resign	Would Not Resign
Was sympathizer	11	81.8	18.2
Was not sympathizer	28	39.3	60.7

Predisposition to Resign:		Past Sympathies With Non-Congress Movement:	
		Sympathizer	Not Sympathizer
Would Resign	20	45.0	55.0
Would Not Resign	19	10.5	89.5

Percentage Distribution Over Total Sample (39)

Past Sympathies with non-Congress Movement		Predisposition to Resign	
Was sympathizer	28.2%	Would Resign	51.3%
Was not sympathizer	71.8%	Would Not Resign	48.7%

Chi-square, 5.72; Contingency Coefficient, 0.36; Level of significance, 0.02.

between other-party sympathizers and factional membership, a significant association did emerge between those who had sympathized with an anti-Congress movement (the Samyukta Maharashtra Samiti) and the two groups under investigation.* It appears that most of the Z.P. Congressmen who had not been sympathetic to this anti-Congress movement were Loyalists and only a tiny proportion were Rebels. A very strong relationship was found, moreover, between Congressmen who had been S.M.S. sympathizers, other-party sympathizers or other-party members, on the one hand, and those respondents who expressed an inclination to

* See Table 6 below for the statistics establishing significance.

113

TABLE 4. *Cross-Classification of Predisposition To Resign From Congress Party By Other-Party Sympathizer*

Frequencies Past Sympathies with Other Party		Percentage Distribution Predisposition to Resign:	
		Would Resign	Would Not Resign
Was Other-Party Sympathizer	12	83.3	16.7
Was Not Other-Party Sympathizer	31	38.7	61.3

Predisposition to Resign		Past Sympathies With Other Party	
		Sympathizer	Not Sympathizer
Would Resign	22	45.5	54.5
Would Not Resign	21	9.5	90.5

Percentage Distribution Over Total Sample (43)

Past Sympathies with Other Party		Predisposition to Resign	
Sympathizers	27.9%	Would Resign	51.2%
Non-Sympathizers	72.1%	Would Not Resign	48.8%

Chi-square, 6.89; Contingency Coefficient, 0.37; Level of Significance, 0.01.

resign from the party if it violated its principles (see Tables 3–5). We may also note that the proportion of Congress respondents who had been members of another party was largest in this district, at 30.2%, which hints at strong tensions within the district organization (see Table 5).

The association between Rebels and S.M.S.-sympathizers is most useful in that it prompts us to compare the current conflict with the great struggle which shook all of Maharashtra (then Bombay State) in 1957. If the factions studied almost ten years after that battle can be traced back to that period, then indeed the

Aurangabad District

TABLE 5. *Cross-Classification of Predisposition To Resign from Congress Party by Other-Party Membership*

Frequencies Past Membership In Other Party		Percentage Distribution Predisposition to Resign:	
		Would Resign	Would Not Resign
Had been member of other party	13	76.9	23.1
Had not been member of other party	30	40.0	60.0

Predisposition to Resign		Past Membership in Other Party	
		Yes	No
Would Resign	22	45.5	54.5
Would Not Resign	21	14.3	85.7

Percentage Distribution Over Total Sample (43)

Past Membership in Other Party		Predisposition to Resign	
Yes	30.2 %	Would Resign	51.2 %
No	69.8 %	Would Not Resign	48.8 %

Chi-square, 4.95; Contingency Coefficient, 0.32; Level of Significance, 0.05.

Rebels (as well as the Loyalists) apparently represent a group with considerable continuity.

A struggle for office very similar to the one under study was waged in 1957, but on a much vaster scale. At the State level, Congress leaders and their followers marshalled their forces into opposing camps for the purpose of deciding who was going to be leader of the Congress Party and thus Chief Minister of the State.

The two contenders were Y. B. Chavan and B. S. Hiray (the latter now deceased). Hiray was originally from a cotton district in the Desh (Dhulia),* had been Vice Chairman of the Maharashtra

* For a number of years before his death, he had his residence in the District of Nasik, which also has considerable cash crop cultivation – in oilseeds, cotton and sugarcane.

The Dynamics of Indian Political Factions

TABLE 6. *Cross-Classification of Factional Alignment By Attitude to Non-Congress Movement (Samyukta Maharashtra)*

Frequencies Attitude to non-Congress movement		Percentage Distribution Factional Alignment:	
		Rebel	Loyalist
Sympathizer	10	50.0	50.0
Not sympathizer	26	15.4	84.6

Factional Alignment		Attitude to non-Congress movement :	
		Sympathizer	Not sympathizer
Rebel	9	55.6	44.4
Loyalist	27	18.5	81.5

Percentage Distribution Over Total Sample (36)

Attitude to non-Congress Movement		Factional Alignment	
Sympathizer	27.8 %	Rebels	25 %
Non-sympathizer	72.2 %	Loyalists	75 %

Chi-square, 4.62; Contingency Coefficient, 0.34; Level of Significance, 0.05.

State Cooperative Bank and was long active in the cooperative field, according to the press.[13] The issue on which the two leaders were divided was whether Gujerat ought to remain a part of Bombay State. The official Congress policy supported the States Reorganization Act, which had brought into being this bi-lingual state. The forces behind the Samyukta Maharashtra Samiti were clamoring for a unilingual state which would exclude the Gujerati-speaking areas. This was the principal issue on which the opposing lines were drawn. However, as I have said earlier (see analysis of Ratnagiri District), there was also an economic aspect to the issue which apparently divided the opposing camps. In Aurangabad, for example, it was learned that Hiray was supported at that time by all the cash crop growers of the Marathwada region.* On the basis of this

* For information regarding the extent of cash crop cultivation in the area, see Table 5 in the Irrigation Commission's Report.[15]

admittedly flimsy evidence, we may tentatively place the ex-Chief Minister of Maharashtra in the camp of the 'Loyalists' – or its equivalent at the State level. In Aurangabad, during 1962, we find him supporting the M.P.C.C. President and supreme leader of the Loyalist group. (In Poona, also, reference was made to Chavan as the backer of one of the important Loyalist leaders. His position in Ratnagiri was not quite clear, and his role in Akola remains to be seen.)

Although there was a controversy in Maharashtra in the early 1960s about decreasing the cash crop acreage to allow for more extensive cultivation of food crops,[14] no one whom I interviewed connected this controversy with the political divisions under investigation here. The possibility is suggested that the 'food versus cash crops' controversy may have been one of the issues agitating State-level leaders at this time – and perhaps even in the earlier dispute. Leaders like Chavan or Hiray often act as spokesmen of important economic interests. Their policy statements, their actions, their political careers and organizational links give us some clues as to the nature of their bases of power and an insight into the dynamics of their policy positions. The statement that 'cash crop growers were behind Hiray in 1957' is, of course, 'one man's opinion'. The fact that Hiray was organizationally linked with the cooperative power structure, however, is a matter of record (see fn. 13), and it gives some weight to the above observation. It is also a fact that Chavan had *no* links with cooperatives at all. The record shows that his political career began in the party organization, and it was from there that he was catapulted into public prominence as Chief Minister of Maharashtra,[16] as national defense minister, and now as India's Home Minister. Although statements made by members of the political elite about their own leaders should be carefully weighed, they assume some credibility when, gathered as they are from disparate parts of the State, they begin to fall into a pattern. Let us take as an example the report of a participant in an M.P.C.C. meeting held at Rahuri in 1965. At that meeting (according to a respondent), someone expressed the opinion that 'Y. B. Chavan could not go against the sugarcane growers' interests (private) because they have him in their pockets'. In the light of the foregoing, this assertion seems to confirm the emerging pattern. (Such statements are not offered – indeed, could not be offered – as conclusive evidence regarding policy positions of top leaders like Chavan. They are simply included as suggestive of certain patterns whose validity is being otherwise demonstrated.) We may therefore say that it is quite possible that Chavan found it necessary to project himself into district politics in Aurangabad. He had no stronghold of his own in Marathwada, and the young State Congress President from Aurangabad (whose appointment Chavan, as leader of the State, no doubt approved) gave the then Chief Minister the kind of support he needed in that region. In the district fight, he might well have backed the Rebel group, which was well established in power there. Yet he chose to throw his weight behind a different group, whose economic and political background we have already discussed. I have hinted at some of the possible reasons for this in Aurangabad. As for the state-level aspect of district politics, this has been more elaborately discussed in the second chapter, reference to which may clarify the nature of the political struggle in this district.

THE BASES OF POLITICAL FACTIONS: A STATISTICAL ANALYSIS

An examination of the findings yielded by discriminant analysis will provide sound evidence in support of the argument presented above for a causal relationship between certain economic interests and the formation of a group of dissidents within the Congress organization in the district.

We shall focus on those characteristics shared by the Rebels which set them apart from the Loyalists. Among the most important distinguishing attributes of the two factors were their relative involvement in the cooperative structure at the district level and their role in the district party organization (Tables 7.1 and 7.2).

POSITION OF REBELS IN LOCAL POWER STRUCTURE: OFFICE IN COOPERATIVE AND PARTY ORGANIZATIONS

The distinguishing feature of the Rebels, in terms of these variables, was their predominance in positions of authority in both the party organization and the cooperative power structure (Table 7.1 and Table C, p. 228). It appears that both these organizations were out of reach of most Loyalists – leaders and followers – at the district level. The Rebel leadership, in fact, may be described as

Aurangabad District

TABLE 7.1. *Discriminant Analysis Findings: Coefficients for Canonical Variable Ranked in Order of Importance*

Combined Variables Cluster Variable	Coefficient
Communications Potential	0.98
Involved in Cooperatives – District	0.98
% Cultivators Serviced by Cooperatives	0.91
Involved in Party – District	*0.51*
Involved in Party – Taluka	0.49
Value of shares owned in cooperatives	0.46
Comments about Z.P. Leadership	0.35
Involved in Government – Village	0.23
Public Electoral Participation	0.23
Distance from Panchayat Samiti	0.12
Voting Preference (majority v. unanimous)	0.10
Average Landholding in Taluka	0.10

TABLE 7.2. *Environment*

Variable	Coefficient
Communications Potential	1.22
% Cultivators Serviced by Cooperatives	0.84
Public Electoral Participation	0.67
Distance from Panchayat Samiti	0.57
Average Landholding in Taluka	*0.53*
Urbanization	0.45
Distance – Bus	0.42
Distance – Z.P.	0.14
Variables Not Entered	
Distance – Railway	
Agricultural Cooperative Activity	
Agricultural Prosperity	
Eligible votes polled by non-Congress candidates	
Total votes polled by non-Congress candidates	

a coalition between members of these two important power spheres. One of the Rebel leaders – who, after the defeat of his group, became Chairman of the Land Development Bank – had been President of the District Congress Committee at the time of the nominations fight, and led the Rebels in that capacity. An older and more respected leader of the dissidents was President of the

119

TABLE 7.3. *Behavior*

Variable	Coefficient
Involved in Party – District	0.74
Involved in Party – Taluka	0.58
Involved in Government – Village	0.56
Involved in Cooperatives – District	*0.50*
Number of Offices – Cooperatives	0.48
Involved in Government – District	0.39
Number of Offices – Government	0.36
Involved in Party – Village	0.34
Involved in Cooperatives – Village	0.22
Number of Spheres – Simultaneous	0.16
Involved in Cooperatives – Taluka	0.09
Variables Not Entered	
Simultaneous Office – Cooperatives	
Simultaneous Office – Party	
Simultaneous Office – Government	
Number of Spheres – Over Time	
Number of Offices – Party	
Involved in Government – Taluka	

TABLE 7.4. *Economic Background*

Variable	Coefficient
Value of shares owned in cooperatives	0.79
Value of houses owned	0.45
Landholding size	0.39
Irrigated landholding size	0.34
Value of landholding	0.23
Variables Not Entered	
Value of machinery owned	
% of acres under cash crops	
Number of acres under cash crops	

District Central Cooperative Bank at the time of this political struggle (and remained in that position until his death a few years later). These, then, were the two top Rebels, and by joining hands they forged into a single political force the power elements of the district Congress organization and the most powerful cooperative credit agency in Aurangabad.

Aurangabad District

TABLE 7.5. *Attitudes*

Variable	Coefficient
Comments about Z.P. leadership	0.72
Voting preference (majority v. unanimous)	*0.64*
Predisposition to resign	0.33
Assessment of M.L.A.	0.28
Caste role in distribution decisions	0.22
Selection of candidates	
Variable Not Entered	
Economic role in distribution decisions	

The two variables mentioned here appeared as powerful discriminators in the analysis of all significant indicators of factional membership, as well as in their own cluster of *behavioral* variables (Tables 7.1 and 7.3). It is interesting to note in this connection that, of the two, authority in district cooperatives had the greater discriminating capacity when examined within the 'combined variables' cluster; on the other hand, when analyzed only with other *behavioral* indices, it was one of the less effective discriminators (though still significant). This simply illustrates the importance of analyzing any given situation from as broad a perspective as possible. The findings of the more inclusive analysis (in each district) ought, of course, to be given greater weight.

The correlation of these two variables with other *behavioral* indicators revealed nothing more profound than that individuals at one level of a particular power sphere tended to be more heavily involved in that sphere than in another, although there was also an intercorrelation between authority in these two organizations. Generally however I found that as group involvement in the district or taluka party organization increased, so did the number of offices held over time by an individual at some level of that organization. The same was true of involvement in district cooperatives and of respondents involved in local government. In other words, there tended to be a specialization of skills acquired by some individuals in particular power spheres (Table II–II.C, Var. Nos. (7, 10, 11), (6, 14), (8, 17), pp. 243, 246).

Rebels, in addition to predominating in the party and cooperative organizations at the district level, were also found in greater

121

numbers at the taluka level of the party structure, as well as in leading positions on their village councils. Loyalists, on the other hand, were distinguished by relative quiescence in these positions (Appendix 2, Table C).

Thus, as far as their organizational base within the district was concerned, there is little question that the Rebels were secure. The fact that this group was defeated is largely due to the power and influence enjoyed by State leadership in district affairs, as we have seen.

THE OBJECTIVE ENVIRONMENT OF POLITICAL ACTORS: POTENTIAL FOR SOCIAL, ECONOMIC AND POLITICAL COMMUNICATION

The *combined variables* factor which so accurately predicted the factional alignment in Aurangabad had an *environmental* dimension as well as the *behavioral* one described above. A very important indicator of factional membership in this district was the potential for communications on a social and economic level (Table 7.2). Dissident Congressmen in this Zilla Parishad lived in areas where the level of education was higher, thus allowing for the use of a greater variety of the available media of exchange; they were also afforded a greater opportunity for economic exchange through fairs, markets and better road facilities.

As this communications potential increased within the Rebels' and Loyalists' talukas, the proportion of cultivators who might have access to a credit cooperative society in the taluka villages also tended to increase (Table I–I.C., Var. Nos. 7 and 13, pp. 237, 240) It was curious, however, that the Rebels were at the same time distinguished by the fact that their talukas were not quite as extensively serviced by cooperatives as were those of the Loyalists (Table C, Var. No. 13, p. 226). That is to say, the proportion of cultivators who might be members of village cooperatives was not as high in Rebels' talukas as it was in those of the Loyalists. This should not necessarily be interpreted to mean that fellow cultivators in a Rebel's taluka received little or less financial assistance from cooperative institutions. If this were the case, then the economic link, which I implicitly posit between this segment of the political elite (the Rebels) and the larger community whose interests it presumably should advance, would be weakened. There is clear indication, however, within the *environmental* cluster, that the Rebels' talukas were very generously serviced indeed. The higher loan activity in the Rebels' talukas is evidenced, first of all, by the mean value of the variable 'agricultural cooperative activity' for each of the factional groups (see Table C, p. 226). This variable is a composite one, derived from factor analysis. It is comprised largely of indicators measuring the amount of loan per member (of cooperative societies) and per acre distributed in each taluka by various lending institutions.* It may be noted that the range of means between Loyalists and Rebels on this variable was quite large, indicating a substantial difference between the two groups in terms of this attribute. That it did not emerge as a significant discriminator is due to the fact that it was significantly correlated with communications potential and highly so with the percentage of cultivators serviced by village cooperatives. Thus it lost some of its discriminating power after the variable 'communications potential' was entered, and was completely eliminated from the analysis when 'percentage of cultivators serviced by cooperatives' was entered in the stepwise discriminant analysis.

Other discriminating indicators identified by the separate analysis of the *environmental* cluster of variables confirmed the greater prevalence of Rebels as it were, at the center of things. Thus, in addition to living in talukas which were afforded greater opportunities for economic and social exchange, they also lived in villages which allowed for greater political communication because they were closer to their taluka headquarters (Table 7.2 and Table C, p. 226). Inasmuch as the distance of villages from the Taluka Panchayat Samiti Headquarters was positively correlated with the distance from a bus station (Table I–I.C., Var. Nos. 1 and 4, pp. 237, 240), we may assume that those Rebels who lived closer to the main taluka town also had available a modern (and, I might add, fairly reliable) means of transport to that town.

Correlations within groups further indicated that areas which had greater communications potential were also more prosperous agriculturally, though, surprisingly, they also tended to have fewer towns and banks, and a smaller urban community (Table I–I.C., Var. Nos. 7 and 9, pp. 237 and 240). Moreover, the talukas in which Aurangabad Rebels lived were characterized, on the whole, by smaller landholdings (Table 7.2 and Table C, p. 226). It is

* For an exact enumeration of the variables comprising this composite factor, see Table E, p. 219.

significant to note in this connection that the loans distributed by cooperative institutions tended to increase as the landholding size decreased (Table I–I.C., Var. Nos. 6 and 8, pp. 237, 240), which suggests that the smaller landowners were favored by the cooperatives. This accords with the finding that the Rebels controlled the cooperatives: it might be expected that they would favor the talukas of smaller landholders, where their own group associates were predominant.

INVESTMENT IN COOPERATIVES AS AN INDEX OF FACTIONAL ALIGNMENTS

Of the two remaining clusters, neither contributed any significant discriminators to the *combined variables* factor, though there was one indicator from the *economic background* cluster which approached significance* in the *combined variables* test. (See Table 7.1.) It was also the only variable among eight in the *economic* cluster which qualified as a significant discriminator of factional alignments in Aurangabad (Table 7.4). This variable was a measure of the value of shares owned by respondents in cooperative institutions. The analysis revealed that Rebels had a bigger financial investment in cooperatives than Loyalists (Table C, p. 226). Still more significant in the context of this study, as a whole, is the fact that, wherever this variable emerged as a discriminator of factional alignment, it was always the Rebels who were found to have a strong financial interest in these institutions. Such an interest was evidenced on an all-district basis and in Poona, as well as in Aurangabad (see Table 8, immediately below). Moreover, in terms of the absolute mean values, the Rebels of both Ratnagiri and Akola were also found to be larger investors in cooperative shares, though for a similar reason as noted above (p. 123) this did not appear as a significant discriminator in either district.

It is also important to note that this indicator was positively correlated (at 0.5) with the value of machinery owned (Table III.C., p. 252). In other words, as the value of a person's investment in a cooperative institution increased, he was also likely to own agri-

* The 'significance' of indicators in any given cluster has been defined in terms of the coefficient for the canonical variable assigned to each indicator in the cluster (see note (*) on page 199, below). All indicators having a value of 0.50 and more were considered 'significant' for purposes of incorporating them in a final test which combined all such 'significant' indicators.

TABLE 8. *Average (Mean) Value of Shares (in Rupees)
in Cooperative Institutions Owned by Factions*

Group (sample size)	Rebels (12)	Loyalists (31)
All Districts	2810	787
Ratnagiri	3201	315
Poona	9252	1048
Aurangabad	2000	808
Akola	2356	830

cultural machinery that was more highly valued. Moreover, as we look at respondents in terms of these features, it appears that a higher investment in cooperatives was likely to be accompanied by a larger plot of irrigated land. This is quite understandable: both the conversion of land to irrigation by bunding or leveling, and the purchase of agricultural equipment necessary to bring water to the land – such as an engine or pump – are rather expensive undertakings, which can be greatly facilitated, for a moderately wealthy cultivator, through the kind of financial help offered by the cooperatives. Finally, the correlations point to a strong link between the value of machinery owned and the number of acres under cash crops (Table III.C p. 252).

The least effective discriminator of all clusters in Aurangabad was the *attitudinal* one (see Table 8). The findings here indicated that Aurangabad Rebels were more readily identifiable by their greater preference for unanimous voting in party meetings (which suggests a stronger disciplinarian attitude), and a rather bleak evaluation of the Zilla Parishad leaders – none of whom, after all, was from their ranks – (Table 7.5 and Table C, p. 226). The latter evaluation is understandable when we take into account the calibre of this leadership, particularly in the case of the Rebels, who were perhaps the more alert group of the two.* Under the circumstances, therefore, it is not surprising to find that those respondents with a low opinion of their officials tended to look up to the M.L.A s with somewhat greater respect.

* In cross-classifying 'factional alignment' with 'relative exposure to news media', a significant relationship was found to exist between these variables. (See Table 9.) The above statement is based on this finding.

The Dynamics of Indian Political Factions

TABLE 9. *Discriminant Analysis Findings: Canonical Correlation– Ranked in Order of Importance*

Variable Cluster	Canonical Correlation	% of Variance Accounted For
Combined Variables	0.86	0.74
Behavior	0.78	0.61
Environment	0.66	0.44
Economic Background	0.36	0.13
Attitudes	0.32	0.10

TABLE 10. *Cross-Classification of Factional Alignment by Exposure to News Media**

Frequencies Exposure to News Media		Percentage distribution Factional Alignment:	
		Rebel	Loyalist
None	4	0.0	100.0
Some	17	5.9	94.1
Most	19	42.1	57.9

		Exposure to News Media:		
Factional Alignment		None	Some	Most
Rebels	9	0.0	11.1	88.9
Loyalists	31	12.9	51.6	35.5

Percentage Distribution Over Total Sample (40)

Exposure to News Media		Factional Alignment	
None	10%	Rebels	22.5%
Some	42%	Loyalists	77.5%
Most	47.5%		

Chi-square, 8.04; Contingency Coefficient, 0.41; Level of Significance, 0.02.

* The categories shown above under 'Exposure to News Media' denote the following:

None: Reads newspapers and listens to radio occasionally, rarely or not at all.

Some: Reads newspapers *or* listens to radio daily or often (several times a week).

Most: Reads newspapers *and* listens to radio daily or often.

126

Aurangabad District

TABLE 11. *Discriminant Analysis Findings: Accuracy of Prediction of Factional Alignment Achieved by Each Variable Cluster (% of Correct Classifications)*

| | Variable Cluster* | | | | | | | | | | | | | | |
| | Environment | | | Behavior | | | Economic background | | | Attitudes | | | Combined variables | | |
Factional Groupings	L	R	T	L	R	T	L	R	T	L	R	T	L	R	T
Actual Membership	31	12	43	31	12	43	31	12	43	31	12	43	31	12	43
Discriminant Analysis Classification	27	9	36	30	9	39	22	6	28	21	9	30	30	11	41
% of Correct Classifications	87	75	84	98	75	90	70	50	65	68	75	70	98	91	95

* The letter headings under each variable cluster represent the following: L, Loyalist; R, Rebel; T, Total (both Rebels and Loyalists).

SUMMARY

A panoramic view of the Aurangabad factional groups based on these findings presents us with a profile of Rebels which differs from others in all respects except one. The dissident Congressmen in this district once again were dominant in the cooperative power structure. From this vantage point, they challenged another group of Congressmen which, in terms of organizational leadership at least, drew its strength from the State level. At the district level, however, the results of the analysis indicated conclusively that the Rebel group controlled the major cooperative institutions.

The link between Rebels and cooperatives was further strengthened by a network of associations which pointed to greater loan activity by cooperatives in Rebels' talukas. The latter were generally distinguished from the Loyalists' areas by the presence of greater opportunities for economic exchange which, incidentally, seemed more evident in areas of more extensive cash crop cultivation. However, these areas of greater economic activity were also – surprisingly – likely to be situated in talukas with fewer urban features.

The Aurangabad dissidents enjoyed not only a strong economic base, but also an enviable political vantage point as top district leaders of the Congress organization. These advantages, however, were overcome (though not without considerable struggle) by intervention from powerful State leaders.

As we conclude our discussion of findings in Aurangabad, we note that a pattern has been discerned in the political divisions here which is similar to that noticed in other Zilla Parishads, even though here it emerged under political, economic and social conditions which varied from those found in other districts. The one element which dissident Congressmen have shared in all districts examined so far has been their activity in positions of authority within the cooperative organizations (and with it, a bias toward the cultivation of commercial crops).*

* For information regarding the proportion of accurate classifications made by each set of test variables, see Table 10.

CHAPTER 7

AKOLA DISTRICT:
FACTIONAL ALIGNMENTS
IN CONDITIONS OF RELATIVE PLENTY
(THE POLITICS OF COTTON)

THE POLITICAL AND ECONOMIC SETTING

The evidence examined thus far has consistently indicated that, under given conditions, there is a definite relationship between activity in cooperative institutions* (which is usually associated with the cultivation of commercial crops) on the one hand, and the pattern of factional alignments on the other.

Akola provides us with a model example of a flourishing cash crop economy as a setting against which to study factional behavior. The entire Vidarbha area, wherein Akola is situated, is in one of the most important cotton tracts in the country.† The economic importance of its principal product is considerable. The cotton textile industry is the single largest manufacturing industry in the country.[1] Textiles also form the most important group of industries in the State of Maharashtra in terms of the productive capital contributed, the value of output and the value added by manufacture.[2] Finally, raw cotton is the most important export item in the District of Akola and provides the raw material for one of the few large-scale industries in the district.[3] Over 40% of the arable land here is under cotton and the proportion of the gross area under cultivation which is devoted to cotton in each taluka ranges from 31% to 55%.[4] In comparison with other districts, respondents here also had the highest proportion of their land under cotton or some other commercial crop, and cooperatives certainly appeared to be an important economic institution to Akola respondents, who had larger cooperative loans, on the average, than respondents in any other district (see Table 3 in Ch. 8, pp. 173–4).

* Particularly those engaged in extending agricultural credit.
† For a more extensive discussion of Vidarbha's economic characteristics, see Chapter 2 above.

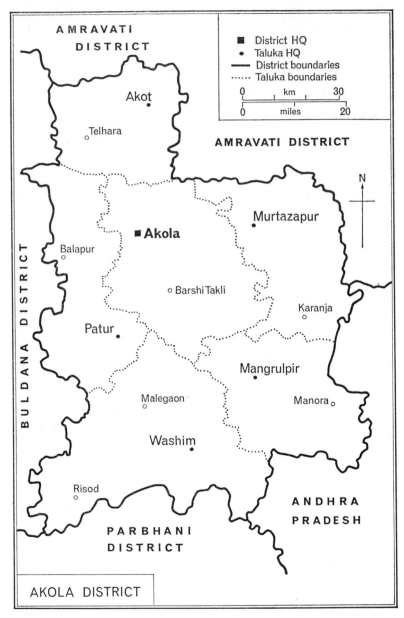

Map 5

It is therefore not surprising to find that the principal hypothesis advanced in this study is substantiated by the analysis of Akola factions. In fact, this prosperous cotton district, where the cooperative banks wielded considerable political power, as we shall see, was the only one of the four studied where the Rebels proved powerful enough to capture the key positions in the Zilla Parishad; indeed, they outnumbered the Loyalist Congressmen in the District Council by an overwhelming margin. There were 35 Rebels as against only 9 Loyalists on this Zilla Parishad, and this sample constitutes an almost complete representation of Congressmen on the body.

For reasons which will be discussed later on, I intend to rely upon this section of the analysis rather heavily in order to demonstrate the association between economic interests and activities and factional membership. A detailed inquiry into the backstage politics of the area will prove very illuminating for our purposes.

VERTICAL LINES OF CONFLICT

The struggle which agitated Akola in 1962 was a three-cornered conflict, involving: (1) State-level leaders against (2) certain regional interests, and (3) powerful rival groups at the district level, one of which had regional links. We are dealing, in effect, with two levels: state and local. At one point of the triangle we find State leaders, who are engaged in conflict with a group of powerful district leaders at a second point. These district leaders, part of a regional alliance, are, in turn, locked in battle with another powerful district-based group, which constitutes the third point of our triangle.

The intensity of feeling which this struggle aroused in the district is attested to by the high level of electoral participation by rural constituents of the Zilla Parishad Councillors. In many of the constituencies, sixty and even seventy percent. or more of the voters cast their ballots on election day.[5] Low proportions in a few of the constituencies brought the average down to 57% which, nevertheless, represented the highest level of voter turnout in any district in the study. However, before we look at the local issues involved, it may be more helpful to try and understand the higher-level conflict which propelled the State leaders into the local struggle.* For the political divisions encountered in Akola in 1962 appear to have been a continuation of an older struggle. Therefore I begin by commenting on that struggle, which had been in process for a while before the factions under study evolved.

Akola did not become a part of Maharashtra until 1956, when the reorganization of state boundaries took place. At that time, the eight districts of Vidarbha† which had been a part of Madhya Pradesh were incorporated in the State of Maharashtra as the Nagpur Division.[6] The region was and is a tremendous asset to Maharashtra. Its rich soils support, as we have seen, an important commercial crop. Oil seeds are another important product which, after processing, yield not only oil for cooking, but a raw material used in the paint and soap industries.[7] Fruit cultivation is also favored here by physical conditions, and Nagpur oranges (another cash crop) are famous in many parts of India. But Vidarbha is also an important food-growing area, and its wheat and millet crop have made an important contribution to the meagre food supply of Maharashtra.‡ In addition, it has tremendous potential for industrial development,[8] and this is just beginning to be exploited.

Vidarbha, however, also brought to Maharashtra the political headaches which had plagued the Government of Madhya Pradesh. The Brahmin community, which had dominated Vidarbha politics during the Nationalist Movement, began – even before independence was achieved – to lose its leading position to the Marwaris.§ This private economic community, followed by a few other minority castes,¶ became the ruling group in Vidarbha (and certainly in Akola) from 1947 on. The Congress Party, providing an organizational base for their economic power, came under their control. Some of the leading government figures in Madhya Pradesh, including the Chief Minister and the Home Minister,

---

* The outlines of this conflict are reconstructed in the pages that follow from information obtained in formal and informal interviews administered in Akola and the other districts. Where possible, this is documented by published primary and secondary sources.

† Akola, Amravati, Bandhara, Buldhana, Chanda, Nagpur, Wardha, Yeotmal.

‡ One respondent, unhappy with his new state citizenship, remarked rather acidly, in response to a question put to him, that he could not help but feel like a Maharashtrian – now that, for the first time in his life, he had experienced scarcity.

§ Since I shall refer to this community several times throughout this chapter, I wish to refer the reader to an earlier note (see p. 14) which commented on the role of ascriptive groups in the context of this study.

¶ Malis, Baris (pan-growers) and Kolis – and some Brahmins as well.

conceived the idea of weakening the hold of this economic community by establishing competitive power centers in bodies of local government, which could be controlled by the State Government and through which the power of this ruling group could be curbed. Thus, the Janpad Sabhas came into being.[9] This took place before the area came under Maharashtra, and these local bodies continued to function until they were displaced by the Zilla Parishads.

So far we have a typical example of a feud between the ministerial and the organizational wing of the party. What is relevant for the district under study at the time of the Presidential nominations, however, is the fact that the private economic community (led by Marwaris) had its organizational base in the Vidarbha Congress. This remained its base after Vidarbha's transfer to Maharashtra. As one might surmise, it is this group which we find in control of the Akola District Congress Committee in 1962, when that Committee exercised its authority to distribute party tickets to aspiring Councillors of the Zilla Parishad.

I have suggested in the foregoing remarks that a Marwari-dominated group was the leading political force in the Vidarbha Congress organization, as well as in Akola District. This, in brief, was the situation which the Maharashtra leadership inherited when Vidarbha became a part of the State. In spite of that, the region constituted a political asset for certain Maharashtra leaders at the time, as well as an economic asset for the State as a whole. We may recall that shortly after the 1956 reorganization, the State leadership was torn by a conflict over the inclusion of the Gujerat districts within the borders of Bombay State (now Maharashtra), which had been effected by the States Reorganisation Act. Y. B. Chavan, who was leading the Congress forces supporting a bilingual Bombay, faced tremendous opposition – not only outside but within the Party as well – and needed all the support he could get. He was able to recruit some of this support from the Vidarbha Congress people* who threw their weight behind Chavan and against Hiray, who was vying with Chavan for leadership of the Congress Party and the Government. We saw, in the analysis of Aurangabad District, that Chavan's opponent (Hiray) was backed

* It is significant to note in this context that the Vidarbha Congress leaders were apparently able to organize impressive popular support for the Congress Party. All but one of the Parliamentary candidates of Congress were elected.[10]

The Dynamics of Indian Political Factions

(in Marathwada, at least) by the cash crop growers and the co-operatives. Our examination of Ratnagiri District revealed that the Congress position on the Samyukta Maharashtra issue was supported by the business interests of Bombay. The Marwari group in Vidarbha, of course, represents the business (industrial and commercial) interests of that area also, and we find that they took a similar position, endorsing the merger advocated by Chavan.

In the legislative assembly election fight, support came in the form of votes. G. B. Khedkar, President of the Vidarbha Pradesh Congress Committee from 1948 to 1958,[11] is said to have given his vote – as a newly elected Member of the Legislative Assembly – to Chavan in 1957. Another man, who had been Vice President of the Vidarbha Pradesh Congress Committee and also a Member of the Legislative Assembly in 1957 similarly supported Chavan.* In 1960, this Chavan supporter became Deputy Minister for Agriculture in the Government of Maharashtra, and the former Vidarbha P.C.C. President became President of the Maharashtra Pradesh Congress Committee in the same year. In 1962, Khedkar was appointed Minister for Rural Development in the Government of Maharashtra, under Chavan.[12] Another Vidarbha Congressman who reportedly backed Chavan later became Minister of Forests, and still another became Minister of Civil Supplies. All of the men to whom I have referred were from Akola District. It may be noted, moreover, that Vidarbha always has been well-represented in the Maharashtra Ministry. The man who succeeded Chavan as Chief Minister when the latter became Defense Minister in the Government of India was from Vidarbha (M. S. Kannamwar from Chanda District). The present Chief Minister (Vasantrao Naik, 1962–71), who succeeded to the highest public post in the State upon the death of Mr Kannamwar is also from the Vidarbha district of Yeotmal.

The Akola politicians who were ostensibly thus rewarded, although supporters of the Marwari group, were themselves chiefly Marathas. The Marwari leaders who constituted the backbone of the Vidarbha Congress organization, were not similarly compensated. They had not been too happy in the Madhya Pradesh fold, and now, too, they did not see many signs that their interests would be better cared for in Maharashtra.

In April 1961, a year before the national, state and local elections were to be held, a deputation of Vidarbha leaders, which included

* Reference here is to M. Vairale.

134

the Marwari strongman from Akola, visited Prime Minister Nehru to present their demand for a separate Vidarbha State.[13] Nehru would not countenance such a demand. Within a few months it was announced that they would contest the forthcoming general elections on the Mahavidarbha issue.[14] In 1957, the people of Vidarbha had been presented with a slate of Congress candidates united on the main election issue. In 1962, however, they were faced with a choice between Congress Party candidates on the one hand, and, on the other, familiar ex-Congressmen running on the separatist ticket of the Nag Vidarbha Andolan Samiti.* Some of the old Vidarbha Congressmen who had been recruited into the Maharashtra Ministry or the leadership ranks of the State Congress organization after 1957 chose to remain with Chavan on this issue. All of them won their legislative seats in Akola except one, who ran in the central stronghold of the Marwari group and was defeated.

On the whole, however, the election results of 1962 constituted a resounding defeat for the Vidarbha separatists – at least in the rural areas of the district. The Zilla Parishad elections remained to be contested, however, and the defeated separatist forces now prepared to enter the field for the fight to control the newly-established district council. The Marwari leader from Akola resigned from the separatist party that had been formed to contest the state elections and within a few months rejoined Congress. The district Congress organization continued to be dominated by separatist leaders or sympathizers.

POWER STRUGGLE IN THE DISTRICT

This was the situation which confronted the political community of Akola as it girded itself for the next political struggle in the district arena. There were many – in and out of Congress – whose sympathies lay with the separatist forces. However, those forces had been soundly defeated in the State elections, and now a powerful local group was poised to deal the final blow to them. The politically wise thing to do – or so it appeared to many – would be to get on the winning bandwagon, and so ensure access to the political and economic benefits which the Z.P. could offer.†

* This was the political party organized to pursue the goal of a separate Vidarbha State.
† This was a sentiment expressed by several respondents.

The Dynamics of Indian Political Factions

The District Congress Committee was thus confronted with a difficult political situation. Its main weapon was control over the distribution of party tickets.* Many of the Rebel respondents said that, having been refused a Congress ticket, they decided to run as independents. Some asserted that pressure had been exerted on them to pledge their support in advance for the Congress-sponsored candidates for office in the Zilla Parishad (whose officials were to be chosen by the new Councillors, following the popular elections). These tactics apparently alienated many people, and we find, possibly because of this, that, out of fifty-odd constituencies which the Congress contested, only 24 candidates were elected on that party's ticket. The remainder won seats as independents or on the Republican Party ticket.† The outcome was that the State Congress Party was placed in a very precarious position in the matter of the coming elections for officers. The dissident Congressmen who had left the party to contest the elections now asked that they be permitted to rejoin – before the Presidential nominations were to be made. The demand was pressed by the leader of the Rebels, who spoke as a Congressman, inasmuch as he had successfully contested for a Z.P. seat on the Congress ticket; and it was addressed to the State leaders through an M.P.C.C. 'observer' sent to Akola (among other districts with similar problems)[15] in an effort to resolve the conflict.

THE ROLE OF STATE LEADERS

At this point State political interests became concerned in the local quarrel. The situation which evolved here can in no way be described as an 'organizational v. ministerial' conflict. Ministers were pitted against Ministers, the State Congress organization against the district organization, and, in the final analysis, the conflict configuration was one of Ministers and State Congress organization leaders against other Ministers and local Congress leaders.

* The decision regarding who was to contest which constituency was also used as a weapon. The Rebel Presidential candidate claimed (and the charge was confirmed by others) that he had been switched from his usual constituency, where he was quite strong, to a less certain one. The election statistics do, in fact, indicate that he won by a narrow margin in that constituency.[16]

† Oddly enough, although this is the party of the scheduled castes, most of those who were given tickets by the Republican Party were Marathas.

Akola District

It appears that some of the Ministers, whose M.L.A. constituencies were in this district and who had been leaders in the Vidarbha Congress Committee, rallied to the support of their old political associates – now that their political positions in the State Government were secure. The choice which faced the top State leaders, however, was a difficult one. The Rebel leader threatened that if the ex-Congressmen were not taken back into the Congress fold, he and his associates would contest the formal election for officers in the general body of the Zilla Parishad, where his group would be assured of victory, since Congress did not hold a majority of the seats there (and even among those it held, it was not assured of total support). This meant, in effect, that the State Congress organization could lose control of one very important district if the Rebel leader carried out his threat. The Congress could hardly afford to lose Akola at a time when it was facing similar problems in other parts of Vidarbha. In any case, the State leaders were not too favorably inclined towards the local Congress leaders, because they had – and continued to have – close relations with the separatist group which had only recently challenged State authority. The Minister who had been an important leader in this district and was a past President of the Vidarbha Pradesh Congress Committee appeared at one point to lend his support to the local Congress leadership. Apparently, however, he came under pressure from the M.P.C.C. President, who reportedly was in favor of accepting the ex-Congressmen rather than losing the district, and from top leaders in the Maharashtra Ministry. Thus, according to the Rebel President, this Minister remained 'neutral' in the last stages of the controversy. And so the prodigal Congressmen were allowed to return to the Party and the Rebel leader won the Congress nomination for the Presidency by a wide margin. (And, of course, he was later easily elected to that office by the general Z.P. membership.)

I have discussed in some detail the various conflicting forces at work in the district's factional struggle in order (1) to demonstrate the weakness of the explanation of factional alignments in terms of the conflict between the organizational and ministerial wings of the Congress Party[17] and (2) more particularly, to further reinforce the proposition that Indian political elites are not always guided by irrational considerations in their political behavior. (In this particular district, actually, this claim can be supported more effectively

The Dynamics of Indian Political Factions

with regard to the leading strata of the elite than the followers –
although circumstantial evidence indicates that the latter also made
rational decisions in the given political conditions.)

It was necessary to identify the leading political actors and
groups which played a role in the main struggles involving the
political community of this district, so that we could understand
that role more clearly against the background of their politico-
economic associations and interests.

CASH CROPS IN AGRICULTURE AND INDUSTRY

It is in this part of the analysis that we are finally able to present
evidence of the links between economic interests and political
behavior, and thus to illustrate the validity of the main hypothesis
in this study.

At the time of the political conflict under investigation, there
were only three large-scale manufacturing factories in Akola, two
producing textiles and one hydrogenated oil.[18] The last-named was
apparently the largest of the three enterprises.* The economic
importance of the industrial sector in this district did not lie in its
capacity as employer: there were only six factory workers per
thousand of total population in Akola, as contrasted to 20 per
thousand for the whole of Maharashtra.[19] However, there was and
is an interdependence here between this sector and agriculture.
The cotton and oil seed produce, which is harvested from 49% of
the total arable area in the district,[20] feeds the local industries.
Approximately two-thirds of the hydrogenated oil produced in
Akola[21] is processed by this one oil mill.[22] I do not have statistics
regarding the exact proportion of textile production which is
undertaken by the two spinning and weaving mills referred to
above. I would venture to guess, however, that these mills probably
process a sizable proportion *of whatever cotton is processed here.*
Although there were three cotton ginning and pressing cooperative
societies organized in the district during 1960–1, they had not yet
started production at the time of the factional dispute under
study.[23] (Nor were they producing in 1965, when I visited the
district.) Hence, all of the cotton processing at the time was done
in the private sector – by the cottage industries or the larger pro-

* This was listed in a Government report on monopolies as one of the top
five enterprises in the country (in 1964) in annual production of milled oil.[24]

138

cessing units. The cottage industry, however, was said to be on the decline, due to competition from the goods manufactured in the mills. As a result of this, many people had to seek alternative employment. Efforts were under way, therefore, to revive the industry by bringing the workers into the cooperative fold.[25] All of this suggests that the larger spinning and weaving units did, indeed, handle most of the cotton processing undertaken in the district.* More importantly, it illustrates the conflict of interests represented by the private as against the cooperative economic sector.

The large oil mill to which I have referred was said to be a Birla enterprise.† It is pertinent – in the context of this study in general, and this district conflict in particular – to point out that the Birla family is reputed to be the wealthiest in the Marwari community, and the second most important business family in India today (after the Tatas).[26]

An important private organization representing the industrial and commercial interests of the area is the Vidarbha Chamber of Commerce. The president of this organization at the time was also a Marwari.[27] The interests of the industrial complex controlled by this family in the jute, cotton and woollen industries together accounted for nearly 60% of the value of their companies' production sales.[28]

Although other examples of the prominent position occupied by the Marwaris in the economy of Vidarbha, and Akola in particular, might be enumerated, sufficient evidence has been presented to document the importance of this business community in the economic affairs of the region.

It may now be recalled that the leading spokesman from Akola for a separate Vidarbha was also a Marwari. He and his associates had established an organizational base in the Congress Party of Vidarbha and were reputed to be the 'ruling group' in the political affairs of the region, from the time Indian independence was attained. It was this leader who stood for a parliamentary constituency in 1962 on the ticket of the Nag Vidarbha Andolan

---

* Much of the cotton produce was exported to the Bombay mills for processing.

† This information was given to me by one of the more knowledgeable respondents in Akola. I have not been able to confirm it, however, through any public sources. Had it been large enough (in assets), it would have been listed among the Birla enterprises in the Monopolies Report. However, its assets were too small for this.

Samiti, the newly-formed party of the separatist forces, and was defeated by the Congress candidate.[29]

The candidate for president of the Zilla Parishad on the Loyalist slate admitted quite freely during his interview that it was this 'prominent' Marwari leader who had brought him into the Congress organization in 1945. From that time there began a long association with this leader and with his group. At their urging, he contested for the municipality and was a municipal councillor from 1945 to 1960, elected twice on the Congress ticket and once on the separatist group ticket.

Although it may be said that this man was associated with the cooperative structure as chairman of his taluka's marketing society, such an association represents more an instance of private interests' efforts to penetrate the cooperatives than a bona fide association. This is deduced from the fact that his association with the leaders of the business community was longer than that with cooperative institutions, particularly at the district level; it is also deduced from the small number of authoritative positions which he held during this association.*

The Rebel leaders, on the other hand, had been closely associated with the cooperative power structure in Akola. The most important Rebel leader, who became President of the Zilla Parishad against considerable odds, had been Secretary of the Akola District Central Cooperative Bank from 1956 to 1959, and Chairman of that Bank from 1959 until the time of his interview, which meant that he had held that position for a period of three years at the time the nominations struggle evolved in 1962, and had been in positions of authority in the most important cooperative bank of the district for a period of six to seven years up to 1962. At about that time he was also elected Chairman of the first cooperative spinning mill established in Akola.

The man who appears by all accounts to have been his chief associate and adviser in this struggle was Vice Chairman of the District Central Cooperative Bank. The latter was a brother-in-law of this top Rebel leader and Secretary of the Bank at the time the field study was being conducted. Another very important Rebel

---

* The latter statement is also descriptive of some of the ministers who had been linked in the past with the leading economic community in Vidarbha, as members and leaders of the Vidarbha Congress. See biographical sketches of the following ministers in the *Times of India Directory*: G. B. Khedkar, M. Vairale, and D. Z. Palaspagar.[30]

leader, who had been an M.L.A., was Secretary of the Bank at the time the presidential elections were held in the Congress Party.

COOPERATIVES AND THE FARMER

The offices held by Rebel leaders in cooperative institutions were positions of great power. There can be little doubt that these organizations have provided services to the Akola farmers – primarily in credit, but also in marketing. In Akola particularly, the opinion seemed to be widespread that the moneylender was on his way out.* However, no hard statistics are available to document this. Indeed a report on rural credit some years ago indicated that institutional sources of credit (including cooperatives) filled only a small proportion of agricultural needs.[31] But this report and follow-up surveys generally did not include any Maharashtra districts in their samples. Moreover, the cooperative movement in Maharashtra is acknowledged as one of the most successful in the country. And much progress has been made in the period following the field studies on which the rural credit survey reports are based.†

As far as Akola is concerned, the cooperative movement has made great strides in the past decade, as well as in the years immediately preceding the factional dispute which is the focus of this study. While one cannot conclusively state that the moneylender's activities have declined, one *can* assert with certainty that the amount of credit disbursed by agricultural credit societies in Akola more than doubled between 1957–8 and 1960–1.[32] Moreover, the number of members enrolled in these societies increased in the same period by almost 50%[33] and their working capital almost tripled.[34]

As far as Vidarbha is concerned, the available information indicates that there was also an increase in the membership and loan activity of the District Central Cooperative Banks between the years 1959–60 and 1960–1.[35]

Thus it can be safely asserted that the cooperative lending institutions, while not necessarily displacing private sources of credit,

---

* It may be noted, however, that such assertions were usually qualified by the statement that the very small landowner still had to depend on the moneylender, as he did not have enough land to offer as security to the cooperative societies.

† For a discussion of the cooperative movement in Maharashtra, see Chapter 2.

have provided an alternative and competitive source for agricultural borrowers. That the cooperative structure, because of financial exigencies or for other reasons, tends to service a limited segment of the agricultural community (namely, the moderately large landowner who usually needs financing for commercial crops) does not necessarily limit the impact of this competition. Indeed, this sector constitutes the better financial risk, compared with the much larger contingent of more risky credit customers – namely the very small landowners or tenants with one or two or five acres of land, who are forced to depend on the moneylender because they do not have large enough landholdings to offer as security to the cooperative lending institution.

THE BASES OF POLITICAL FACTIONS: A STATISTICAL
ANALYSIS

For reasons which will be set forth immediately below, the statistical findings only indirectly hinted at a relationship between the cooperative organization and the nature of factional alignments. However, the above inquiry into the background of the political struggle in this district in 1962 and the network of associations and interests between one group and the other has, I believe, conclusively traced the conflict to essentially economic roots.

One reason which may account for the inconclusive nature of the findings here can be traced back to the state-regional conflict to which I referred earlier. As I indicated, the district factions observed here were, in effect, extensions of this larger struggle. The national and state elections held in 1962 did not produce a compromise between the opposing forces. In that sense, the conflict remained partially unresolved, at least as far as the separatist elements were concerned. Though defeated, they did not abandon their efforts to secure or retain control in other political arenas. Because of this, the political calculations of some of the respondents under study here had apparently been thrown into a temporary state of confusion. Thus I found that some of the Rebel respondents had had political associations which would almost certainly range them in the camp of the Loyalists. This political uncertainty may partly explain the weakness of the findings.

In addition, one or two of the aggregate characteristics of Akola respondents will give us a clue as to why factions do not appear to

Akola District

TABLE 1. *Frequencies Indicating Level of Political Ambition Displayed by Respondents in Each District*

Variable: Political Ambition	Frequencies in			
	Ratnagiri	Akola	Poona	Aurangabad
Respondent was not inclined originally to contest 1962 Z.P. elections but was persuaded to do so (or idea suggested to him) by others	36	25	20	17
Respondent wanted to contest 1962 elections	17	23	23	29
Total	53	48	43	46

be so well-formed in this district. For one thing, the level of political ambition seems to be rather low here (see Table 1). However, as may be seen from this table, it was still lower in Ratnagiri which, nevertheless, had well-defined factional groupings. I mention this characteristic because it assumes more meaning when considered in conjunction with another relevant attribute exhibited by respondents in Akola. The extent of involvement in the total power structure was lower here than in any other district (see Table 3, p. 172). While the reasons for this can be traced to the nature of the factional alignment itself, it nevertheless indicates that one or both of the groups contained many men who had few of the political skills which are acquired while holding political office. Whatever the reasons, their generally limited participation in positions of political responsibility indicates that they had only briefly, if at all, experienced the specialized process of political socialization which political recruits undergo in such positions of authority. In these circumstances, they may not have had time to become familiar with the political symbols, signs and personnel through which information about and recognition of one's interests are registered. It is possible, then, that this state of affairs coincided with other conditions to bring about apparently blurred lines of factional divisions.

The fact remains that the results of the discriminant analysis do not lend themselves readily to an intelligible interpretation, insofar

143

The Dynamics of Indian Political Factions

as the main hypothesis of this study is concerned. I therefore intend to rely, in part, on another type of statistic, which is descriptive rather than inferential in nature.*

I would also like to emphasize the importance of the non-statistical analysis which preceded this section. Particularly in view of the possibility that the rank-and-file followers of each group may be less privy to the inner councils of the top leadership in this district than in any other, I believe that more insights have been gained into the nature of the factional struggle here by scrutinizing the characteristics and associational patterns of the top level leadership.

THE DISSIDENTS EXCLUDED FROM THE DISTRICT CONGRESS

Analysis by cross-tabulation indicated a significant association between involvement in the party structure and the factional alignments in this district. This confirmed an earlier observation that Rebels had generally held no office in the party organization or at most one, while the Loyalists tended to have held two or more offices in the party over a period of time (see Table 2). Thus the assertion that the victorious Rebels were the men who had opposed the district party organization assumes a credible basis in this association. Many of the complaints voiced by the dissidents, in fact, indicated that they were disenchanted with the Congress organization because of the favoritism it showed in all its dealings generally, but particularly at election time, in the distribution of tickets. It appears then that many rallied behind the Rebel leadership to defeat the organization men.

As I have stated, it is difficult to establish conclusively whether the Rebels were deliberately excluded from the party organization or whether they had not considered the Congress a useful political association before the establishment of the Zilla Parishads. The fact remains, however, that the Rebel group was made up of relative newcomers to the party. A significant association is revealed between the year respondents joined Congress and the direction of their factional loyalties. Of those who had joined the party between 1947 and 1957, 92% were Rebels. However, *none* of the Loyalists had joined Congress after 1957. Of approximately one-third of the

* I refer to chi-square and the contingency coefficient.

144

TABLE 2. *Cross-Classification of Factional Alignment by Number of Offices Held in Congress Party*

Frequencies		Percentage Distribution Factional Alignment	
Number of Offices Held in Party		Rebel	Loyalist
None	27	81.5	18.5
One	13	92.3	7.7
Two or more	4	25.0	75.0

		Number of Offices Held in Party:		
Factional Alignment		None	One	Two or More
Rebel	35	62.9	34.3	2.9
Loyalist	9	55.6	11.1	33.3

Percentage Distribution Over Total Sample (44)

Number of Offices Held in Party		Factional Alignment	
None	61.4	Rebels	79.5
One	29.5	Loyalists	20.5
Two or more	9.1		

Chi-square, 8.68; Contingency Coefficient, 0.41; Level of Significance, 0.02.

respondents who had enrolled in the party in the years following 1957, *all* were Rebels (Table 3). This does not mean, however, that the Rebel group was made up of younger men. Both Rebels and Loyalists were a mixed group, age-wise. Although most members among the younger respondents (aged 30 to 44) tended to be Rebels (who outnumbered the Loyalists in a ratio of 35:9), as many as two-thirds of the small Loyalist group were also of this younger age group. And, finally, almost half of the Rebels were between the ages of 45 and 74 (Table 4).

Another significant association indicates that non-involvement in the party power structure in Akola, more than in any other district, hindered one's chances of holding positions of authority

145

TABLE 3. *Cross-Classification of Factional Alignment by Period of Enrolment in Congress Party*

Year Joined Party	Frequencies	Percentage Distribution Factional Alignment	
		Rebel	Loyalist
By 1947	15	53.3	46.7
By 1957	13	92.3	7.7
After 1957	12	100.0	0.0

Factional Alignment		Year Joined Party:		
		By 1947	By 1957	After 1957
Rebel	32	25.0	37.5	37.5
Loyalist	8	87.5	12.5	0.0

Percentage Distribution Over Total Sample (40)

Year Joined Party		Factional Alignment	
By 1947	37.5	Rebel	80
By 1957	32.5	Loyalist	20
After 1957	30.0		

Chi-square, 10.90; Contingency Coefficient, 0.46; Level of Significance, 0.01.

in other power centers. Thus, over 40% of those not holding or having held office in the party organization had held no office in any of the other spheres of the local power structure (Table 5). Almost all of those who had held some office in the party, on the other hand, were also found to have been involved in one or more of the other power spheres. About three-fourths of all respondents, however, had held no office at all in the party. And as we have seen, it was largely the Rebel group which was thus divorced from the Congress organization (see Table 2).

TABLE 4. *Cross-Classification of Factional Alignment by Age*

Age	Frequencies	Percentage Distribution Factional Alignment:	
		Rebel	Loyalist
Up to 34	8	87.5	12.5
35 to 44	16	68.8	31.2
45 to 54	14	100.0	0.0
55 to 74	6	50.0	50.0

Factional Alignment		Age:			
		To 34	35–44	45–54	55–74
Rebel	35	20.0	31.4	40.0	8.6
Loyalist	9	11.1	55.5	0.0	33.3

Percentage Distribution Over Total Sample (44)

Age		Factional Alignment	
To 34	18.2	Rebel	79.5
35–44	36.4	Loyalist	20.5
45–54	31.8		
55–74	13.6		

Chi-square, 8.28; Contingency Coefficient, 0.40; Level of Significance, 0.02.

COOPERATIVES, LOCAL GOVERNMENT AND POLITICAL POWER

There was also a large proportion of respondents (69%) who had held no office in cooperative institutions (Table 6). Here, also, we find that non-involvement in this sphere hindered one's chances of assuming office in the other power spheres, while, on the other hand, an office in this organization almost guaranteed multiple involvement in the other power spheres, slightly more so than involvement in the party organization (see Tables 5 and 6).

Finally, we find that of the much larger proportion who *were* involved in the local government sphere (61%), only two-thirds or so had been extensively involved in the total power structure

TABLE 5. *Cross-Classification of Involvement in All Spheres by Involvement in Party Organization*

Office Held in Party Organization	Frequencies	Percentage Distribution Office Held in Various Spheres		
		In No Sphere	In One Sphere	In More Than One Sphere
Not held	34	41.2	41.2	17.6
Held	12	0.0	8.3	92.7

Office Held in Various Spheres		Office Held in Party Organization	
		Not Held	Held
In no sphere	14	100.0	0.0
In one sphere	15	93.3	6.7
In more than one sphere	17	35.3	64.7

Percentage Distribution Over Total Sample (46)

Office Held in Party Organization		Office Held in Various Spheres	
Not held	73.9	In no sphere	30.4
Held	26.1	In one sphere	32.6
		In more than one sphere	37.0

Chi-square, 21.02; Contingency Coefficient, 0.56; Level of Significance, 0.001.

(Table 7). It may be noted by contrast that over 90% of those involved in either the party organization or the cooperative sphere had also tended to hold or to have held office in one or both of the other two local power spheres. Thus, while respondents might have been more active in the governing institutions of their district, this did not ensure their participation in other power spheres as strongly as their involvement in the party or the cooperative organizations (see Tables 5, 6 and 7).

Akola District

The above findings are substantiated or complemented by the results of the discriminant analysis. For example, the *combined variables* test revealed that Rebels were more intensively involved in local government, holding two offices at a time, at one or more levels (village, taluka or district). Loyalists, on the other hand, were particularly evident in village panchayats or in local government at an intermediate level (Table 8.1 and Table D, p. 231). A sight check of Loyalists' interviews indicated that the period in which these offices were held was after 1962, so that we are dealing here with offices held in the three-tier 'panchayati raj' structure of local government.

The only significance attributable to this finding is that the Loyalists, while losing the nomination fight, were yet strong enough to command positions of authority – for four out of nine in their group – on bodies of some weight within the Zilla Parishad (either in the district body or in the Panchayat Samiti,* which is subordinate to the Zilla Parishad). The residual strength of the group is further attested to by the fact that one of the most important leaders of the Loyalists – their presidential candidate – was able, in spite of his defeat, to command a post on the new district body.

The separate analysis of *behavioral* variables served to illustrate the low level of political activity among Akola respondents, most of whom were dissident Congressmen. Rebels were found to be significantly less involved in the party organization at the taluka level (Table 8.3 and Table D, p. 231). This is understandable in view of the fact that they were generally excluded (either by accident or design) from the party organization as a whole. What was more surprising, however, in a district where the cooperative bank president led the Rebel group to victory, was that his followers were not extensively involved in cooperative office. It appears that in this district of politically-shy cultivators, it was not necessary for the political leader to win support through the spoils of office. The banks may have satisfied a good many people through their loan activities. It is pertinent to note, for example, that almost three-quarters of Akola cultivators in respondents' talukas had access to

* Akola, as part of the Nagpur Division (Vidarbha), is the only district (of the four) where the Panchayat Samiti's jurisdiction is not coterminous with the taluka unit. Talukas in Akola cover a larger territory than similar units in districts outside Vidarbha. The Akola talukas were therefore demarcated so that each encompassed two or three Panchayat Samitis.

TABLE 6. *Cross-Classification of Involvement In All Spheres By Involvement In Cooperative Organization*

		Percentage Distribution Office Held in Various Spheres		
Office Held in Cooperative Organization	Frequencies	In No Sphere	In One Sphere	In More Than One Sphere
Not held	33	42.4	39.4	18.2
Held	15	0.0	6.7	93.3

		Office Held in Cooperative	
Office Held in Various Spheres		Not held	Held
In no sphere	14	100.0	0.0
In one sphere	14	92.9	7.1
In more than one sphere	20	30.0	70.0

Percentage Distribution Over Total Sample (48)

Office Held in Cooperative Organization		Office Held in Various Spheres	
Not held	68.8	In no sphere	29.2
Held	31.3	In one sphere	29.2
		In more than one sphere	41.7

Chi-square, 24.13; Contingency Coefficient, 0.58; Level of Significance, 0.001.

village agricultural credit cooperative societies (see Table D, p. 230 below, Variable No. 13, under 'Rebels and Loyalists'). This proportion was higher than in any other district (see Table 3, p. 172). We have already noted that the value of loans secured by Congressmen in this district was also the highest of all. Moreover, the loan activity engaged in by cooperatives at the district and lower levels was very high (see Table 3, p. 172). The cooperatives, it would appear, had done their 'homework' well. Economic benefits to the

Akola District

		Percentage Distribution Office Held in Various Spheres		
Frequencies Office Held in Local Government		In No Sphere	In One Sphere	In More Than One Sphere
Not held	20	70.0	30.0	0.0
Held	31	0.0	32.3	67.7

		Office Held in Local Government	
Office Held in Various Spheres		Not held	Held
In no sphere	14	100.0	0.0
In one sphere	16	37.5	62.5
In more than one sphere	21	0.0	100.0

Percentage Distribution Over Total Sample (51)

Office Held in Local Government		Office Held in Various Spheres	
Not held	39.2	In no sphere	27.5
Held	60.8	In one sphere	31.4
		In more than one sphere	41.2

Chi-square, 35.27; Contingency Coefficient, 0.64; Level of Significance, 0.001.

people at large (in the form of loans) proved a more effective currency here than political benefits (in the form of cooperative office, for example) in ensuring widespread support for the Rebel leader.

Finally, Rebels were found to be intensively involved in the power structure as a whole (Table 8.3 and Table D, p. 231). It

The Dynamics of Indian Political Factions

TABLE 8.1. *Discriminant Analysis Findings: Coefficient for Canonical Variable Ranked in Order of Importance*

Combined Variables Cluster Variables	Coefficient
Simultaneous Office – Government	1.15
Involvement in Government – Taluka	0.87
Involvement in Government – Village	0.86
Caste role in distribution decisions	*0.53*
Number of Spheres – Simultaneous	0.44
Distance – Z.P.	0.42
Distance – Bus	0.34
Irrigated landholding size	0.28
Value of machinery owned	0.27
Loan distribution machinery	0.18
Number of Offices – Cooperatives	0.17
Involved in Party – Taluka	0.12
Variable Not Entered Value of houses owned	

TABLE 8.2. *Environment*

Variables	Coefficient
Distance – Z.P.	0.69
Distance – Bus	*0.55*
Public electoral participation	0.44
Agricultural prosperity	0.36
% Cultivators serviced by cooperatives	0.32
Distance – Panchayat Samiti	0.14
Variables Not Entered Distance – Railway Average landholding in taluka Communications potential Agricultural cooperative activity Urbanization Eligible votes polled by non-Congress candidates Total votes polled by non-Congress candidates	

Akola District

TABLE 8.3. *Behavior*

Variables	Coefficient
Simultaneous Office – Government	1.35
Involved in Government – Village	0.99
Involved in Government – Taluka	0.98
Number of Spheres – Simultaneous	0.70
Involved in Party – Taluka	0.54
Number of Offices – Cooperatives	*0.50*
Involved in Cooperatives – Village	0.25
Involved in Party – District	0.23
Involved in Government – District	0.18
Variables Not Entered	
Simultaneous Office – Cooperatives	
Simultaneous Office – Party	
Number of Spheres – Over Time	
Number of Offices – Party	
Number of Offices – Government	
Involved in Party – Village	
Involved in Cooperatives – Taluka	
Involved in Cooperatives – District	

TABLE 8.4. *Economic Background*

Variables	Coefficient
Value of machinery owned	0.95
Value of houses owned	0.71
Irrigated landholding size	*0.69*
Value of shares (in cooperatives)	0.40
% of acres under cash crops	0.40
Value of landholding	0.38
Value of loans (from cooperatives)	0.34
Variables Not Entered	
Landholding size	
Number of acres under cash crops	

153

TABLE 8.5. *Attitudes*

Variables	Coefficient
Caste role in distribution decisions	1.13
Loan distribution machinery	*0.80*
Comments about Z.P. leadership	0.49
Economic role in distribution decisions	0.27
Voting preference (majority v. unanimous)	0.12
Evaluation of M.L.A.	0.12
Predisposition to resign	0.12
Variable Not Entered Selection of Candidates	

should be pointed out that this does not contradict the earlier assertion that Akola respondents were on the whole politically quiescent. The intensive involvement of Rebels mentioned here refers to a relatively small proportion of the group and represents the leading stratum of the dissident Congressmen. Moreover, it refers to offices held simultaneously – at a given point in time – in two different spheres of the local power structure. The earlier reference was to a lack of extensive involvement, that is, *over a period of time*.

SOME SOCIAL AND ECONOMIC FACTORS

The environmental and personal economic background of respondents contributed no significant indicators of factional alignment to the *combined variables* cluster (Table 8.1). Both were highly unreliable discriminators in Akola.* These findings, therefore, ought to be viewed with particular caution.

The analysis of *environmental* variables indicated that Rebels were distinguishable from Loyalists on the basis of the distance separating their villages from Zilla Parishad headquarters and from bus transportation (Table 8.2 and Table D, p. 229). Rebels tended to be further away from the center of political activity in their district, and were apt to be more discouraged from traveling to this center owing to the relative inaccessibility of an inexpensive

* See Chapter 3, above, and Table A, p.53.

and quick means of transportation. This may account, in part, for the fact that Rebels were so little involved in the affairs of the district. But while it may suggest a reason for the lack of activity at the district level, it still does not explain their equally poor showing at lower levels, where travel might be less of an obstacle to political activity.

The economic background of respondents was the poorest predictor of factional alignments in Akola (see Table 9). One economic indicator which distinguished between the two groups was the value of machinery owned (Table 8.4). Unlike Rebels in most other districts (except Ratnagiri), however, the average value of agricultural equipment owned by Akola dissidents was lower than that owned by Loyalists (Table D, p. 230). This might be difficult to explain, if it were found to be the case in a district like Poona, where the cultivation of sugarcane requires the use of expensive irrigation machinery. But in Poona, we may recall, the Rebels' machinery was worth about four times as much as that of the Loyalists. In Aurangabad, where sugarcane was a secondary cash crop, the difference in the value of machinery owned, while significant, was not as great. However in Akola the principal commercial crop is cotton, which in this district is largely a dry crop.[36] Hence the need for expensive engines and pumps is not as great. Moreover, it should be noted that Akola is in an area which has adequate and reliable rainfall.[37] Therefore the pressure for irrigation has not been as great as in certain areas of the Deccan. As a result, the need (and hence the expenditure) for irrigation equipment is less critical on the whole.

The two remaining economic indicators place the Rebels, as usual, in the higher rungs of the economic ladder. We find that Rebels here generally owned houses which were worth significantly more than those of Loyalists. And Akola dissidents also were likely to own larger irrigated landholdings than the Loyalists (although overall, as compared with irrigated plots in other districts, the average size of such a tract was low here, for the reasons referred to above). (See Table 8.4 and Table D, p. 230).

While the size of respondent's landholding did not prove to be a significant discriminator in Akola, a pertinent observation is in order about this variable. It ought to be noted that the size of landholding owned by Akola respondents was, on the average, larger than that of respondents in any other district (see Table 3,

TABLE 9. *Discriminant Analysis Findings: Canonical Correlation Ranked in Order of Importance*

Variable Cluster	Canonical Correlation	% of Variance Accounted For
Combined Variables	0.72	0.52
Attitudes	0.60	0.36
Behavior	0.51	0.26
Environment	0.47	0.22
Economic Background	0.37	0.14

p. 173). Secondly, there were *no* small landlords at all among the respondents here. Almost 70% owned over 50 acres of land, and the remaining were medium-sized landlords, with holdings of 16 to 50 acres. Only one man's holding ranged between 6 and 15 acres. And *no one owned five acres or less*.[38]

SOME SOCIAL AND POLITICAL ATTITUDES
OF DISSIDENTS

Finally, we may consider the *attitudinal* variables which contributed one significant indicator to the *combined variables* test (Tables 8.5 and 8.1). According to this, Rebels in Akola shared the conviction that caste played no role in the distribution of benefits by the Zilla Parishad (Table, p. 233). This was of interest only because in one way, at least, caste *had* – according to some respondents – played a role in the politics of this multi-caste district (see Table 8). Forty-two per cent. of those interviewed had complained that caste was a governing factor (among others) in the selection of Congress candidates to contest a seat in the Z.P. As almost half the Congressmen ran as independents (and joined or rejoined the party after they had been elected to the Z.P.) (see Table 11), this complaint may suggest that the 'rebellion' was, at least in part, due to dissatisfaction with the party's nominating practices.* Thus, the dissi-

---

* Once again, I should like to anticipate comments noting an apparent inconsistency in my position regarding the factor of caste as a political determinant. Let it be noted that I do not claim anywhere in this study that caste plays a limited role or none at all *in all aspects of political behavior*. The nominating process is one sphere of political activity where I might concede (with qualifications)

dent Congressmen – now at the helm of government – were perhaps eager to stress the view that the Rebel leadership was not guided by such considerations in the distribution of benefits to the people.

The analysis of *attitudinal* variables by themselves revealed that Rebels were distinguished by one other attitude, which was far more easy to interpret. Rebels in Akola voiced a clear opposition to the notion of turning over to the Zilla Parishad the authority enjoyed by the cooperative banks and societies in the matter of distributing loans.* (See Table 8.5 and Table D, p. 233.) This would support the hypothesis that the Rebels had a vested interest in the cooperative structure and therefore did not want to relinquish authority in cooperatives to a body like the Zilla Parishad, over which they might not be able to exercise sustained control in coming years.

SUMMARY

It may be said in conclusion that the profile of the rank-and-file Akola Rebels was somewhat blurred compared with other districts. But certain features do emerge from the statistical findings. Rebels were either newcomers to the Congress or had been deliberately or accidentally excluded from the district party organization. Their involvement with the cooperatives in positions of authority was also small – a feature which certainly constitutes a deviation from the pattern of Rebel profiles in other districts. Akola Rebels, however, did follow the general pattern in that they were in some respects economically better off than Loyalists.

that caste plays a role. It is not an emotion-bound role, however. Rather, considerations of caste by political leaders in such instances are likely to be motivated by rational calculations about voting support and not by emotionalism. Election data may be interpreted as illustrative of such 'rational calculations'. Thus I usually found in checking election statistics that each party seemingly tried to match the caste or community identity of its candidate with that of the contending parties' candidates. Thus, while I do not wish to discount entirely the role of caste, I would suggest that claims regarding the role of caste in politics ought to be made with perhaps a greater sense of discrimination among different sectors of political activity, e.g., nominations, factionalism, policymaking at various levels, distribution of benefits, and so on.

* Perhaps I ought to note that the plausibility of such a move suggests itself in the first place because there are now four different agencies empowered to distribute loans in a district: the central cooperative bank, the land development bank (both of these being cooperatives), the District Collector's Office and the Zilla Parishad, through its Panchayat Samitis. The first two agencies, however, carry the bulk of credit distribution, as far as institutional agencies are concerned.

TABLE 10. *Indices of Multiplicity of Castes in the Akola*
Zilla Parishad and in the District of Akola

Caste composition of Zilla Parishad		
Caste category	Frequency	%
Depressed and other backward classes	2 ⎫	
Intermediate castes (Malis, Kolis, Telis, etc.)	19 ⎭	41
Marathas	30	59
Brahmins	—	—
Total	51	100

Caste composition of Akola District (as of 1931)*		
Caste category	Frequency	%
Depressed and other backward classes	103,083	14
Intermediate castes (Malis, Kolis, Telis, Sonars, etc.) and non-Hindus (Muslims, Jains, etc.)	186,325	25
Mehra (cotton-weavers)	148,027	20
Kunbi (agriculturists)	136,324	19
Maratha	109,055	15
Brahmin	29,851	4
Total	712,665	100

* SOURCE: *Census of India – 1931 – Volume XII, Part II, Central Provinces & Berar* – Nagpur: 1932, pp. 274 ff.

This early Census had to be relied upon for the district as a whole because reliable caste information is not available after that year.

The 'Mehra' and 'Kunbi' categories were not included among the 'Intermediate Castes' here as it is believed that, with the passage of years, these were incorporated in the Maratha caste whose occupational classification is given as 'soldier' in the 1931 Census. This conjecture is offered in view of the fact that there was not a single respondent in the Akola Zilla Parishad who gave 'Mehra' as his caste. As will be seen from the table above, this was the largest single caste in 1931. It seems unlikely, therefore, that their representatives would not appear in the Zilla Parishad membership. As far as the 'Kunbi' category is concerned, it was noted during the interviews that many respondents gave their caste as 'Maratha-Kunbi' while others identified their caste simply as 'Maratha'.

Thus, if we combine the Mehra, Kunbi and Maratha categories from the 1931 Census, we find that their proportion of the total population of the district is 54%. This would correspond more closely with the representation of the Maratha caste in the Zilla Parishad.

All of the above, of course, is pure conjecture and would have to be confirmed by more detailed study of the district's caste composition.

Akola District

TABLE 11. *Frequencies Indicating whether Congressmen Interviewed in 1965 had Contested 1962 Z.P. Elections as Independents or on the Congress Ticket*

Label Under Which Congressmen Contested 1962 Elections to the Zilla Parishad	Frequencies	%
Independent	18	46
Congress Party	21	54
Total	39	100

TABLE 12. *Discriminant Analysis Findings: Accuracy of Prediction of Factional Alignment Achieved by Each Variable Cluster (% of Correct Classifications)*

	Environ-ment			Behavior			Economic back-ground			Attitudes			Combined Variables		
Factional Groupings ...	L	R	T	L	R	T	L	R	T	L	R	T	L	R	T
Actual Membership Discriminant Analysis	9	35	44	9	35	44	9	35	44	9	35	44	9	35	44
Classification	8	27	35	4	31	35	4	24	28	8	29	37	7	33	40
% of Correct Classifications	88	77	80	44	88	80	44	68	64	88	83	84	77	94	90

Variable Cluster

* The letter headings under each variable cluster represent the following: L, Loyalist; R, Rebel; T, Total (both Rebels and Loyalists).

Some general characteristics of Akola serve to support our proposition. Thus we find that, in a district which had the largest proportion of moderately large landowners, where about half the land cultivated was under cotton, an important commercial crop, and where the cooperative banks were very active, the Rebel group predominated and was able to gain control of the Zilla Parishad.

Moreover, the background of the leaders within each faction (and their associates at the local or higher levels) reveals a pattern of economic interests and associations which parallels the one posited in my central thesis. Similarly, the interrelationship of district political alignments with regional and state politics further supports my contentions about the role of economic interests in factional behavior.

To repeat then, the general outlines of the Akola factions had not hardened to the extent that they had in some of the other districts. We have examined some of the reasons why this appeared to be so, particularly at the rank-and-file level. At the same time, we have noted that the features of the leadership strata were considerably better-defined.*

* For information regarding the proportion of accurate classifications made by each set of test variables, see Table 12.

CHAPTER 8

ALL DISTRICTS: SOME COMPARISONS

The general hypothesis regarding the economic nature of factional groups was tested once again on members of each faction which, in the final analysis to be discussed here, included all the Rebels and all the Loyalists from the four districts, pooled together in their respective groups. In this chapter, we will be examining the characteristics of these rival groups as derived from this last series of discriminant analyses. Perhaps I ought to preface this discussion with a general observation (made earlier in Chapter 3) regarding the effectiveness of the variable clusters used as tests of discrimination and prediction of factional alignments. I would remind the reader that these tests do not compare well, on the whole, with equivalent tests applied separately in each district, specifically in regard to discriminating strength and predictive scope. With this *caveat* in mind, we may proceed to the interpretation of the findings yielded by this analysis.

As in the individual districts, so too on the all-district level, the cluster of *combined variables* proved to be the most powerful discriminator of Rebels and Loyalists. The strongest single predictor within this cluster was an indicator of the average size of landholding owned by cultivators in the respective talukas of respondents (Table 1.1).* It should be noted that the variable which thus proved most effective in identifying factional membership was an *environmental* one, with an *economic* connotation, and not one directly descriptive of the individual respondent. This finding indicated that Rebels generally lived in talukas where the average

* This is a composite variable yielded by factor analysis, and its component indicators are listed below:
Agricultural laborers/Total cultivators
Hired workers/Family workers
Number of households with landholding of 50 acres and over
Percentage of agricultural land owned by the 50-plus class of landlord
Gross area sown per agricultural worker (laborer and cultivator)
Net area sown per cultivator
Number of tractors in taluka.

6   161

The Dynamics of Indian Political Factions

TABLE 1.1. *Discriminant Analysis Findings: Coefficients for Canonical Variable Ranked in Order of Importance*

Combined Variables Cluster Variable	Coefficient
Average landholding in taluka	0.61
Public electoral participation	0.49
Distance – Railway	0.47
Eligible votes polled by non-Congress candidates	0.46
Value of shares owned (in cooperatives)	0.45
Size of landholding	0.40
Involved in Party – District level	0.39
Caste role in distribution decisions	0.37
% cultivators serviced by cooperatives	0.36
Number of Offices – Party	0.22
Simultaneous Office – Government	0.20
Value of machinery owned	0.19
Involved in Government – District level	0.08
% of acres under cash crops	0.07

TABLE 1.2. *Environment*

Variable	Coefficient
Average landholding in taluka	1.02
Eligible votes polled by non-Congress candidates	0.71
Distance – Railway	0.64
% cultivators serviced by cooperatives	0.62
Public electoral participation	*0.54*
Agricultural prosperity	0.48
Distance – Bus	0.38
Distance – Z.P.	0.35
Total Votes Polled by non-Congress Candidates	0.32
Agricultural cooperative activity	0.19
Communications potential	0.15
Urbanization	0.08
Distance – Panchayat Samiti	0.04

landholding was larger than that in Loyalists' talukas (Table E, p. 232). In other words, Rebels (and Loyalists) could be identified most often in terms of this particular feature of their respective talukas. The claim may be advanced, therefore, that some degree of homogeneity exists in the environment of the observed groups.

TABLE 1.3. *Behavior*

Variable	Coefficient
Number of Offices – Party	0.87
Simultaneous Office – Government	0.83
Involved in Party – District	0.72
Involved in Government – District	*0.59*
Involved in Party – Village	0.42
Involved in Cooperatives – Village	0.40
Simultaneous Office – Cooperatives	0.40
Involved in Government – Taluka	0.38
Involved in Government – Village	0.36
Involved in Cooperatives – Taluka	0.23
Involved in Party – Taluka	0.21
Number of Spheres – Various	0.18
Involved in Cooperatives – District	0.18
Number of Offices – Government	0.04
Simultaneous Office – All Spheres	0.04
Simultaneous Office – Party	0.03
Number of Offices – Cooperatives	0.03

TABLE 1.4. *Economic Background*

Variable	Coefficient
Size of landholding	0.79
Value of machinery owned	0.60
Value of shares owned (in cooperatives)	*0.56*
Value of landholding owned	0.43
% of acres under cash crops	0.35
Irrigated landholding size	0.35
Number of acres under cash crops	0.28
Value of loans (from cooperatives)	0.22
Value of houses owned	0.13

TABLE 1.5. *Attitudes*

Variable	Coefficient
Caste role in distribution decisions	*0.57*
Loan distribution	0.46
Voting preference (majority v. unanimous)	0.38
Predisposition to resign	0.34
Economic role in distribution decisions	0.18
Comments about Z.P. leadership	0.13
Selection of candidates	0.12
Evaluation of M.L.A.	0.08

The Dynamics of Indian Political Factions

This characteristic, it might also be noted, points toward a possible community of economic interests among the members of the larger political community within which the respondent functions. The latter observation is supported by another *environmental* characteristic, which indicated that Rebels came from talukas where the percentage of cultivators serviced by village agricultural credit cooperatives was higher than that in Loyalists' talukas* (Table E, p. 232). This is the first intimation of a link between Rebels and cooperative institutions provided at the all-district level. Moreover, we find that, within each group, this ecological characteristic was positively correlated with one other, indicating that the more agriculturally prosperous areas† had more cultivators serviced by cooperatives (Table I–I-E, pp. 237, 242). A positive correlation was also found between this variable and two others: (1) urbanization and (2) the potential for communication on a social and economic basis.‡ That is to say, in areas where more cultivators were serviced by village cooperatives, there was also likely to be a larger number of towns, with more banks in them, a larger urban population and thus a larger number of non-agricultural workers. In addition, areas served by village agricultural credit cooperatives were likely to offer more opportunities for transactions of an economic or social nature. This possibility was defined in terms of a larger number of roads, post offices,

* The predictive capacity of '% cultivators serviced by cooperatives' was established in the test of the *environmental* rather than the *combined variables* cluster. (See Table 1.2.)

† 'Agricultural prosperity' was another one of the composite variables yielded by factor analysis. Its component indicators were:
Average land revenue per acre
Average land revenue collected per cultivator
Number of irrigation machines per acre
Percentage of acreage under cash crops.

‡ The component indicators of each of these two factors are listed below:
Urbanization: % of urban to total population; % of workers not working on land; number of banks in taluka; number of towns in taluka.
Communications Potential: % of villages connected by road; % of villages served by a post office; % of villages in which fair held annually; % of villages in which weekly market held.
% of literacy among rural males in taluka
Rural male literates in taluka/Rural male literates in district
Rural male literates in taluka/Rural male literates in State
% of literates among rural male cultivators in taluka
Rural male literate cultivators in taluka/Rural male literate cultivators in district
% of villages without a middle or high school.

All Districts

annual fairs and weekly markets in the villages of such areas, and by the relatively higher level of literacy, not only among the village menfolk in general, but among the rural male cultivators as well.*

Finally, a direct relation was found between the average size of landholding in respondents' talukas and the proportion of land cultivated by respondents under cash crops. In other words, the bigger cash crop growers among respondents in each group tended to be found in talukas where the average size of landholding was larger. Moreover, such cash crop cultivators were also likely to be found in areas which were more extensively serviced by village credit cooperatives (Table V.E.1 and 2, pp. 268–9).

Other ecological variables proved to be significant discriminators of factional alignment. However, since we are now dealing with economic characteristics, I turn for a moment to indicators of respondents' personal economic status, following a discussion of which we shall return to the remaining environmental indices.

Variables defining respondents' own *economic* background identified the Rebels as the more affluent group of the two (Table 1.4 and Table E, p. 233). Thus, their landholdings were larger than those of Loyalists,† and they owned agricultural equipment which was more valuable than that owned by the rival group members. It is particularly significant to note in the context of this study that this characteristic (i.e., the value of machinery owned) was positively correlated with the value of loans taken from cooperative institutions by a respondent. Still more pertinent is the fact that Rebels could be distinguished from Loyalists by their larger investment (in the form of shares owned) in cooperative institutions. This establishes more concretely the existence of an economic interest on the part of the Rebels in cooperatives. Indeed, it was most striking to find that the average rupee investment in such shares

* Although some of the items mentioned here might also be construed as indices of urbanization, the factor analysis of this set of taluka-level variables distinguished between two factors which are here entitled 'Urbanization' and 'Communications Potential'. In a broad sense, of course, we may interpret all of these as attributes of an urban or 'urbanizing' environment, but they do constitute different facets of such an environment.

† Please note, however, that the range of landholdings of *all* the respondents together indicates that there is a group of cultivators which is not at all (or very poorly) represented in these local governing bodies. The group to which I refer is that of the very large landholders, owning 150 to 200 acres or more (see p. 232, Variable No. 14). In addition, the very small landowner is very poorly represented (see Table 2).

165

The Dynamics of Indian Political Factions

TABLE 2. *Frequency of Landholdings in Different Size Categories*

Landholding Size (acres)	No. of Acres Owned:				
	All Districts	Ratnagiri	Akola	Poona	Aurangabad
Up to 5	10	8	—	1	1
6 to 15	28	16	1	11	—
16 to 25	23	4	6	6	7
26 to 50	34	3	10	7	14
Over 50	83	9	33	15	26
Total	178	40	50	40	48

was more than three times that of Loyalists (see Table 8, p. 125, above).

Our discussion so far has distinguished between Rebels and Loyalists on the basis of certain *economic* characteristics and/or interests of respondents and their areas of origin. (In this instance, the area referred to as the 'area of origin' is the taluka.) However, certain political and social characteristics of respondents' area of operations also emerged as significant discriminators between the groups. One such variable has been interpreted here as a measure of the level of political awareness or political participation of the residents in the respondent's electoral constituency.* This recorded the number of votes polled by all the candidates in a given constituency (during the elections of the Zilla Parishad members), as a proportion of the total eligible votes.† This finding revealed that there was a larger turnout of voters in Rebels' constituencies than in those of the Loyalists (p. 232). Closely related to this was yet another political variable which also emerged as an independent predictor of factional membership. This was the percentage of votes cast in the Z.P. popular elections for other-party candidates

* It may be noted that the areal unit here is the constituency rather than the taluka. The radius of operations is thus smaller here, and may encompass no more than 35,000 people.[1] The population of the average taluka, on the other hand, is generally around 100,000.

† The coefficient for canonical variable of this indicator placed it just at the threshold of 'significance' as a predictor in the 'combined variables' test (Table 1.1). Within its own cluster of *environmental* variables, however, it emerged as a 'significant' predictor (Table 1.2). (See note on p. 199, below.)

or for independents (Table 1.2). It was found once again that this percentage was greater in Rebels' constituencies than in those of Loyalists (p. 232). Votes thus cast could be construed as votes against Congress.

Another *environment* variable which distinguished between Rebels and Loyalists was a measure of the distance between the respondent's place of residence and a railway station (Table 1.2).* According to this finding, it appears that members of the Rebel group were, on the average, located further from this means of transportation than were Loyalists (p. 232). This would seem to conflict with the broadly 'urban' nature of Rebels' environment which we described earlier. The apparent conflict may be resolved if we consider the following points.

To begin with, we ought to bear in mind that the concept of urbanization is extremely complex, and there is no consensus in the social sciences about the indices which ought to be used to measure it.[2] Hence, a mental qualification ought to be registered when encountering references to 'urbanization', 'urban environment', 'urbanizing influences' and so forth – a qualification to the effect that these are tentative conceptualizations. As far as the explicit 'urbanization' factor used here is concerned, all that can be stated is that no predictive association was found between it and factional membership. An association *was* found to exist within each group, however, between indices of urbanization or an 'urbanizing environment' and certain distinctive environmental traits of Rebels (and Loyalists). Thus Rebels were identifiable by the fact that there were more cultivators serviced by cooperatives in their talukas (Table 1.2, and Table E, p. 232), and the correlations, within groups, indicated that as this incidence increased in a given area, so did the level of urbanization and the communications potential (Table I–I.E, pp. 237, 242). On the other hand, the distance from rail transportation, which might be considered an auxiliary index of 'urbanization', identified Rebels as deficient in this respect ('Table 1.2, and Table E, p. 232).

Let me remind the reader, however, that the ecological units with which we are concerned vary in size. Urbanization, average size of landholding and percentage of cultivators serviced by village cooperatives are all aggregate measures describing taluka charac-

---

* It may be noted that the environmental unit to which reference is made here is the village (or town) in which the respondent resides.

teristics. Distance from railways, on the other hand, refers to an ecological unit which is more intimately descriptive of the respondent's environment – namely, his village. All these characteristics may be viewed as possible influences operating on the respondent over a wider or narrower radius. In these circumstances, it is not inconceivable that the stimuli issuing from the environment (whether village, constituency or taluka) may differ. No claim is made here about the relative weight of influence from smaller as against larger areas. The relevance of different stimuli is simply acknowledged.

Hence the apparent contradiction between 'urban' and 'non-urban' characteristics noted above may be most satisfactorily resolved if we accept the fact that Rebels' villages are 'deficient' in one 'urban' feature (namely, proximity to rail transportation), while the broader area within which they function exposes the Rebel to a somewhat more urbanized environment.

We may now look at some of the political aspects of the rival groups' environment. Here we note that the Rebel is characteristically found in areas where voting participation is high and coupled with disaffection vis-a-vis the Congress Party (Table 1.2 and Table E, p. 232). This probably generates a favorable climate for dissidence within Congress, inasmuch as we find that the incidence of Rebels is usually greater in such areas. The configuration of characteristics and associations described in the preceding paragraphs defines a situation where disaffection with Congress seems to lie largely in 'urbanizing' areas and fans out through the communications network provided by village roads, markets, fairs, post offices and the facilities of nearby towns. In such areas voting participation by the general public is high, as is the vote for non-Congress candidates and the incidence of rebellion within the Congress Party.

In the light of the fact that Rebel Congressmen, on the whole, project an image of relative affluence compared with the Loyalists, the question may be raised why these Congressmen should be dissatisfied with the party, when their well-being seemingly coincides with membership in that very party. Several factors may help to explain this apparent inconsistency between 'conditions of action' and actual behavior (defined in terms of their Rebel or Loyalist status).

Let us remember first of all that in every Zilla Parishad studied here, district or state leaders – either within the party or in

168

government – attempted to block the Rebel group and its leaders from positions of authority in the newly established local governing bodies. These bodies, through their elected officers, control the distribution among the talukas of a district of a large variety of material and non-material goods and services, including fertilizers, seeds and certain building materials. They also influence the appointment of teachers and allocate funds for the construction of schools, village roads, small-scale irrigation projects and for horticultural loans.* Certainly, if an individual such as the Rebel described here wishes to retain or improve the level of his economic status, his efforts could only be aided by control of such positions of authority.

The findings yielded by the analysis of *behavioral* variables complement the observations made in the preceding paragraph. In general, it appears that Rebels may have been excluded from two spheres of the local power structure: the party and local government. Thus we find that Rebels usually held few offices in the party organization (although at one level – the district – they were predominant) (Table E, p. 234). From our examination of individual districts, we know that the areas where they were predominant at this level were Ratnagiri and Aurangabad. We might recall further, however, that in Ratnagiri the district party leader was ineffectual and the dominant political power was a State Minister. In Aurangabad, again, the district party leadership was effectively countered by the State Party head who was from that district. In the remaining two districts – Akola and Poona – the Rebels, as we saw, were quite effectively excluded from the party organization (in Akola from all levels and in Poona from the district level).

We find, further, that the Rebels were characteristically sparse in positions of authority in district local government (though at any point in time they might be found to hold two or more offices in local governing bodies, generally at the village and/or taluka level) (Table 1.3 and Table E, p. 234).

Excluded thus from the more explicitly political centers of power and authority, this group, in spite of their relative affluence,

* Decisions regarding horticultural loans, the building of schools, village roads and small-scale irrigation projects were statutorily within the jurisdiction of the Zilla Parishad or its agencies.[3] The remaining items, while not *technically* under the control of the Zilla Parishad, had, through convention and practice, passed into the hands of the Zilla Parishad officials, according to many knowledgeable people interviewed (within and outside the Z.P.), including some of the officials themselves.

may have rebelled against the dominant elements of authority in their respective districts, whether these were party-based or government-based. We are assuming, after all, that individuals will act – at a minimum – to protect, if not to improve, their economic status.

The remaining cluster of variables – *attitudes* – contributed only one significant discriminator between the rival groups, though it does not lend itself to a very plausible interpretation of factional alignment (Table 1.5). According to this finding, Rebels more than Loyalists feel that caste considerations play no role at all in decisions taken by the Zilla Parishad regarding the distribution of various benefits. They also tend to reject the possibility that these decision-makers might be guided by economic interests in allocating benefits (Table IV–IV.E, pp. 255, 259). One might have expected that, as internal critics of Congress, Rebels would express some dissatisfaction with the Loyalist-dominated Council's distribution policies. Several things might account for the fact that they do not. One reason may be found in the fact that almost half of all Rebels are from one district – Akola. In this district, as we have seen, Rebels have captured control of the Zilla Parishad.* Hence, they would have no serious complaints about their Council's distribution policy.† Secondly, as far as Congressmen – whether dissident or not – are concerned, distribution is likely to be 'fair', perhaps even generous, as compared to allocations made to non-Congress constituencies. (This feeling was expressed by a number of independent or other-party members of the Zilla Parishads.)

In general, then, the findings discussed above have largely supported the fundamental hypothesis advanced in this study. The particular configuration of circumstances and conditions characterizing factional alignments within each district has been discussed at length in the preceding chapters. In this concluding section, I should like to draw upon the profiles sketched in those chapters to highlight some of the distinctive features of factional groupings by way of comparison and contrast between districts.

Some interesting questions are suggested by the findings. It is curious, for example, that the Rebel group defeated the Loyalists in only one district, Akola. Why was this group victorious in this

---

* In effect, the district Congress organization was out of power here. The Congress, then, was represented by the opponents of that contingent.

† See discussion on this particular question in Chapter 7, pp. 156–7 above.

All Districts

particular district, and why in this district alone? How is it that the dissident Congressmen, who had been numerically strong in all four districts during the final stages of the struggle, were unable ultimately to defeat the Loyalist forces in Ratnagiri, Poona and Aurangabad? Some of the immediate causes have been discussed in the analyses of individual districts. Thus we found that in Aurangabad and Ratnagiri effective pressure was brought to bear on the dissidents from State-based political forces. In Poona a strong district leader, backed by State political forces, was able to defeat the Rebel group. However, State forces were also arrayed against the Rebel group in Akola. Yet the latter proved resilient enough to counter these effectively. One is compelled to ask why this was so.

Some of the questions posed here may be answered or clarified if we take note of certain features which Ratnagiri, Poona and Aurangabad respondents shared in common, compared with those in Akola. Or there may be elements in the Akola configuration which are absent from the other districts. Then, too, we may consider the fact that Ratnagiri was one of the districts where the Rebel element was strong (though defeated by the Loyalist group). It might therefore be of interest to look for common features in Akola and Ratnagiri, in contrast to similarities observed in Aurangabad and Poona. Different general properties may distinguish the total sample of respondents in each district. Or perhaps we may find that there are group features which vary from district to district.

Let us look first at some of the broad features which characterized the districts in which the Loyalists won, as against attributes of the respondents in Akola, where the Rebels were the victors.

In terms of landholding size and number of acres under cash crops, the respondents in the three districts controlled by the Loyalist faction were considerably behind the Akola respondents. As a region, also, Akola was better off economically. Thus, its level of agricultural prosperity exceeded by far that of any other district. The average landholding in its talukas ranked largest of all. And a larger proportion of its cultivators were serviced by cooperatives. As far as the respondents were concerned, we may say that their economic status accorded with the overall level of prosperity in the district (Table 3).

All this suggests that the sense of community in economic interests may have been strongest among Akola respondents, by

171

The Dynamics of Indian Political Factions

TABLE 3. *Districts Ranked According to Mean Values of Total Sample, Listed Within Each Variable Cluster*

	Rank (Mean Values Appear in Parentheses under District Name)*			
Variable Title (*Environment*)	1	2	3	4
Distance – Panchayat Samiti	Abad.	Poona	Akola	Ratn.
(miles)	(13)	(11.6)	(10.9)	(9.7)
Distance – Zilla Parishad	Ratn.	Abad.	Akola	Poona
(miles)	(77.6)	(42.4)	(40.2)	(37)
Distance – Railway	Ratn.	Abad.	Poona	Akola
(miles)	(83)	(27)	(22)	(12)
Distance – Bus	Abad.	Akola	Ratn.	Poona
(miles)	(8)	(7)	(5)	(2)
Public Electoral Participation	Akola	Poona	Abad.	Ratn.
(%)	(57)	(41)	(37)	(26)
Average landholding – Tq.	Akola	Abad.	Poona	Ratn.
(factor score)	(−1.42)	(−0.60)	(0.23)	(0.82)
Communications Potential	Ratn.	Akola	Poona	Abad.
(factor score)	(0.30)	(0.20)	(0.06)	(−0.56)
Agric. Coop. Activity	Abad.	Akola	Poona	Ratn.
(factor score)	(−0.47)	(−0.01)	(0.10)	(0.44)
Urbanization	Akola	Poona	Ratn.	Abad.
(factor score)	(0.47)	(0.18)	(0.01)	(−0.24)
Agricultural prosperity	Akola	Abad.	Poona	Ratn.
(factor score)	(−1.42)	(−0.28)	(0.38)	(0.54)
Eligible votes polled by	Akola	Poona	Abad.	Ratn.
non-Congress candidates (%)	(23.40)	(12.25)	(10.67)	(6.63)
Total votes polled by	Akola	Poona	Ratn.	Abad.
non-Congress candidates (%)	(41.47)	(31.02)	(24.66)	(23.89)
Cultivators Serviced by Village	Akola	Ratn.	Poona	Abad.
Credit (Agric.) Cooperatives (%)	(75.23)	(62.36)	(49.37)	(43.42)
(*Behavior*)				
Spheres – Simultaneous	Poona	Ratn.	Abad.	Akola
(no.)	(2.85)	(2.76)	(2.60)	(2.20)
Simultaneous Offices – Coops.	Poona	Ratn.	Abad.	Akola
(no.)	(2.32)	(2.30)	(1.95)	(1.81)
Simultaneous Offices – Party	Poona	Abad.	Ratn.	Akola
(no.)	(2.02)	(1.77)	(1.54)	(1.39)
Simultaneous Offices – Govt.	Ratn.	Poona	Akola	Abad.
(no.)	(2.06)	(1.97)	(1.91)	(1.86)
Spheres – Over Time	Poona	Ratn.	Abad.	Akola
(no.)	(3.07)	(3.03)	(3.0)	(2.45)
Cooperative Offices – Over Time	Poona	Ratn.	Abad.	Akola
(no.)	(2.92)	(2.64)	(2.35)	(2.04)

172

TABLE 3. (*Continued*)

Variable Title (*Behavior*)	Rank (Mean Values Appear in Parentheses under District Name)*			
	1	2	3	4
Party Offices – Over Time	Poona	Abad.	Ratn.	Akola
(no.)	(2.32)	(2.19)	(1.75)	(1.50)
Government Offices – Over Time	Ratn.	Poona	Akola	Abad.
(no.)	(2.39)	(2.22)	(2.20)	(2.07)
Party Offices – Village	Poona	Ratn.	Akola	Abad.
(graded according to level)	(5.25)	(3.12)	(3.04)	(2.63)
Party Offices – Taluka	Abad.	Poona	Ratn.	Akola
(graded according to level)	(10.30)	(10)	(5.85)	(4.18)
Party Offices – District	Poona	Abad.	Ratn.	Akola
(graded according to level)	(11)	(9)	(7.06)	(4.64)
Cooperative Offices – Village	Poona	Ratn.	Abad.	Akola
(graded according to level)	(6)	(4.94)	(3.79)	(2.36)
Cooperative Offices – Taluka	Ratn.	Poona	Abad.	Akola
(graded according to level)	(8.88)	(7.67)	(6.12)	(5.09)
Cooperative Offices – District	Abad.	Ratn.	Poona	Akola
(graded according to level)	(12.16)	(11.91)	(11.26)	(10.09)
Government Offices – Taluka	Ratn.	Akola	Abad.	Poona
(graded according to level)	(74.69)	(56.27)	(51.60)	(49.0)
Government Offices – District	Poona	Ratn.	Abad.	Akola
(graded according to level)	(90.60)	(63.06)	(36.72)	(35.91)
Government Offices – Village	Poona	Akola	Abad.	Ratn.
(graded according to level)	(16.20)	(14.82)	(13.65)	(13.61)
(*Economic Background*)				
Size of landholding	Akola	Poona	Abad.	Ratn.
(acres)	(145)	(100)	(58)	(34)
Size of irrigated landholding	Poona	Abad.	Ratn.	Akola
(acres)	(17)	(11)	(3.7)	(3.5)
Value of landholding	Akola	Poona	Abad.	Ratn.
(rupees) ('000s)	(120)	(112)	(79)	(39.5)
Value of machinery	Poona	Akola	Abad.	Ratn.
(rupees) ('000s)	(10)	(5.6)	(5.2)	(0.65)
Value of houses	Ratn.	Akola	Abad.	Poona
(rupees) ('000s)	(27)	(23)	(21)	(19)
Acres under cash crops	Akola	Ratn.	Abad.	Poona
(%)	(51)	(45)	(32)	(19)
Acres under cash crops	Akola	Abad.	Ratn.	Poona
(no.)	(67)	(21)	(16)	(11)
Value of shares in cooperatives	Poona	Akola	Abad.	Ratn.
(rupees)	(3100)	(2000)	(1100)	(300)

173

TABLE 3. (*Continued*)

Variable Title (*Economic Background*)	Rank (Mean Values Appear in Parentheses under District Name)*			
	1	2	3	4
Value of loans in cooperatives (rupees)	Akola (4600)	Poona (4270)	Abad. (4250)	Ratn. (230)
(*Attitudes*)				
Predisposition to resign (range: No – 4; Yes – 1)	Abad. (2.64)	Poona (2.43)	Ratn. (2.29)	Akola (2.02)
Voting preference (range: Unanimous – 4; Majority – 1)	Poona (2.37)	Ratn. (2.34)	Abad. (2.31)	Akola (1.76)
Comments about Z.P. leadership (range: Favorable – 5; Unfavorable – 1)	Poona (3.94)	Ratn. (3.90)	Akola (3.74)	Abad. (3.60)
Evaluation of M.L.A. status (range: Z.P. officials rated highest – 7; M.L.A. rated highest – 1)	Abad. (6.76)	Poona (5.71)	Ratn. (5.33)	Akola (4.70)
Caste role in distribution (range: no role – 4; improper role – 1)	Poona (3.70)	Ratn. (3.67)	Abad. (3.61)	Akola (3.55)
Economic role in distribution (range: no role – 4; improper role – 1)	Ratn. (3.57)	Poona (3.18)	Akola (3.09)	Abad. (3.0)
Selection of candidates (range: proper – 3; improper – 1)	Ratn. (1.93)	Poona (1.82)	Akola (1.18)	Abad. (1) (very small sample)
Control of loan distribution machinery (of cooperatives) (range: Z.P. should control – 3; Z.P. should not control – 1)	Abad. (2.14) (very small sample)	Akola (1.60)	Poona (1.58)	Ratn. (1.52)

* The values under column 1 are *always* the higher ones and those under column 4 the lower ones.

virtue of their high individual stake. Hence the motivation to protect or promote these interests would also have been more deeply felt than in other districts. The fact that such indices of personal economic interest as 'landholding size' did not discriminate between factional groups in this district does not lessen the significance of the fact that Akola respondents, as a whole, were the larger landowners and cash crop growers and probably, therefore, had a stronger economic motivation for political action.

Akola respondents were further distinguished by other broad environmental characteristics which were somewhat muted in most of the remaining districts. The communications potential, in particular, was quite high in this district. This meant, in effect, that the proportion of literates in the rural population was higher and, moreover, that a fairly large percentage (relative to the other districts) of the rural population, and of the cultivators as well, had attained levels of education above mere literacy. The possibility of communicating was thus increased by educational levels. But other channels of communication were also open to them. Roads, markets, fairs and post offices provided more facilities for economic and social exchange here than in other districts. Akola respondents were also aided in their communications by the fact that they did not have to travel as far as did respondents in other districts to reach the political headquarters of the block or the district. By the same token, they were also more readily accessible to district and block political leaders. In addition, Akola was the most urbanized district in terms of population and urban facilities, such as banks, which may have further enhanced socio-economic exchange between rural and urban areas. (See Table 3 for statistics on the above statements.)

It appears from the foregoing that the Akola respondents whose social and economic bases were essentially rural in nature were exposed, more than the average respondent in any of the other districts, to urban or urbanizing influences, as evidenced by the communications and urbanization factors and by the relative proximity to political centers of activity. This is significant in the context of the argument developed earlier (see Chapter 2). There we saw that the interests of the private economic community are largely based in the urban areas. Assuming that this was so in Akola as well, we may infer that the rural-based economic interests in Akola had more avenues of contact with this urban sphere of operations than in any other district.

Another singular feature noted in Akola concerned the larger political community, which was found to be the most politically active, at least as far as participation in public elections was con-

175

The Dynamics of Indian Political Factions

cerned. Close to 60% of the voters cast their ballots in the Zilla Parishad elections. The highest proportion attained in the other districts was around 40% – in Poona and Aurangabad; as little as 26% of the electorate voted in the Ratnagiri elections. (See Table 3.) The poorer showing in Poona and Aurangabad may be attributable to the lower literacy levels there. In Ratnagiri the very low vote count was explained by many respondents and others interviewed there by the fact that the elections were held during the monsoon season, when the roads were largely impassable and access to the polling booths was severely limited.

Not only were Akola voters more active but they also expressed the greatest opposition to the Congress Party.* This dissatisfaction in the larger political community was also reflected among Congress Councillors of the Zilla Parishad. On the whole, the Akola Congressmen seemed the least committed to the party. They exhibited a stronger inclination than any other group of respondents to resign from Congress. More of them expressed a preference for majority voting than in any other district which suggests some dissatisfaction with the conventional voting procedure followed in party meetings (*viz.* unanimous voting). Moreover, the selection of candidates by the Party was considered improper, on the whole, by Akola Congressmen. (See Table 3.)

Some of these characteristics of Akola respondents and their environment suggest that the amount of communication among respondents, and between respondents and their constituents or neighbors, was greater than in most other districts. In such circumstances, of course, organization for political (or other) purposes is greatly facilitated. The particular configuration of traits which we encountered in Akola is unique. Personal economic wealth, a strong bias toward cash crop cultivation – encouraged by cooperative financing – and agricultural prosperity in the district, were combined with popular opposition to Congress and a considerable capacity for communication among respondents and rural citizens at large. These conditions allowed Rebel leaders to weld together representatives of common economic interests, fueled by a common

---

* A point of clarification may be in order here. It ought to be understood that the opposition vote referred to here was not from the urban areas. We are, after all, dealing here with strictly rural constituencies and rural representatives. Those references to respondents from 'urban areas' are merely descriptive of their larger environment – of the taluka in which they reside – and not of their constituencies.

dissatisfaction with district Congress policies and actions, not only in the general public but among the smaller political elite. One or more of these general features were lacking in the total sample of respondents in each of the remaining districts.

The finding that Rebels, on the whole, were excluded from positions of authority in the Congress organization of Akola also supports the assertion that many Congressmen here may have felt alienated from the party organization. And the disclosure that many Rebels were newcomers to this political sphere accords well with the observation that Akola respondents did not feel highly committed to the Congress Party. In the other districts, respondents seemed generally more devoted to the party. Aurangabad respondents, especially, expressed great reluctance to resign from Congress under any hypothetical circumstances; in Poona they were hesitant to label as improper the process of selecting Congress candidates. A similar reticence – more akin to ambivalence, perhaps – was found among Ratnagiri respondents regarding their commitment to the party organization. The fact that none of these attitudinal attributes distinguished between Rebels and Loyalists in Poona and Aurangabad (as they did in Ratnagiri) suggests that potential 'rebels' were disinclined to challenge Congress authority. This may have contributed, in part, to the Loyalist victory, in these districts (and conversely, their near defeat in Ratnagiri).

In Ratnagiri, although respondents as a whole were moderate in their commitment to the party, the Rebels were distinguished by a weaker sense of obligation to the Congress. In this and other aspects, Ratnagiri was an anomaly. Here was a district where the Rebel element was quite strong. Hence the possibility presents itself that Ratnagiri and Akola respondents shared a comparable setting. In some respects, this was indeed the case. The communications potential here was the highest of all. Literacy and higher educational levels were particularly notable in this district. In this respect, Akola and Ratnagiri respondents far outdistanced their counterparts in Poona and Aurangabad. The Ratnagiri Rebels, moreover, resembled the Akola respondents as a whole in their weaker commitment to the party organization. They were involved in cooperatives here, of course, as in every other district. Some of these characteristics among respondents in general, and dissidents in particular, may account for the higher incidence of Rebels in this district. (See Table 3.)

However, there were too many other elements lacking from the configuration which resulted in victory in Akola. In sharp contrast to the latter district, Ratnagiri respondents were very poor. Their landholdings were the smallest of all. On the average, only 34 acres were owned by the respondents here, as against 145 acres in Akola. The value of the landholding and agricultural equipment owned by the average Ratnagiri Councillor was the lowest of all the districts. Moreover, cooperatives – which constituted the main base of operations among dissidents in other districts – were very weak in Ratnagiri. Not only is this conceded in official publications,[4] but it was also reflected in the very low value of shares owned by Ratnagiri respondents compared with other Councillors (Table 3). In addition, the agricultural cooperative activity (which measured the value of loans distributed by cooperatives) was lowest in Ratnagiri. The average landholding in Ratnagiri's talukas was also lower than in any of the other talukas examined here. These economic deficiencies were reflected in the general agricultural economy as well; Ratnagiri was found to be the least prosperous of all districts. Finally, public electoral participation as well as opposition to Congress (in terms of the non-Congress vote) were lowest in this district. Thus some of the most important elements required to forge a strong force to challenge the entrenched Congress leadership were lacking. Although there was an attempt to rally behind the head of the cooperative bank in the district, his weak leadership and the weakness of the cooperative movement in the district as a whole vitiated much of the power potential of the cooperative base and frustrated the efforts of this group to assert their leadership. The fact that the level of economic development in the district was generally low naturally limited the amount of support which could be drawn from economic interests. It is particularly relevant to recall at this point that these very same dissident forces did manage to secure control of the top posts in the Zilla Parishad in the 1967 elections, only to be ousted from the Party. Intervention by State-level leaders could not be withstood by the Ratnagiri dissidents at this time, as it had been by the Akola Rebels in 1962. I would maintain that the economic inadequacies of the Ratnagiri dissidents probably accounted for their defeat both in 1962 and in 1967.

Poona respondents owned the highest value of shares in cooperative institutions of all the districts studied, and their economic

All Districts

background suggested considerable agricultural wealth. These were important elements in the 'winning' configuration of Akola characteristics. Yet, as we know, the Poona dissidents lost their bid for power in the 1962 elections. The cooperative organization, as a political base, draws much of its strength from a prosperous cash crop economy. In Akola, not only was this type of cultivation extensive throughout the district;[5] it was so among the Councillors also. Thus, about 67 acres were cultivated under cotton (or some other commercial crop) by the average respondent in Akola. Only 11 acres were thus cultivated in Poona. (See Table 3.) An examination of the overall cropping pattern in the latter district[6] further reveals that the bulk of cash crop cultivation was limited to a much smaller tract of land in each taluka and to only a handful of talukas. Thus, the political strength which could be derived from a cooperative base was limited to a few talukas. The average loan activity was also much smaller here than in Akola. Poona's communications potential and level of urbanization were also rather low. So that in Poona all of these elements were lacking from the pattern which distinguished Akola (see Table 3). This may account, in part, for the defeat of the dissident group here.

In Aurangabad, where the Rebels waged a powerful struggle against the Loyalist group, the conditions were again inadequate to ensure their victory. The respondents here were the least inclined to resign from the Congress and their loyalty to the party was reflected in the larger voting public. Opposition to Congress, in terms of the votes polled by non-Congress candidates, was the lowest of all districts (see Table 3). In general, the public seemed to be apathetic to political affairs, and the proportion of voters who participated in the 1962 Z.P. elections was considerably lower than in Akola. This lack of political emotion was possibly associated with the very low communications potential which characterized this district. Aurangabad, in fact, ranked lowest of all districts in respect of this factor (see Table 3). The low level of education reflected by this characteristic was apparent in the incompetence displayed by most of the Councillors here, and particularly by the elected officers of the Zilla Parishad (with the exception of the Vice President who had had higher education). The general lack of political drive in the electorate, together with the inadequate conditions for communication, may have combined to weaken the political advantage which Aurangabad dissidents enjoyed through

179

control of the district party organization and the major cooperative institutions. Thus we find once again that intervention by State-level political leaders proved effective in countering the power of the dissident group in Aurangabad.

As we have seen here and in Chapter 3, the combination of factors which could explain political alignments differed from district to district, as did the capacity of the various tests to explain and predict group differences. It might be interesting to speculate on the significance of such irregularities for research strategy.

Both in the separate district analyses and on an all-district basis, it was found that the *combined variables* cluster was always the most effective discriminator between factional alignments. In each of the districts, significant predictors in this *combined* cluster were usually representative of at least two or more sets of characteristics. On an all-district level, however, only one variable, representative of one cluster, emerged as a strong predictor. Five other variables – to which secondary importance was assigned* – were also interpreted as significant predictors in this test. Three out of these five were again drawn from the *environmental* cluster. The question arises why, of the four categories of variables included in this final test, only the *environmental* variables retained their discriminating and predictive capacity at this all-inclusive level. And why did the *behavioral* variables, which in individual districts had been among the best predictors and discriminators of factional differences, rank lowest in these capacities on an all-district basis?

A possible explanation of the first question may lie in the fact that, unlike the *behavioral* traits, the broad *environmental* influences impinging on the Rebels (and Loyalists) remained rather stable for each group as a whole. Thus a large proportion of the Rebels – viewed as a single unit – lived in areas where the average landholding was large compared with that of Loyalists. This is not to say that in every district the average landholding size was greater in the Rebels' talukas than in the Loyalists' talukas. Only in Poona was this the case. It does appear, however, that the total Rebel sample was concentrated in areas where the average landholding size in their talukas was large (for example, in Akola and Aurangabad). A similar observation may be made about public

---

* Coefficients for the canonical variable ranging from 0.40 to 0.49 were considered as predictors of secondary importance in the all-district analysis only. (See note (*) on page 199, below.)

electoral participation and opposition votes vis-a-vis Congress, both of which emerged as significant predictors (at the secondary level of importance). As we have seen, the public vote and the vote for non-Congress candidates were highest in Akola, where the Rebels predominated. Yet within the district these percentages were somewhat lower in the areas of the dissidents, compared with those of the Loyalists. The differences were not so great, however, as to qualify these variables as predictors within the district. That these and other *environmental* characteristics thus assumed importance in the all-district analysis, but not in individual districts, may serve to reinforce an earlier observation that a configuration of general features characteristic of a district and its respondents had optimal value in the analysis of factional alignments, rather than any single factor. (The greater strength of the *combined variables* cluster in each district also supports this view.)

The all-district analysis was able to consider, simultaneously, features in the four districts' environments which were maximally dissimilar, and the dissimilarities were measurable by single indices in the case of each respondent. However, while a single score measured public electoral participation or landholding size in the taluka, for example, there were several indices of involvement in the cooperative or party or governmental structure of authority. Although Rebels were generally involved in the cooperative authority structure, there were no significant indicators in the final analysis (which combined groups from all districts) which demonstrated this. The reason is that the nature of involvement in cooperatives varied. Office may have been held at any one or more of three levels, each of which was denoted separately. Or a respondent may have held posts over time or simultaneously. Thus, any one or more of five variables may have indicated activity in offices of the cooperative organization. In the all-district analysis Rebels from Aurangabad, who were heavily involved in *district-level* cooperatives, were combined with Poona Rebels, whose cooperative base was at the *taluka* level, with Akola Rebels who were *not* very *active in cooperatives*, and finally, with Ratnagiri Rebels, who, like the Aurangabad dissidents, were linked with *district* cooperatives. Hence, the all-district analysis could not reveal differences which had been significant in individual districts.

Another observation which lends itself to speculation is the following. As we have seen, the *combined variables* cluster was

TABLE 4. *Discriminant Analysis Findings: Canonical Correlation –*
Ranked in Order of Importance

Variable Cluster	Canonical Correlation	% of Variance Accounted For
Combined Variables	0.50	0.25
Environment	0.41	0.17
Economic Background	0.36	0.13
Attitudes	0.35	0.12
Behavior	0.32	0.10

extremely effective in explaining the bases of factional alignments within each district. Thus the variance explained by this cluster ranged from 52% to 74%, which constituted the highest range of explained variances, compared with any other variable cluster used in each of the four districts. However on an all-district basis this cluster, although more effective than any of the individual clusters used at this inclusive level, was not nearly as precise in discriminating capacity as it had proved in the separate district analyses. If we relate this observation to the fact that in this cluster only *environmental* variables were significant, certain inferences may be drawn. With regard to the latter observation we may conclude that, in attempting to analyze higher-level units such as the state,* regional rather than individual traits provide the more efficient interpreters of political behavior. All the individual indicators at this inclusive level were poor predictors, compared with environmental measures.

However, the fact remains that the *environmental* cluster registered a relatively low discriminating capacity. This prompts us to seek alternative approaches in interpreting State politics. It would appear that the analysis of coalesced samples is not as instructive as we might wish. It is quite possible, of course, that State-level politics could be explained in terms of variables other than those used here. However, another worthwhile solution to the problem may be to confine the analysis to the individual districts (provided they are broadly representative of the State). This is largely the

---

* The assumption is made here that these areas, collectively, are representative of the State to a large extent (see pp. 4–5 above).

All Districts

TABLE 5. *Discriminant Analysis Findings: Accuracy of Prediction of Factional Alignment (% of Correct Classifications) Achieved by Each Variable Cluster*

| | Variable Cluster* | | | | | | | | | | | | | | |
| | Environment | | | Behavior | | | Economic Background | | | Attitudes | | | Combined Variables | | |
Factional Groupings	L	R	T	L	R	T	L	R	T	L	R	T	L	R	T
Actual Membership	87	73	160	87	73	160	87	73	160	87	73	160	87	73	160
Discriminant Analysis Classification	68	49	117	54	42	96	67	43	110	54	50	104	68	53	121
% of Correct Classifications	78	67	73	62	57	60	77	60	69	62	68	65	78	73	76

* The letter headings under each variable cluster represent the following: L, Loyalist; R, Rebel; T, Total (both Rebels and Loyalists).

approach followed in this study and it has thereby been possible to isolate significant determinants which may be relevant to each representative area of the State. It is from these districts – or districts such as these – that top government and party leaders come after all. And it is in these areas that the important rural issues, requiring action at the State level, arise. The type of investigation conducted in each district also illustrates the importance – indeed the necessity – of combining statistical with quasi-journalistic methods of investigation. A fusion of these approaches may yield both intelligible and sound results. The statistical method validates and renders more comprehensible seemingly disconnected on-the-spot reports, while the intuitive analytical approach may elucidate skeletal statistical findings. *

* For information regarding the relative ability of variable clusters to discriminate between groups on an all-district basis (shown in terms of the variance accounted for by each test cluster), see Table 4 above. In addition, Table 5 indicates the proportion of accurate classifications made by each set of test variables.

CHAPTER 9

CONCLUSION

In the preceding chapters we have been examining some of the conditions within which factions develop, conditions which may determine the particular direction and form of factional alignments. The broad political setting in which the groups evolved is characterized by a dominant political party organization which is linked in a relationship of mutual dependence with the Government of Maharashtra. These two organizations are the major structural components of the political system in the State of Maharashtra. They specialize in – but do not monopolize – the adaptive and integrative activities which are crucial to the effective functioning of the political system. To the extent that these political structures are interdependent, factional behavior within or between them may be reflected in both. Insofar as factions are disruptive of a given condition of harmony within or between these political organizations, the existence of such factions may be expected to have repercussions on the stability of the political system of Maharashtra as a whole, or on any of its component parts.

The analysis presented in this study has been guided by several considerations which are interrelated. In providing an explanation of factional alignments which has been closely reasoned and empirically demonstrated, I have attempted to establish that Indian politics – in at least one important state of the nation – are defined in a rational pattern. Evidence has been advanced to show that the 'factional' behavior of political actors corresponds, on the whole, with rational (or calculable) economic interests; that it is not determined by 'irrational' (that is, emotional) and often unpredictable personal loyalties which may be based almost exclusively on feelings of awe, respect or devotion to a leader because of his charismatic qualities, or on feelings of loyalty evoked by caste or community ties or by family links.

Moreover, I have argued that these rational considerations of economic interests, although they are causal factors, are not solely

184

Conclusion

responsible for political divisions of the type examined here. The friction is generated, in part at least, by the incompatibility of ideas and related practices sanctioned by the politico-economic philosophy of the nation. Specifically, it has been proposed, and I trust illustrated, that the economic principle of the 'mixed enterprise' has provided fertile ground upon which the conflict between economic interests has flourished. To the extent that this principle allows for the coexistence – on an equal basis – of private (individual) and 'public' (collective) economic organizations, it sanctions economic practices and institutional forms which are inimical to the integrity of one another (as long as they have the potential for functioning on a one-to-one basis).*

Thus, contrary to the widespread feeling that Indian politicians are motivated only by personal gain (toward which end personal loyalties are exploited), and that ideology is ignored where such 'selfish' interests are concerned, it is claimed here that ideological preferences *do* play a role in political behavior *in so far as they are interlinked with consideration of personal interest.*†

The fundamental proposition with which this study has been concerned is that political behavior in Maharashtra – more specifically, factionalism – can be traced to economic origins, whether ideological or material. The empirical analysis has probed the material foundations. The general type of dichotomy which has been posited, in terms of policy orientation, is between a preference for private, individual forms of economic enterprise and a prefer-

* I do not wish to imply here that the two forms of economic organization cannot coexist under any circumstances. What I do assert is that one or the other must be accepted as dominant in the political and economic culture, and so practised.

† In effect, I reject assumptions that conceive of 'realistic' and 'idealistic' considerations as mutually exclusive determinants of political behavior. Neither a Marxian nor a Hegelian point of view provides, in and of itself, an adequate understanding of the multi-dimensional nature of human behavior. Rather, I would contend that these philosophical views of man complement one another.

Within the context of this study I would maintain that both ideology *and* economic (material) conditions and interests combine, in an *interactive* pattern, to influence behavior. Thus, I would not claim that the Rebels' 'leftist' policy orientation (which inclines them toward a collective form of economic organization) has developed separately from their rational economic interests and the objective conditions of their environment. Nor would I allege that the pattern of economic interests and conditions has consistently and independently determined the direction of the groups' ideological preferences for individual or collective forms of economic organization.

ence for collective forms. At the district level, this dichotomy is reflected in the political breach between those associated with cooperatives and those unconnected with them, on the whole, and apparently linked with interests in the private economic community. Although respondents in the various districts have differed in terms of many conditions of action and motivating patterns, the one factor which has held constant throughout has been the association of dissident Z.P. Congressmen with cooperatives; at the same time, the group supporting and supported by the dominant Congress leadership of the area examined has invariably had some liaison with private economic interests.

A few projections may be attempted now of the prospects for stability in the political system of Maharashtra. We have seen that the conflict within districts has arisen wherever cooperative-based economic interests have intruded or threatened to intrude into the economic arena of the private entrepreneur. Thus the stability which the Congress-dominated government has enjoyed in Maharashtra may be adversely affected if cooperative-based groups capture the Zilla Parishads and press their claims on the State Government from wide areas of rural Maharashtra. The critical question is whether many such groups can, indeed, assume controlling positions of authority in rural district government.

Our examination of these groupings indicates that cooperative institutions are successful as political instruments only if there exists a complex nexus of conditions. These include a fairly high level of agricultural prosperity in a district where cooperatives can provide their services to a large and somewhat evenly dispersed community of moderately prosperous cash crop cultivators. These cultivators would own fairly large tracts of agricultural land which would permit them to secure their own food needs, while at the same time allowing them to set aside land and capital for the cultivation of profitable commercial crops.

Moreover, the findings suggest that cooperative leadership is more apt to succeed in its political aims if conditions permit access, for purposes of organization, to political functionaries over a wide arena of operations. Higher levels of education and a working network of communications are some of the conditions which greatly facilitate political organization here (as elsewhere).

On the basis of the findings stated here, we may assume further that these rural economic interests, in launching their challenge,

Conclusion

will encounter opposition within the district and/or from higher levels of authority. In such circumstances, their goals may be more easily attainable if they can elicit the tacit or active cooperation of the political community at large. The support of the public may constitute merely a protest vote against the opponents of the cooperative-based group, or it may be a manifestation of genuine sympathy for the group as representative of common interests. In either case, such a sentiment may be generated or (if it already exists) brought into play only through appropriate channels of communication.

Another broad ecological characteristic of areas where the cooperative-based political group has been successful in the past, and might be in the future, is the general level of urbanization. In Akola, for example, the general setting of the rural political feud was more urban in nature than in any other district studied. At the very least, we may say that this factor probably increases the potential for interaction between rural and urban interests. If we accept the proposition that their interests, at the moment, are antagonistic, then that interaction is more likely than not to be accompanied by some friction.

Thus, as urbanization spreads, as general education increases, and as new avenues of communication are opened, the possibility that rural-based interests will come into contact with the urban-based economic interests will increase, thereby creating or extending one of the preconditions of conflict. That is to say, the *arenas* of conflict may be expected to widen as this trend develops.

On the other hand, we ought to bear in mind that there are certain physical and other limitations imposed on the development of preconditions for future 'rebel' success. The cultivation of commercial crops which at this point seems to coincide with cooperative institutions, is limited not only by financial considerations but by physical conditions as well. Cotton, for example, cannot be profitably cultivated on just any type of soil. To a certain extent this is true of sugarcane also. So that the expansion of commercial crops will necessarily be limited to certain areas. The individual field studies of Poona (and to a certain extent, Aurangabad) indicated that this kind of localization weakens the political thrust of the cooperative-based interest group. If we carry such an analogy over to the State level, we may infer that to the extent that cooperative-based power is confined to limited areas of cash crop cultivation, to that extent it will be circumscribed.

So even if cooperative institutions continue to expand and increase their loan activities, as they have done in the past several decades, they may not be able to increase their political power commensurately in the rural areas as long as their physical sphere of effective activity is narrowly restricted. However, if they can extend their political base through an important agricultural area, they will have considerable leverage, like that which the localized industrial community has and is able to exercise at this point. Vidarbha is such an agricultural area, and a crucial one at that. Indeed, the top Maharashtrian leadership felt constrained to confer important positions of authority in the State Government to Vidarbha leaders in order to ensure their support in 1957 and thereafter. The economic importance of this area is perhaps second only to that of the Bombay–Poona industrial complex in Western Maharashtra.

If at some time in the future the political power of these interests can be consolidated in the Zilla Parishads of Vidarbha, the Government of Maharashtra may well be faced with a crisis, as it tries to accommodate conflicting pressures from different economic interests in the State. Thus, for example, cooperative-based interests in Vidarbha, which now function largely in the credit sphere, may press for a more enthusiastic promotion by the Government of cooperative marketing and processing facilities to handle the large cotton and fruit produce. Much of this is now processed and distributed by Bombay business enterprises. If such pressures are brought to bear on the Government, the private textile and fruit canning industries (and any other industries similarly affected), together with commercial trading interests, may be expected to attempt to block these demands and their implementation. The convergence of conflicting pressures on the Government of Maharashtra may be expected to produce considerable strife within the inner councils of government and party, and to weaken the stability of both these political structures and of the political system of Maharashtra as a whole. The event which is more likely to precipitate a convulsive crisis in the Congress Party (reverberating through the political system at large) is the capture of the Zilla Parishads by the cooperative power structure. This would reinforce the economic foundation of these rural interests with the

Conclusion

cement of political power and governmental authority. In these circumstances the Government of Maharashtra, buffeted by conflicting forces, may have to adopt and implement a more decisive socialist program of action, or retrench from the present course of tentative support for the cooperatives, and perhaps even abolish the Zilla Parishads.

A NOTE ON METHODOLOGY

I shall set forth in this section the essential steps followed in processing the data collected. The two basic stages involved were (1) reducing the data to manageable proportions, and (2) analyzing them. As I have indicated earlier, the information on which the foregoing analysis is based was gathered through a uniformly structured interview administered to popularly elected district councillors and from published official sources. References to the latter will be found throughout this work – in the text and in the tables appended to the preceding chapters. The interview schedule used will be found immediately following this Note).* The material gathered through this interview and from other sources was supplemented by much background information obtained through unstructured interviews with respondents and others (journalists or civil servants, for example) regarding the intricate details of local politics.

Some comments are in order now regarding the nature of the interview schedule in relation to the study as defined herein. An examination of this schedule will reveal a very lengthy document indeed, which yielded several volumes of data from the districts covered in the study. The number of variables extracted from this material alone totalled two hundred and eighty-five. In addition I used forty-two environmental measures, compiled from official (printed or mimeographed) sources. (See Table A below, pp. 209–10.) It is therefore necessary to explain the procedure by which I ultimately selected only forty-seven variables for testing by the principal analytical method used.

The original emphasis of the study was to be the nature of 'emerging leadership' in these new bodies of local government and the relationships of the local elected officials and members of the

* The interview schedule was translated into Marathi from an original English draft. The translation was then checked against the English version to ensure correspondence in meaning. The interview was administered in Marathi by a Marathi-speaking Maharashtrian colleague.

Appendix 1

Councils, on the one hand, with appointed officials on the same bodies, as well as with the local assembly representatives and party leaders, on the other. (The excessive breadth of scope reflects the optimism of the uninitiated in Indian field studies.)

The nature of factional alignments as a significant area of investigation presented itself shortly before the field survey was undertaken, and it proved to be a most promising one in the course of the first field trip in Aurangabad. New lines of questioning were perceived in this district which could yield information regarding the nature of the factional dispute. Hence the interview schedule as it appears now incorporates some changes made primarily in the course of the Aurangabad field trip. In the remaining districts, also, questions were dropped – either because they were considered peripheral or irrelevant to the focus of the study as it had taken shape, or because little reliable information could be obtained from respondents owing to their apparent inability to understand certain questions. The appended interview schedule is a revised version of the original, and the variables which are enumerated in Table B at the end of this section are derived entirely from data obtained through the revised interview schedule. Strictly speaking, the field work conducted here might be considered more in the nature of a pilot study, in view of this fact. However, it should be noted that the interview-derived variables used in the discriminant analysis were based on answers to questions which were uniformly administered to all respondents, starting from the first field survey.

What follows is a description of the two basic steps used in processing the data collected.

STEP I. REDUCING OF DATA TO MANAGEABLE PROPORTIONS

As indicated elsewhere, a limitation was imposed upon the number of variables to be used in the final analysis, for technical reasons. Only a small number of variables (relative to the total available) could therefore be drawn upon for the main analysis. Several criteria were used in selecting these; some were logically dictated by the analytical focus and goals or again by technical necessity, and others were defined by statistical tests.

One technical problem involved inadequate sampling due to changes made in the interview schedule by the addition of questions (or for other reasons). Those variables for which the district sample was very poor were usually dropped. Beyond that, a broad criterion used to decide upon the initial elimination of variables was established by reference to the theoretical framework within which the study was conceived. Thus the first standard applied concerned the relevance of a variable to the issue of factional alignment in terms of those environmental and individual characteristics subsumed under the four categories set forth in Table C below. Those variables considered (by reference to the above yardstick) to be potentially relevant to the subject under study were cross-classified with factional alignment (that is, with the dichotomous variable comprising the categories 'Rebel' and 'Loyalist').

The cross-classification technique is a correlating procedure suitable for qualitative data.[1] It measures the degree of association between two or more variables, and it provides a test of significance (chi-square) by which that association may be evaluated. The elimination or inclusion of variables so tested was decided upon on the basis of the following criteria:

1. Those variables which were not significantly associated (at a level of 0.05 or more) with factional alignment in at least one area (that is, on an all-district basis or district-wise) were *generally* excluded from the discriminant analysis tests.*

2. Those variables which fell in any one of the four categories employed in this study as empirically ascertainable measures of factional alignment (see Table C below) were subjected to examination by discriminant analysis, even where, in a few cases, they were not significantly associated with factional alignment or approached significance (at 0.10) in the cross-classification test.

3. Finally, certain variables which were significantly associated with factional alignment, or which approached significance in at least one area, were nevertheless deleted from the discriminant analysis tests. In such cases, the main reason for deletion was that other variables were available to measure the same or a similar

---

* Where it was felt that duplication or unnecessary elaboration of a category might have been introduced by any variable or variables, these were also excluded. For example, with regard to the behavioral indices, the variables specifying the particular spheres of authority in which a respondent held office, either simultaneously or over time (see Variables 47–54 in Table B below), were considered redundant because other variables were incorporated which indicated simultaneous involvement (or involvement over time) in two or more spheres or in any one sphere. Furthermore, because there was a relatively large number of indices in the behavioral category, the variables referred to above were deleted.

Appendix 1

characteristic. Thus, for example, the variable 'exposure to news media' (see Variable 8 in Table B below) was considered an index of urbanizing influences to which a respondent might have been exposed. As other variables were available to gauge this characteristic it was not included in the discriminant analysis, for the sake of economy. Those variables derived from the interview data and considered for analysis by cross-tabulation or discriminant testing are enumerated in Table B below. The first part of this table lists the variables which were cross-classified with factional alignment and identifies those which (1) were significantly associated, (2) approached significance, or (3) were not significantly associated. The final column further indicates which among these were subsequently used in the discriminant tests.

The second part lists variables which were not cross-classified with factional alignment but were nevertheless used in the final analysis. They were entirely quantitative measures. Hence they could not be used in the cross-classification tests unless the values were grouped in gross categories. This was attempted with the 'size of landholding' variable. However it was considered an unnecessarily cumbersome task to do the same with all of these variables. The large number of digits in certain variables, for example, made the collapsing of categories technically inefficient, as an additional transformation of such a measure would have been required before proceeding with the cross-classification tests. In view of the fact that only a small number of variables was involved in this category, it was decided to test all of them directly in the discriminant analysis.*

In addition to variables derived from interview data, however, I compiled forty-two aggregate measures descriptive of the taluka from which respondent came. They were reduced to a total of six clusters by factor analysis. This is a procedure (or rather a set of procedures) used to analyze the intercorrelations within a given set of variables.[2] The application of this technique may vary, depending on the user and the nature of his study. Here it was used to determine whether there might be a small number of 'factors'

---

* For an enumeration of those variables which were neither cross-classified with factional alignment nor used in the final analysis, please see Mary C. Carras, *The Dynamics of Political Factions: A Study of District Councils (Zilla Parishads) in the State of Maharashtra.* (*Dissertation* in South Asia Regional Studies, University of Pennsylvania, 1969.) These were excluded largely because they were not of immediate relevance to the study of factional alignments as that study was designed.

underlying the forty-two measures of social and economic attributes characteristic of the respondents' areas of origin. It allowed us, in effect, to combine or 'factor' a number of measures and examine them as though they constituted a single variable.

Once these common factors were extracted it was necessary to devise a general measure – or factor score – which represented an average of the combined measures. The procedure used was one which converted each 'raw' score for a respondent on a given variable* into a standard score. This score was then weighted (or multiplied) by the factor loading† for each variable in a given 'factor' which had registered a significant factor loading.‡ Thus if there were three such variables in a given factor, the standard score of respondent 'i' on *each* of the three variables was multiplied by the factor loading for that variable. The three products were added and then divided by the number of variables used, so that an average normalized cluster score was obtained for each individual.§

Finally, a rough estimation of the independence of clusters or factors was made by checking the intercorrelations between variables of one cluster and those of another. This simply provided an additional check on the selection of optimal factors.

Of the forty-two measures initially subjected to factor analysis, ten were subsequently dropped. The reasons for eliminating these variables were mainly of two kinds. The utility of measures which were highly loaded on a number of factors was considerably reduced, since one purpose of applying the factor analytic technique is to obtain, as far as possible, factorially 'pure' measures. Hence, where it was found that variables were 'factorially complex' they were eliminated. Another reason in the case of two variables was

* Each respondent 'i' from taluka 'j' was given the score of variable 'x' descriptive of that particular taluka.

† This statistic is conceptually similar to the correlation coefficient. Each factor loading expresses the correlation between a particular variable and a given factor.

‡ It has been estimated that loadings greater than 0.29 are significant at the 0.05 level. Hence, only loadings of 0.30 and over are generally used to select the component variables of a factor cluster.[3] I used loadings of 0.40 and over.

§ It has been validly demonstrated by W. S. Robinson that ecological correlations cannot be properly used as substitutes for individual correlations, and that when they are thus used the result is an 'ecological fallacy'.[4] It is submitted here that these measures are *not* used as substitutes for individual measures. Other valid uses can be made of such correlations. The case for such usage has been convincingly argued by Herbert Menzel.[5]

that while these were highly correlated with each other (at over 0.9), they were very poorly correlated with all other variables. Thus, while they appeared as a 'pure' factor in the matrix of factor loadings, they were in effect a single measure rather than a factor.

Of the six factors yielded, only five were used in the final analysis. It was decided to eliminate the sixth factor partly because I was not satisfied that it was a conceptually meaningful factor* and partly because two of the three variables in this cluster loaded highly with other factors. The factors which were ultimately used in the discriminant analysis appear in Table D at the end of this Note. (The table is a reproduction of the matrix used to obtain factor scores. The cluster within each factor is shown in bold type. The variable titles corresponding to each number appear in Table A below, and the factor clusters, identified in terms of their component indices, also appear below in Table E.)

STEP II. APPLICATION OF DISCRIMINANT
ANALYSIS TECHNIQUE

I have described above the various procedures used to reduce to more manageable proportions the number of variables derived from interviews and official sources. Now, we shall examine the analytical technique used to determine whether selected variables could be considered reliable discriminators between members of the two factional groups under analysis.

Discriminant analysis was the procedure used to establish the cohesiveness (or general homogeneity) of each group, as well as the distinctiveness of one vis-a-vis the other. This technique is suited to this purpose inasmuch as it tests the significance of the group differences and permits us to examine the nature of the differences found.[6]

Before an exposition of the analytical method is undertaken, it is very important to note, in terms of operational procedure, that the data must undergo a standardization process before being submitted to discriminant analysis. The standardization procedure

---

* The three variables in the eliminated cluster, which I had tentatively labeled 'Rural Backwardness', were: (1) percentage of matriculates among rural male literate cultivators in taluka; (2) number of infant deaths as percentage of total deaths in taluka; and (3) percentage of villages not electrified.

The Dynamics of Indian Political Factions

projects the measures on to a single plane where they can be validly compared. For example, the range of measures for one variable – such as 'size of individual landholding' – may be from 1 to 200, while the scores of composite variables derived from factor analysis may range from − 0.9 to 0.9. The standardization procedure simply gives us a single scale on which the real distance from one point to anothei with regard to variable 'X' is analogous to the real distance between two points for variable 'Y', providing us with measures which are comparable.

A special feature of discriminant analysis which particularly commends it for use in a study of this type is that it can be applied in a research design where the dependent variable is categorical and the independent variables are continuous (interval).* The dependent variable referred to here, of course, is 'factional alignment', a dichotomous variable with two categories: Rebel and Loyalist.† Although discriminant analysis resembles the analysis of variance technique in some ways,‡ it differs from the latter in that it does not test the significance of the relationship between independent, interval variables in one or more groups of randomly classified respondents. The groups in an analysis of variance experiment do not signify dimensions of a dependent test space (as in the former technique). We may view them, geometrically, as existing on a single plane. Discriminant analysis, on the other hand, tests the relative effect of independent variables on a multi- or two-dimensional dependent variable, and it predicts the respondent's group (or category within the dependent variable) on the basis of his scores on a set of predictive measures. That is to say, it tests whether the observed groups may have come from a single population rather than two (or more). Toward this end, a 'discriminant function' is computed which transforms the 'predictor' (independent) measures for each individual into a single discriminant score which can be located along a single line for members of both groups. Thus it reduces a multi-dimensional predictor space (in

* Although interval variables are generally more desirable, the method is being experimentally applied to variables that include qualitative measures. It is the equivalent of multidimensional, partial and multiple correlation for categories as dependent variables.

† Discriminant analysis may be undertaken also where the categorical dependent variable has more than two classifications.

‡ Statistics such as between-groups and within-groups variance and error, as well as the F-ratio, are used in both techniques.

Appendix 1

this study defined by 47 variables, or rather by sub-sets thereof) to a single dimension, divided into two regions.*

A brief description is set forth below (in substantive rather than mathematical language) of those among the various procedures comprising the discriminant analysis technique which I feel are most relevant for an understanding of the method.

One of the first important steps in the procedure involves the testing of each variable with a view to determining the extent to which it contributes a statistically significant difference between the two groups (i.e., the two sets of scores).† Then a set of computations is performed for each variable in a step-wise fashion; among other things, these computations result at each step in the elimination or inclusion of some variables, depending on their tested ability to contribute to differences between the groups. A test of the homogeneity of group means is also executed at each step on the basis of the variables which have been included up to that point. Ultimately, the step-wise process culminates in an optimal discriminant function and in the identification of each individual by means of a score which places him on one or the other side of some mid-point‡ on the line constituting the discriminant function.§

Broadly speaking, the underlying procedure involved here is similar to multiple regression techniques (often referred to as multiple correlation).[7] Multiple regression essentially orders the independent variables in terms of how well each of them will *predict* variance in some dependent variable (which, however, may not be categorical). It then enables the researcher to make a prediction regarding a dependent variable from several variables considered *simultaneously*. Multiple correlation, on the other hand, analyzes the relations between one set of measures and a single variable. In general we may say that regression analysis focusses on *predictors*, whereas in correlation analysis it is the *strength* of relationship that is measured and tested for significance.

Canonical correlation (relevant to discriminant analysis) is a type of multiple correlation technique which is used for studying the

---

* A single discriminant function is obtainable only in the case of a two-group discriminant analysis, because the number of functions is always equal to: (1) the number of groups minus one; or (2) the number of variables, whichever is smaller.[8]

† The level of significance is established by application of the F test.

‡ This is exactly at the mid-point between group means, the latter representing, roughly speaking, an average composite characteristic of each group.

§ All of the statistical findings in this analysis were significant at the 0.05 level.

interrelations between two sets of measurements made on the same subjects. In canonical correlation however (in its general application) both the dependent *and* independent variables are multiple, whereas in multiple regression (and correlation) there is a single dependent variable. For a study of this type, where the dependent variable is a single one and the number of independent variables is multiple in both groups, discriminant analysis constitutes a special case of the canonical correlation method.

The canonical correlation coefficient indicates the highest correlation possible between two sets of variables (one independent, the other dependent). What this analysis tells us, basically, is that the correlation between given pairs of independent variables is significantly related to the correlation between given pairs of dependent variables, and that these pairs of independent and dependent variables are combined in such a way as to make the correlation between components of the two sets maximal.[9]

The predictor measures for group '1' are tested for relationship against the dependent variable categories. The same is done with the measures for group '2' (in a simultaneous procedure). In each case, of course, the dependent variable categories are the same. The dependent variable is, in effect, treated twice, as though it constituted two dependent variables, thereby satisfying one of the conditions of canonical correlation analysis (namely, that both independent and dependent variables should be multiple).

In geometrical terms, the canonical correlation can be considered as a measure of the extent to which individuals occupy the same relative positions in the predictor space (that is, in the space defined by the independent variable measures) as they do in the test space (that is, in the space defined by the dependent variable). (Although the predictor and test spaces are conceptually distinct, empirically they are the same.)

A 'canonical variable' is derived from the correlation procedures at each step, reducing the set of measures represented by significant variables in each group to one. This canonical variable is continually modified as another variable is introduced and correlated with the canonical variable. Having produced a new set of canonical variables, the problem at each step is to find two sets of weights which will maximize the correlation between these derived canonical variables. The problem as defined here, where there is a single dependent variable, is one of multiple regression.[10]

Appendix 1

Finally, when all the variables have been exhausted in the stepwise discriminant analysis, a canonical correlation coefficient is computed, from which it is possible to estimate the proportion of variance between groups contributed by the canonical variable. This statistic is used in the same way in which a regular correlation coefficient might be used, where we would simply square its value in order to estimate the variance contributed by the correlated variables. (In this case, the correlated variables would be the two canonical variates representing each of the two group measures.) In addition, there is computed a set of 'coefficients for the canonical variable' which serve as weights for the individual variable scores. Through these an individual's score can be computed, telling us whether he is a member of one or the other group. We may consider this coefficient for the canonical variable as a type of regression coefficient which enables us to predict the location of an individual on the discriminant function line. The higher the value of this coefficient, the more effective it will be in discriminating between groups, and on the basis of this figure the variables may be ranked in the order of their predictive strength.*

The results obtained in applying this technique were highly satisfactory (though I am fully aware of the possibility of error, given the lack of extensive experimentation with the method of discriminant analysis). Although this is a technique that is widely used in the field of industrial marketing, it has not enjoyed much vogue in the social sciences (with the exception of the educational and psychological fields.)

I have purposely outlined in some detail the basic steps and statistical concepts used in this method of analysis in the hope of encouraging others – particularly social scientists in the South Asian field – to experiment with discriminant analysis.

* Upon examination of the several district-chapter tables listing the coefficients for the canonical variable, it will be noted that a dividing line is drawn below variables registering a coefficient of 0.50 and over. Although technically speaking all variables which had a coefficient above zero could be considered significant at the 0.05 level, only those coefficients of 0.50 or over were considered 'significant' for purposes of inclusion in the 'combined variables' test. This cutoff point simply serves to distinguish between stronger and weaker predictors, at an approximate midpoint in the average range of coefficients. A cutoff point was useful for the purpose of limiting the number of variables (within each of the four categories) to be used in the final ('combined variables') tests. Such a limitation was desirable for a more efficient application of discriminant analysis, given the sample sizes dealt with.

199

The Dynamics of Indian Political Factions

1. Name

2. Identification Number

3. Address

4. Sex

5. Date of birth or age

6. Religion

7. Caste: Sub-caste:

8. Kul (clan)

9. Gharana (traditional title of authority, e.g. Patil, Deshmukh, Desai, etc.)

10. Languages known: Speak   Read   Write
    (a) Mother tongue:
    (b) Other Indian language(s)
    (c) English

11. (a) What was the last year of education completed?
    (b) In what year was your education completed?
    (c) Where did you get your education?
        In village: Number of years –
        In city or town: Number of years –

12. What was the occupation of your grandfather, father and yourself:
                              Grandfather   Father   Self
    (a) Primary occupation
    (b) Secondary occupation

13. (a) What is the name of your home village?   Population:
    (b) How far is your village from:
        Taluka Headquarters –
        District Headquarters –

14. What is the caste-wise breakdown of the population of your:
                                  Village   Constituency
    Brahman
    Maratha   Adivasi
    Mali   Balutedar
    Harijan   Other

15. (a) What is your total annual income (gross or net)?
    (b) Is your family joint or nuclear?
    (c) If nuclear, when did the split occur?
    (d) How many members are there in your family?

Appendix 1

16. (a) Private property owned and valuation:
   (1) Land   Value (Rs.)
       Number of acres
       Number of acres irrigated
       When bought
   (2) Houses
       How many owned?
       When or by whom built?
   (3) Wells (number)
   (4) Vehicles   Value
       Car
       Jeep
       Bullock cart
       Other
   (5) Machinery
       Tractor
       Oil engine   Duster
       Spray pump   Other
   (6) Animals
       Bullocks   Goats
       Cows   Sheep
       Buffalo   Poultry
       Horses   Other
   (7) Store(s): (Describe)
   (8) Shares and/or savings in:
       (i) private company or factory
       (ii) cooperative society
       (iii) Government savings certificates, bonds, etc.
   (9) Insurance
   (b) What do you produce on your land?
       Name of crop:
       No. of Acres:
       Average Annual Yield (quintals or other):
                                      Selling Price
       Proportion Sold:
       Proportion Kept For Household Use:
   (c) Total Annual Expenditure on Following Items:
       (1) Agricultural – Seeds   Fuel for engines
                     Fertilizers   Land revenue and cess
                     Insecticides   Water rate
                     Wages   Other
                     Transport to market
       (2) Household
       (3) Political
       (4) Travel
       (5) Other

The Dynamics of Indian Political Factions

(*d*) To whom do you sell your product?
   (1) Cooperative society
   (2) Private trader
   (3) Consumer
   (4) Other

17. (*a*) Of what party are you a member?
   (*b*) In what year did you join that party?   Why?
   Who brought you into the party?
   (*c*) Did you ever leave that party?   Why?
   Have you since rejoined that party?
   (*d*) Did you ever join any other party or parties?   Why?
   If you did not join, were you ever a sympathizer of any other party or parties?

18. Did you ever take part in the Nationalist Movement? In what way?

19. (*a*) Do you now hold, or have you ever held, a position of authority in your present party? In any other party? Please name that position, the party and the period (from when to when).
   (*b*) Have you ever held any position of authority in any political association (other than a political party)? (Describe.)
   (*c*) Before being elected to the Zilla Parishad, had you ever held a government post (from village level, e.g., patwari, or higher)?
   (*d*) Did you ever contest any election for public office?

20. Are you a member or office-bearer in any of the societies listed below?
Professional (medical, legal, educational)
Industrial (workers' union, etc.)
Agricultural (farmers' union, etc.)
Trade association
Labor
Civic Association
Religious (temple trustee, etc.)
Cooperatives (please indicate level, e.g., village, taluka or district; and approximate number of members)

21. (*a*) How many times a month and for what purpose do you generally go to:
   (i) your village
   (ii) taluka (or block) headquarters
   (iii) district headquarters
   (iv) Bombay (or Nagpur – in Vidarbha)
   (*b*) Have your wife or other members of your family visited these places?
   (*c*) Have you ever traveled outside Maharashtra?
   Where?   When?
   (*d*) Have you ever traveled outside India?
   Where?   When?
   (*e*) Have your wife or other members of your family traveled outside Maharashtra or India?

Appendix 1

22. (a) Did you yourself initially consider contesting the Zilla Parishad election or did someone suggest this to you? If the latter, who?

(b) What do you think of the system for selection of candidates?

(c) Did you yourself take part in your election campaign? How did you campaign? (i) Did you travel by foot, jeep, car or bullock cart? (ii) Did you hold public meetings or go from house to house? (iii) Who, among the political leaders, came to campaign for you? (iv) What costs did you incur in your campaign? (v) In your campaign speeches, what issues did you stress?

(d) How many other candidates opposed you in the elections? What was the caste of each? What was their party? (If independent, what was their political inclination, if any?) What was the approximate percentage of votes polled by each?

(e) Did you have any hopes at the time you contested that you might be nominated to the office you now hold? (Asked only of office-bearers)

23. How and when (before or after your election) did you become familiar with the Zilla Parishads Act? Did you read the Act in the original, or hear lectures about it, or come to know of it in informal conversations?

24. When, as a member of the Zilla Parishad, you must consider 'serving the needs of your area', what area do you usually have in mind: your village, constituency, taluka or district?

25. Name the country of the following world leaders:

Johnson	U Thant
Kosygin	Soekarno
Wilson	Nasser
Mao Tse-tung	
(or Chou En-lai)	

26. Who is the President of the All-India Congress Committee?
Minister of Rural Development in Maharashtra?
President of your District Congress Committee?
President of your Taluka Congress Committee?

27. (a) Do you read the newspaper daily? Which one(s)? Do you subscribe to any newspaper?

(b) Do you listen to radio news? How many times a day? a week? a month? Do you listen at home or at the Gram Panchayat office?

28. For whom did you vote in the Congress Party Presidential elections? In the Zilla Parishad Presidential elections?

29. Were you affected by the Land Reform laws (e.g., the Land Ceilings Act and the Tenancy Act)? If you were, did you lose or gain land? How many acres?

30. (a) Were discussions held on the Fourth Five Year Plan at the Gram Panchayat level, Panchayat Samiti level and/or Zilla Parishad level? What were some of the suggestions made? Did you propose any priorities?

203

The Dynamics of Indian Political Factions

(b) With regard to village public contribution:

(i) Have there been any works completed through public con-tributions? What works?

(ii) Is collection of public contribution generally easy or difficult?

(iii) Have you ever solicited public contribution in your village?

31. What was the purpose of the Act establishing the Zilla Parishads? Has that purpose been fulfilled?

32. Some of the other purposes of the Act were:

(i) to awaken the public's consciousness in public affairs

(ii) to create new leadership, in terms of outlook as well as source of recruitment.

Have these purposes been fulfilled?

(NOTE: With regard to the above question, 'new outlook' was explained to the Respondent in terms of the tendency of the 'new leaders' to use, and to actively encourage the use of, new methods of agriculture, as well as the use of facilities offered by the Panchayat Samiti and the Zilla Parishad, to campaign for social and economic improvements, and so on.)

33. What are the shortcomings in the ways in which the Act is being implemented?

34. (a) How would you rank yourself (in your village and constituency) in terms of wealth? If you do not rank first, what is the occupation of the man who does rank first?

(b) Was your father a 'village leader'? Was he a big landlord, a trader or moneylender?

(c) Are Zilla Parishad members mostly from the richer classes, the middle classes or the poor classes?

35. (a) Is Congress strengthened as a result of the establishment and functioning of the Zilla Parishads?

(b) Is Congress likely to win the next elections because of the exist-ence of the Zilla Parishads, or will it lose strength because of them? Or will the existence of the Zilla Parishads have no effect on the elections?

36. (a) (Regarding the economic relation with the State Government.) What proportion of the Zilla Parishad Budget consists of State funds and what proportion consists of Zilla Parishad's own funds?

(b) (Regarding the political relationship with the State Government.) Are you familiar with the issue regarding the seating of Members of the Legislative Assembly on the Zilla Parishads? If you are, do you think the Zilla Parishads are likely to win out on this controversy?

37. Should the Zilla Parishads be given additional subjects to administer, such as revenue, police, forests, higher education?

38. Should the Zilla Parishads be given additional authority to administer the subjects they do have? For example:

Appendix 1

(a) Should they have the authority to appoint, dismiss, transfer, and/or promote Class I, II, III and IV officers and servants?

(b) With regard to the Department of Cooperation:

(i) Should the Zilla Parishad have representation on the major district-level cooperative banks?

(ii) Should policy decisions in regard to the distribution of loans by cooperative societies and banks be made by the Cooperative Committee of the Zilla Parishad?

39. Does the Zilla Parishad have the power to reappropriate funds in the District Fund from one major head to another? If not, should it have this power?

40. On what basis is the distribution of funds (both State and Zilla Parishad) made at the time of the formulation of the budget? Is it on the basis of: population; needs; equality; other?

41. (a) Does caste play any role in decisions taken at Zilla Parishad Committee meetings?

(b) Does economic interest play any role in such decisions?

42. Can you suggest any means by which the Zilla Parishad's own income can be increased?

(a) Would you be in favor of increasing land cess?

(b) Would you be in favor of imposing a progressive agricultural income tax?

(c) Have you any other suggestions?

43. How many times a month (a year) do you tour your constituency?

44. Who is the more important person, politically, when comparing:

(a) the Member of the Legislative Assembly with the Zilla Parishad Committee Chairman?

(b) the Member of the Legislative Assembly with the Zilla Parishad President?

That is, if both went to a Minister with conflicting demands, of equal merit, whose demand is most likely to be heard?

45. (a) What type of people come to you to put forth their demands: Farmers, teachers, gram sevaks (village level workers), others?

(b) Who comes in the greatest number?

(c) Do farmers who come have individual or collective demands?

46. (a) Should the backward castes be given aid toward their advancement?

(b) Is the economic and educational aid being given to them now sufficient?

(c) Should the method of distribution be changed? That is, should aid be given in kind or in cash?

47. Do you think the caste system should be retained and just its bad features eliminated? Or should it be completely destroyed? What, if any, are its good features? What, if any, are its bad features?

The Dynamics of Indian Political Factions

Are you in favor of inter-caste marriage? Has there ever been such a marriage in your family?

48. The following is a list of fundamental rights guaranteed to the Indian citizen by the Constitution. Please rank them in the order of importance to you:

Right to equality
Freedom of speech
Freedom of religion
Right to property
Constitutional remedies (e.g., right to move Supreme Court to enforce fundamental rights)
Right against exploitation (e.g., the prohibition of forced labor and employment of child labor in factory)
Right to conserve one's distinct language or culture (i.e., cultural and educational rights)

49. (a) Should there be strong opposition parties in the Zilla Parishad?
(b) What would be the benefit of having an opposition party in the Zilla Parishad?

50. Why are opposition parties so weak in this district?

51. What, if any, are your goals in life?

52. Do you approve of the unanimous voting method for reaching decisions now prevailing in the party? Why?

If not, has anyone suggested majority voting? If not, why not?

53. (a) Which of the following economic needs do you consider the most urgent, from the point of view of your constituency:

Improved seeds and fertilizer
Implements
Agricultural loans
Technical advice
Irrigation facilities
Better road links for marketing
Storage facilities
Drinking water supply
Other

(b) Which of the following social needs do you consider most urgent from the point of view of your constituents?

More schools and teachers
Better housing
Adult education
Family planning
Social propaganda, e.g., for uplift of women, untouchables, etc.
Education of public regarding political rights and duties

Appendix 1

54. (a) Do you think that the State Government's distribution of expenditures among the various districts is fair or not?

(b) Do you think that the distribution of expenditure by the Zilla Parishad among the various talukas (or blocks) is fair or not?

55. Do you think that the developmental needs of your constituency are being adequately met? Is distribution fair, even though inadequate, or is it unfair?

56. Who is the most politically powerful leader in your district?

57. What is the distinctive feature of democracy? Is it the method and machinery used to reach decisions in which the people or people's representatives participate? Or is it the content of the economic and social program of the government insofar as it is oriented towards benefiting the majority of the people?

58. Which of the following characteristics do you consider most essential for a model political leader (please rank):

Integrity
Kindness
Intelligence
Impartiality
Capacity for getting along with people
Ability to wield influence among constituents
Ability to influence other leaders, either at district or state level
Ability to command respect
Ability to ensure and promote the economic welfare of his constituents

59. (a) Which is the most important domestic problem facing: India? Maharashtra? Your district? Your constituency?

(b) Which is the most important international problem facing India?

60. (a) Are you going to remain in politics?

(b) Do you intend to contest the next elections? In the Zilla Parishad, Legislative Assembly or Parliament?

61. (a) Do you think that your party is liable to go against the principles or policies which had attracted you to that party?

(b) If it did, would you be prepared to resign?

(c) On which principle or policy would you resign?

62. What public service have you performed for the people in the course of your public career, before being elected to the Zilla Parishad?

The Dynamics of Indian Political Factions

List of Districts, Talukas, and Taluka and/or Panchayat Samiti Headquarters

District	Taluka	Taluka Headquarters	Panchayat Samiti Headquarters
Ratnagiri	Mandangad	(Both Taluka and Panchayat Samiti Headquarters are located in the same town which is named after the Taluka)	
	Dapoli		
	Khed		
	Chiplun		
	Guhagar		
	Sangameshwar		
	Ratnagiri		
	Lanja		
	Rajapur		
	Deogad		
	Kankaoli		
	Malwan		
	Kudal		
	Sawantwadi		
	Vengurla		
Poona	Junnar	(Both Taluka and Panchayat Samiti Headquarters are located in the same town which, with the following exceptions, is named after the Taluka)	
	Ambegaon		
	Khed		
	Sirur		
	Mulshi	Paud	Paud
	Dhond		
	Purandhar	Saswad	Saswad
	Velhe (Mahal)		
	Bhor		
	Baramati		
	Indapur		
	Haveli		
Aurangabad	Kannad	(Both Taluka and Panchayat Samiti Headquarters are located in the same town which is named after the Taluka)	
	Khuldabad (Mahal)		
	Vaijapur		
	Gangapur		
	Paithan		
	Soegaon (Mahal)		
	Sillod		
	Bhokardan		
	Jafferabad (Mahal)		
	Jalna		
	Ambad		
Akola	Akot	Akot	Akot
			Telhara
	Akola	Akola	Akola
			Barshi Takli
	Balapur	Balapur	Balapur
			Patur
	Washim	Washim	Washim
			Malegaon
			Risod
	Mangrulpir	Mangrulpir	Mangrulpir
			Manora
	Murtazapur	Murtazapur	Murtazapur
			Karanja

208

Appendix 1

TABLE A. *List of Taluka-level Variables*

1. % of villages connected by road
2. % of villages served by a post office
3. % of villages in which fair held annually
4. % of villages in which weekly market held
5. % of urban to total population
6. % of workers not working on land
7. Number of banks
8. Number of towns
9. Average amount of loan per member distributed by primary (village) agricultural credit society
10. Average amount of loan per acre (net) distributed in taluka by (village) agricultural credit society
11. Average amount of loan per rural male cultivator (aged 15–59) distributed by district-level bank
12. Average amount of loan per acre sown (net) distributed by district-level cooperative bank
13. % of rural male cultivators (aged 15–59) who may be members of primary (village) agricultural credit society
14. % of villages served by primary agricultural credit cooperatives
15. % of literates among rural males in taluka
16. Rural male literates in taluka/rural male literates in district
17. Rural male literates in taluka/rural male literates in State
18. % of literates among rural male cultivators in taluka
19. Rural male literate cultivators in taluka/rural male literate cultivators in district
20. % of matriculates among rural male literates in taluka
21. Matriculated rural male literates in taluka/matriculated rural male literates in district
22. % of matriculates among rural male literate cultivators in taluka
23. Matriculated rural male literate cultivators in taluka/matriculated rural male literate cultivators in district
24. Number of persons (rural) served per medical facility
25. % of villages with inadequate drinking water
26. Infant deaths as % of total deaths in taluka
27. % of villages without primary school
28. % of villages not electrified
29. % of villages without a middle or high school
30. Agricultural laborers/total cultivators
31. Hired workers/family workers
32. Number of households with landholding of 50 acres and over

209

The Dynamics of Indian Political Factions

TABLE A. (*Continued*)

33. % of agricultural land owned by 50-plus class of landholders
34. Gross area sown per agricultural worker (laborer and cultivator)
35. Net area sown per cultivator
36. % of gross cropped to total geographical area
37. % of irrigated to gross cropped area
38. Number of tractors in taluka
39. Average land revenue per acre
40. Average land revenue collected per cultivator
41. Number of irrigation machines per acre
42. % of acreage under cash crops

NOTE: Variables numbered 12, 13, 20, 21, 23–25, 27, 36 and 37, above, were eliminated by factor analysis. The sources for the thirty-two taluka-level variables remaining after factor analysis are as follows:

Variable No.	Source
1–8, 15–19, 22, 27–35, 38–42	Census of India 1961 (compiled by the Maharashtra Census Office):

District Census Handbook – Ratnagiri (Bombay: 1964)
District Census Handbook – Akola (Bombay: 1964)
District Census Handbook – Aurangabad (Bombay: 1964)
District Census Handbook – Poona (Bombay: 1966)

9–10, 14, 26 Bureau of Economics and Statistics, Government of Maharashtra:
District Statistical Abstract of Ratnagiri District – 1961–62
District Statistical Abstract of Akola District – 1961–62
District Statistical Abstract of Aurangabad District – 1961–62
Socio-Economic Review and District Statistical Abstract of Poona District – 1962–63 and 1963–64

11 In connection with the variable entitled 'Amount of loan per male rural cultivator (aged 15–59) distributed by a district-level bank', two items of information were required. Each is shown below, followed by the source for each district:
(*a*) Amount of loan distributed by a district-level bank.
Ratnagiri: District Central Cooperative Bank,
Annual Report, 1966 (Marathi)
Aurangabad: District Land Development Bank,
Annual Report, 1964–65 (Marathi)
Poona: District Land Development Bank,
'*Note on Working of Poona District Land Development Bank*,' – Statement VII (mimeo.)
Akola: (No information available on distribution of loans, on a taluka-wise basis, by district-level cooperative banks)
(*b*) Number of rural male cultivators (aged 15–59):
Census of India 1961 (Compiled by the Maharashtra Census Office):
District Census Handbook – Ratnagiri (Bombay: 1964)
District Census Handbook – Aurangabad (Bombay: 1964)
District Census Handbook – Poona (Bombay: 1966)

Appendix 1

TABLE B. *Variables derived from interview data*

Part A. *Variables cross-classified with factional alignment*

Variable no.	Variable title	Significant association	Significance approached	Not significantly associated	Used in discriminant analysis Yes	Used in discriminant analysis No
1	Caste			×		×
2	Gharana*			×		×
3	Formal education			×		×
4	Occupation			×		×
5	Size of Landholding†	Poona (0.05)				×
6	No. of years in Urban Center			×		×
7	Extent of travel			×		×
8	Exposure to news media	Abad.‡ (0.02)	Akola			×
9	Spheres – Simultaneous	Abad. (0.01)			×	
10	Cooperatives – Simultaneous		Ratn.		×	
11	Party – Simultaneous	Akola (0.05)			×	
12	Local Govt. – Simultaneous	A.D. (0.01) Poona (0.001)			×	
13	Spheres – Various			×		×
14	No. of off. – Cooperatives	Abad. (0.05)	Ratn.		×	
15	No. of off. – Party	Abad. (0.01)			×	
16	No. of off. – Government			×		×
17	Village office – Party			×		×
18	Tq. office – Party		Abad.		×	
19	District office – Party	Abad. (0.001)	A.D.		×	

211

TABLE B. *Part A* (*continued*)

Variable no.	Variable title	Significant association	Signifi-cance approached	Not significantly associated	Used in discriminant analysis Yes	No
20	Village office – Cooperatives				×	×
21	Tq. office – Cooperatives				×	×
22	District office – Cooperatives	A.D. (0.05) Abad. (0.001)			×	
23	Village office – Government				×	×
24	Tq. office – Government				×	×
25	District office – Government				×	×
26	Contested as Independent	A.D. (0.001)				×
27	Other-Party Member		Ratn. Abad.			×
28	Other-Party Sympathizer		Abad.			×
29	Non-Congress Movement Sympathizer	Abad. (0.05)				×
30	Party Would Go Against Principles			×		×
31	Predisposition to Resign	A.D. (0.05)			×	
32	Voting Preference (majority v. unanimous)		A.D.		×	
33	Comments about Z.P. Leadership			×	×	
34	Assessment of M.L.A.	Poona (0.02)			×	
35	Caste role		A.D. Akola		×	

Appendix 1

TABLE B. *Part A (continued)*

Variable no.	Variable title	Significant association	Significance approached	Not significantly associated	Used in discriminant analysis — Yes	No
36	Economic role		Abad.		×	
37	Selection of Candidates	A.D. (0.01) Ratn. (0.02)			×	
38	Polit. Ambition (1962 – wanted to run)			×		×
39	Polit. Ambition (1967 – intended to run)			×		×
40	Loan Distribution Machinery	A.D. (0.05)			×	
41	Knowledge of Z.P. Budget			×		×
42	Knowledge of Reappropriation Provision			×		×
43	Knowledge of Act			×		×
44	Knowledge of World Leaders			×		×
45	Level of Understanding	Poona (0.05)				×
46	Participation in Educational Association	A.D. (0.01)	Poona			×
47	Simultaneous – Govt. and Party			×		×
48	Simultaneous – Govt. and Coop.			×		×
49	Simultaneous – Party and Coop.	Abad. (0.01)				×
50	Over time – Govt. & Pty Off.			×		×
51	Over time – Govt. and Coop.			×		×

TABLE B. *Part A (continued)*

Variable no.	Variable title	Significant association	Significance approached	Not significantly associated	Used in discriminant analysis Yes	No
52	Over time – Party and Coop.	Abad. (0.01)				×
53	Simult. – Coop., Pty and Govt.			×		×
54	Over time – Coop., Pty and Govt.			×		×
55	Party office held	Abad. (0.05)				×
56	Coop. office held	Abad. (0.01)				×
57	Govt. office held		Poona			×
58	Official status			×		×
59	Age			×		×
60	D.C.C. Pres. Powerful	Abad. (0.05)				×
61	Coop. Bank Pres. – Powerful			×		×
62	Minister – Powerful	A.D. (0.01)				×
63	Public Electoral Participation	A.D. (0.01)	Poona		×	
64	Dissatisfied with Act			×		×
65	Dissatisfied with State Govt.	Ratn. (0.05)				×
66	Dissatisfied with Z.P. Administration			×		×
67	Additional Substantive Authority Required			×		×
68	Additional Administrative Authority Required			×		×
69	Additional Authority Over Class I Officers			×		×

Appendix 1

TABLE B. *Part A (continued)*

Variable no.	Variable title	Significant association	Significance approached	Not significantly associated	Used in discriminant analysis Yes	No
70	Participation in Civic Association			×		×
71	Year Joined Party	Akola (0.01)	Poona			×

Part B. *Variables which were not cross-classified with factional alignment but were used in discriminant analysis*

72 Size of landholding (acres)
73 Size of irrigated landholding (acres)
74 Value of landholding (rupees)
75 Value of machinery owned
76 Value of houses owned
77 Percentage of acres under cash crops
78 Number of acres under cash crops
79 Value of shares in cooperative institutions
80 Value of loans from cooperative institutions

* Refers to household title, e.g., Patil, Deshmukh, Desai, etc.
† This was cross-classified in categorical form, e.g., small, medium, large. It was used in discriminant analysis in interval form. See Variable No. 72 below.
‡ The following abbreviations are used: 'Abad.' for Aurangabad; 'Ratn.' for Ratnagiri; 'A.D.' for All Districts.

TABLE C. *Variables used in discriminant analysis classified according to category**

Environment

1. Distance (of respondent's village) from Panchayat Samiti Head-quarters.
2. Distance (of respondent's village) from Zilla Parishad Headquarters
3. Distance (of respondent's village) from railway station
4. Distance (of respondent's village) from bus station
5. Public electoral participation (votes polled by Congress candidate in respondent's constituency as percentage of total votes polled)
6. Average landholding in taluka†
7. Communications potential
8. Agricultural cooperative activity

215

TABLE C. (*Continued*)

9. Urbanization
10. Agricultural prosperity
11. Percentage of eligible votes polled by non-Congress candidates
12. Percentage of total votes polled by non-Congress candidates
13. Percentage of cultivators serviced by village cooperatives in respondent's taluka

Economic background

1. Size of landholding
2. Size of irrigated landholding
3. Value of landholding
4. Value of machinery owned
5. Value of houses owned
6. Percentage of acres under cash crops
7. Number of acres under cash crops
8. Value of shares in cooperative institutions
9. Value of loans from cooperative institutions

Behavior (involvement in local power structure)

1. Spheres – Simultaneous (Number of spheres in which offices held at one time, that is, in cooperatives, political party or government)
2. Simultaneous – Cooperatives (number of offices held at one time in this sphere)
3. Simultaneous – Party (number of offices held at one time in this sphere)
4. Simultaneous – Government (number of offices held at one time in this sphere)
5. Spheres – Various (number of spheres in which offices held at various times)
6. Number of offices (held at various times) in cooperatives
7. Number of offices (held at various times) in party
8. Number of offices (held at various times) in government
9. Whether or not party office held: village level
10. Whether or not party office held: taluka level
11. Whether or not party office held: district level
12. Whether or not cooperative office held: village level
13. Whether or not cooperative office held: taluka level
14. Whether or not cooperative office held: district level
15. Whether or not government office held: village level
16. Whether or not government office held: taluka level
17. Whether or not government office held: district level

216

Appendix 1

TABLE C. (*Continued*)

Attitudes

1. Whether or not respondent would resign from the Congress Party under hypothetical conditions
2. Whether respondent prefers majority to unanimous voting procedure in Congress Party meetings
3. Comments regarding Zilla Parishad leadership
4. Evaluation of M.L.A. (Member of Legislative Assembly) vis-a-vis the Zilla Parishad elected official
5. Evaluation of caste role in Z.P. distribution decisions
6. Evaluation of role of economic interests in Z.P. distribution decisions
7. Evaluation of the process for selecting Congress candidates
8. Whether or not cooperatives' loan distribution machinery should be turned over to the Z.P.

EXPLANATORY NOTE: With regard to the category *economic background*, the measures used for Variable Nos. 1, 3, 6 and 7 may refer either to joint or individual landholdings. For those respondents whose families were joint in nature, I have used only the information on joint landholdings. For the nuclear families, the individual holding size was the score used. I justify this procedure on the following ground. The most significant social unit at the lowest level from which an individual may derive political strength would be the family. In this instance, I was interested in the economic facet of such a unit, as represented by respondent. Landholding size is essentially a 'family' measure of an economic nature. The important characteristic I wished to consider, then, was the size of landholding controlled by respondent's family. If respondent was a member of a joint family, then the joint landholding was important for my purposes. If it was nuclear, then the individual landholding was the measure I would be interested in. Whether that family was joint or individual was not relevant, *per se*, to a study of this type.

With regard to the category *behavior*, I have assumed that the political party, a representative governing body and agricultural cooperatives are all vehicles providing (potentially or in actuality) access to material benefits. It was in terms of such benefits that respondents tended to define the issue at stake toward which political action might be oriented. Merely for purposes of identification, I have referred to these three organizations collectively as a 'power structure', and to each as a 'sphere' of the power structure. I use the word 'structure' to convey the idea that their respective members regularly interact with each other in roles of authority graded hierarchically and horizontally within each organization, in a stable pattern over time; and they may interact across organizations in a similar way, although this is less formalized and less stable over time. I recognize that there are many difficulties inherent in this definition of a 'power structure'. But I wish to emphasize again that I am using the concept purely for descriptive purposes.

* These categories and their component elements constitute the operational definitions of empirical measures of political integration. (In this study, they are used as measures of group cohesion.) (See Chapter 3 above, pages 46–8, for further clarification.)

† Variables 6–10 were derived by factor analysis. For a list of their component indices, see Table E below.

217

TABLE D. *Matrix of Factor Loadings Identifying Optimal Factors Extracted*

Varimax rotation

1	2	3	4	5	6
		% of variance			
19.773	21.838	10.770	10.003	10.333	6.396
		Rotated factor loadings			

Variable no.*	Average size of landholding	Communications potential	Agricultural cooperative activity	Urbanization	Agricultural prosperity	Rural backwardness
1	0.576	**0.656**	0.167	0.120	−0.296	−0.091
2	0.213	**0.856**	0.014	0.014	−0.291	−0.127
3	0.267	**0.578**	−0.244	0.314	−0.401	0.431
4	−0.432	**0.573**	−0.321	0.180	−0.152	0.171
5	−0.245	0.056	−0.041	**0.901**	0.174	−0.029
6	0.140	0.189	−0.042	**0.869**	−0.079	−0.012
7	−0.095	0.241	−0.030	**0.667**	−0.068	−0.452
8	−0.002	0.124	0.084	**0.626**	0.147	0.346
9	−0.395	−0.139	**−0.800**	−0.017	−0.041	0.109
10	−0.062	0.083	**−0.773**	0.076	−0.042	0.038
11	−0.138	0.058	**−0.639**	−0.133	0.261	−0.136
14	−0.230	0.559	**−0.482**	0.127	−0.435	0.318
15	0.168	**0.879**	0.268	0.124	0.220	−0.134
16	0.069	**0.771**	−0.365	−0.001	0.246	−0.063
17	0.148	**0.858**	0.295	0.149	0.216	−0.083
18	−0.242	**0.859**	0.085	0.120	0.371	−0.136
19	−0.039	**0.792**	−0.405	0.001	0.129	−0.102
22	0.170	0.250	−0.011	0.139	−0.063	**−0.683**
26	−0.223	−0.233	−0.530	0.241	0.190	**0.481**
28	−0.071	−0.452	0.102	−0.314	0.054	**−0.495**
29	−0.009	**−0.819**	−0.075	−0.211	0.106	−0.039
30	**−0.804**	0.050	−0.106	0.101	0.521	−0.028
31	**−0.721**	−0.080	−0.129	−0.121	−0.018	−0.124
32	**−0.914**	−0.082	−0.047	0.051	−0.046	0.061
33	**−0.945**	−0.065	−0.078	0.039	0.131	0.126
34	**−0.557**	−0.352	−0.502	0.150	0.044	0.365
35	**−0.811**	−0.148	−0.309	0.125	0.389	0.156
38	**−0.549**	0.087	−0.131	0.453	0.407	0.102
39	0.096	0.239	−0.375	0.050	**0.569**	−0.277
40	−0.567	0.091	−0.052	0.250	**0.720**	0.111
41	−0.328	0.026	0.032	0.041	**0.767**	0.230
42	−0.755	0.092	−0.252	−0.008	**0.472**	−0.024

* See Table A for variable titles.

Appendix 1

TABLE E. *Factor clusters*

1. Communications potential (Potential for Communication on a Social and Economic Level)
   (a) % of villages connected by road
   (b) % of villages served by a post office
   (c) % of villages in which fair held annually
   (d) % of villages in which weekly market held
   (e) % of literacy among rural males in taluka
   (f) Rural male literates in taluka/rural male literates in district
   (g) Rural male literates in taluka/rural male literates in State
   (h) % of literacy among rural male cultivators in taluka
   (i) Rural male literate cultivators in taluka/rural male literate cultivators in district
   (j) % of villages without a middle or high school

2. Urbanization
   (a) % of urban to total population
   (b) % of workers not working on land
   (c) Number of banks
   (d) Number of towns

3. Agricultural credit cooperative activity
   (a) Average amount of loan per member distributed by primary (village) agricultural credit society
   (b) Average amount of loan per acre distributed by primary (village) agricultural credit society
   (c) Average amount of loan per rural male cultivator (aged 15–59) distributed by district-level bank
   (d) % of villages served by primary agricultural credit cooperatives

4. Average size of landholding
   (a) Agricultural laborers/total cultivators
   (b) Hired workers/family workers
   (c) Number of households with landholding of 50 acres and over
   (d) % of agricultural land owned by 50-plus class of landholders
   (e) Gross area sown per agricultural worker (laborer and cultivator)
   (f) Net area sown per cultivator
   (g) Number of tractors in taluka

5. Agricultural prosperity
   (a) Average land revenue per acre
   (b) Average land revenue collected per cultivator
   (c) Number of irrigation machines per acre
   (d) % of acreage under cash crops

219

DISTRICT-WISE AND ALL-DISTRICT TABLES SHOWING ABSOLUTE GROUP MEANS OF VARIABLES USED IN DISCRIMINANT ANALYSIS

TABLE A. *Ratnagiri*

Group Means of Variables Used in Discriminant Analysis, According to Variable Cluster

Variable No. and Title (within each cluster)	REBELS	Sample Size	LOYALISTS	Sample Size	Total Sample: 33 Total Rebel Sample: 16 Total Loyalist Sample: 17 REBELS and LOYALISTS	Sample Size
(Environment)						
1. Distance – Panchayat Samiti (miles)	9.69	16	9.70	17	9.70	33
2. Distance – Zilla Parishad (miles)	64.75	16	89.82	17	77.67	33
3. Distance – Railway (miles)	90.44	16	75.47	17	82.73	33
4. Distance – Bus (miles)	5.69	16	4.00	17	4.82	33
5. Public electoral participation (votes cast as % of eligible voters in respondent's constituency)	26.71	10	25.06	11	25.82	21
6. Average landholding in taluka*	0.81	16	0.83	17	0.82	33
7. Communications potential	−0.21	16	0.78	17	0.30	33
8. Agricultural cooperative activity	0.53	16	0.35	17	0.44	33
9. Urbanization	0.08	16	−0.04	17	0.01	33
10. Agricultural Prosperity	0.68	16	0.40	17	0.54	33

11. Total valid votes polled by non-Congress candidates (%)	7.23	16	6.07	17	6.63	33
12. Total votes polled by non-Congress candidates (%)	26.14	16	23.26	17	24.66	33
13. % of cultivators serviced by village cooperatives in taluka	64.17	16	59.67	17	62.36	33
(Economic Background)						
14. Landholding size (acres)	29.08	12	38.43	14	34.11	26
15. Irrigated landholding size (acres)	5.50	4	0.0	2	3.66	6
16. Value of landholding (rupees)	54,750.00	2	9,000.00	1	39,500.00	3
17. Value of machinery (rupees – 'ooos)	0.00	10	1.30	10	0.65	20
18. Value of houses (rupees)	30,266.50	3	25,100.00	5	27,037.50	8
19. % of acres under cash crops	51.00	8	39.5	9	44.9	17
20. Number of acres under cash crops	9.87	8	21.3	10	16.2	18
21. Value of shares in coops. (rupees)	319.6	14	315.4	17	317.3	31
22. Value of loans from coops. (rupees)	0.0	12	416.6	15	231.48	27
(Attitudes)†						
23. Predisposition to resign	1.78	14	2.70	17	2.29	31
24. Voting preference (majority v. unanimous)	1.78	14	2.87	15	2.34	29
25. Comments about Z.P. leadership	3.73	15	4.07	15	3.90	30
26. Evaluation of M.L.A.	5.09	11	4.81	16	5.33	27

* The minus signs yielded in the factor-scoring process do not always correspond with a low range. Hence, the variable scores may be read with the following in mind:

A minus score (and a lower score in general) indicates a higher value for the following factors: Average Landholding in Taluka. Agricultural Cooperative Activity. Agricultural Prosperity.

A minus score (and a lower score in general) indicates a lower value for the following factors: Urbanization. Communications Potential.

TABLE A. (Continued)

Variable No. and Title (within each cluster)	REBELS	Sample Size	LOYALISTS	Sample Size	REBELS and LOYALISTS	Sample Size
27. Caste role in distribution decisions	3.86	14	3.50	16	3.67	30
28. Economic role in distribution decisions	3.61	13	3.53	15	3.57	28
29. Selection of candidates	1.57	14	2.25	16	1.93	30
30. Loan distribution machinery	1.60	15	1.43	14	1.52	29
(Behavior)						
31. Simultaneous Office – No. of Spheres	3.0	16	2.53	17	2.76	33
32. Simultaneous Office – Cooperatives	2.87	16	1.76	17	2.30	33
33. Simultaneous Office – Party	1.62	16	1.47	17	1.54	33
34. Simultaneous Office – Government	2.06	16	2.06	17	2.06	33
35. No. of Spheres – Various times	3.31	16	2.76	17	3.03	33
36. No. of Offices – Cooperatives	3.19	16	2.12	17	2.64	33
37. No. of Offices – Party	1.69	16	1.76	17	1.73	33
38. No. of Offices – Government	2.50	16	2.29	17	2.39	33
39. Involved in Party Office – Village	3.50	16	2.76	17	3.12	33
40. Involved in Party Office – Taluka	4.75	16	6.88	17	5.85	33
41. Involved in Party Office – District	8.50	16	5.70	17	7.06	33
42. Involved in Cooperatives – Village	5.37	16	4.53	17	4.94	33
43. Involved in Cooperatives – Taluka	11.0	16	6.88	17	8.88	33
44. Involved in Cooperatives – District	13.5	16	10.41	17	11.91	33
45. Involved in Government – Taluka	73.0	16	76.29	17	74.69	33
46. Involved in Government – District	33.0	16	91.35	17	63.06	33
47. Involved in Government – Village	13.0	16	14.17	17	13.61	33

† Please see note (†) on pages 235–6, below, for coding classifications used for each variable in this cluster.

TABLE B. *Poona*

Group Means of Variables Used in Discriminant Analysis, According to Variable Cluster

Variable No. and Title (within each cluster)	REBELS	Sample Size	LOYALISTS	Sample Size	Total Sample: 40 Total Rebel Sample: 10 Total Loyalist Sample: 30 REBELS and LOYALISTS	Sample Size
(Environment)						
1. Distance – Panchayat Samiti (miles)	12.80	10	11.30	30	11.67	40
2. Distance – Zilla Parishad (miles)	26.80	10	40.53	30	37.10	40
3. Distance – Railway (miles)	11.90	10	25.33	30	21.90	40
4. Distance – Bus (miles)	1.20	10	2.67	30	2.30	40
5. Public electoral participation (votes cast as % of eligible voters in respondent's constituency)	44.26	7	39.50	22	40.65	29
6. Average landholding in taluka*	0.13	10	0.27	30	0.23	40
7. Communications potential	0.49	10	−0.08	30	0.06	40
8. Agricultural cooperative activity	−0.19	10	0.19	30	0.10	40
9. Urbanization	0.81	10	−0.03	30	0.18	40

* The minus signs yielded in the factor scoring process do not always correspond with a low range. Hence, the variable scores may be read with the following in mind:

A minus score (and a lower score in general) indicates a higher value for the following factors: Average Landholding in Taluka. Agricultural Cooperative Activity. Agricultural Prosperity.

A minus score (and a lower score in general) indicates a lower value for the following factors: Urbanization. Communications Potential.

TABLE B. (*Continued*)

Variable No. and Title (within each cluster)	REBELS	Sample Size	LOYALISTS	Sample Size	REBELS and LOYALISTS	Sample Size
10. Agricultural prosperity	0.33	10	0.40	30	0.38	40
11. Total valid votes polled by non-Congress candidates (%)	13.52	10	11.69	30	12.15	40
12. Total votes polled by non-Congress candidates (%)	30.79	10	31.09	30	31.02	40
13. % of cultivators serviced by village cooperatives in taluka	48.96	10	49.51	30	49.37	40
(*Economic Background*)						
14. Landholding size (acres)	251.80	10	49.13	30	99.80	40
15. Irrigated landholding size (acres)	35.90	10	8.92	25	16.63	35
16. Value of landholding (rupees)	198,044.00	9	76,236.00	22	111,600.00	31
17. Value of machinery (rupees – '000s)	21.62	8	5.90	20	10.39	28
18. Value of houses (rupees)	26,687.50	8	16,275.00	20	19,250.00	28
19. % of acres under cash crops	18.94	9	18.50	24	18.62	33
20. Number of acres under cash crops	18.33	9	8.62	24	11.27	33
21. Value of shares in coops. (rupees)	9,252.89	9	1,047.96	27	3,099.19	36
22. Value of loans from coops. (rupees)	10,214.28	7	2,459.13	23	4,268.67	30
(*Attitudes*)†						
23. Predisposition to resign	2.22	9	2.50	26	2.43	35
24. Voting preference (majority v. unanimous)	1.89	9	2.56	23	2.37	32

25. Comments about Z.P. leadership	4.11	9	3.87	23	3.94	32
26. Evaluation of M.L.A.	7.0	10	5.09	21	5.71	31
27. Caste role in distribution decisions	3.62	8	3.74	19	3.70	27
28. Economic role in distribution decisions	3.22	9	3.16	25	3.18	34
29. Selection of candidates	1.43	7	1.95	21	1.82	28
30. Loan distribution machinery	1.33	6	1.83	6	1.58	12
(Behavior)						
31. Simultaneous Office – No. of Spheres	3.20	10	2.73	30	2.85	40
32. Simultaneous Office – Cooperatives	2.50	10	2.27	30	2.32	40
33. Simultaneous Office – Party	2.30	10	1.93	30	2.02	40
34. Simultaneous Office – Government	2.50	10	1.80	30	1.97	40
35. No. of Spheres – Various times	3.30	10	3.0	30	3.07	40
36. No. of Offices – Cooperatives	2.90	10	2.93	30	2.92	40
37. No. of Offices – Party	2.60	10	2.23	30	2.32	40
38. No. of Offices – Government	2.70	10	2.07	30	2.22	40
39. Involved in Party Office – Village	7.0	10	4.67	30	5.25	40
40. Involved in Party Office – Taluka	13.0	10	9.0	30	10.0	40
41. Involved in Party Office – District	13.0	10	10.33	30	11.0	40
42. Involved in Cooperatives – Village	8.0	10	5.33	30	6.0	40
43. Involved in Cooperatives – Taluka	9.0	10	7.21	29	7.67	39
44. Involved in Cooperatives – District	13.0	10	10.65	29	11.26	39
45. Involved in Government – Taluka	77.80	10	39.40	30	49.0	40
46. Involved in Government – District	103.40	10	86.33	30	90.60	40
47. Involved in Government – Village	20.20	10	14.87	30	16.20	40

† Please see note (†) on pages 235–6, below, for coding classifications used for each variable in this cluster.

TABLE C. *Aurangabad*

Group Means of Variables Used in Discriminant Analysis, According to Variable Cluster

Total Sample: 43
Total Rebel Sample: 12
Total Loyalist Sample: 31

Variable No. and Title (within each cluster)	REBELS	Sample Size	LOYALISTS	Sample Size	REBELS and LOYALISTS	Sample Size
(Environment)						
1. Distance – Panchayat Samiti (miles)	11.75	12	13.87	31	13.28	43
2. Distance – Zilla Parishad (miles)	49.75	12	39.61	31	42.44	43
3. Distance – Railway (miles)	35.58	12	23.45	31	26.84	43
4. Distance – Bus (miles)	10.50	12	7.22	31	8.14	43
5. Public electoral participation (votes cast as % of eligible votes in respondent's constituency)	36.21	3	36.76	19	36.68	22
6. Average landholding in taluka*	−0.46	12	−0.66	31	−0.60	43
7. Communications potential	−0.46	12	−0.60	31	−0.56	43
8. Agricultural cooperative activity	−0.71	12	−0.38	31	−0.47	43
9. Urbanization	−0.51	12	−0.13	31	−0.24	43
10. Agricultural prosperity	−0.27	12	−0.28	31	−0.28	43
11. Total valid votes polled by non-Congress candidates (%)	5.45	12	12.69	31	10.67	43
12. Total votes polled by non-Congress candidates (%)	13.07	12	28.07	31	23.89	43
13. % cultivators serviced by village cooperatives in taluka	41.58	12	44.14	31	43.42	43

(Economic Background*)

14. Landholding size (acres)	57.58	12	58.97	31	58.58	43
15. Irrigated landholding size (acres)	13.50	12	9.96	23	11.17	35
16. Value of landholding (rupees)	68,925.00	10	83,039.62	29	79,420.49	39
17. Value of machinery (rupees – 'ooos)	6.90	10	4.57	28	5.18	38
18. Value of houses (rupees)	13,450.00	10	23,816.67	30	21,225.00	40
19. % of acres under cash crops	39.05	10	29.58	30	31.95	40
20. Number of acres under cash crops	21.90	10	21.90	29	21.90	39
21. Value of shares in coops. (rupees)	1,999.50	10	808.00	31	1,098.61	41
22. Value of loans from coops. (rupees)	15,000.00	2	666.67	6	4,250.00	8
(Attitudes)†						
23. Predisposition to resign	2.08	12	2.89	27	2.64	39
24. Voting preference (majority v. unanimous)	2.36	11	2.28	21	2.31	32
25. Comments about Z.P leadership	3.09	11	3.79	29	3.60	40
26. Evaluation of M.L.A	6.64	11	6.81	26	6.76	37
27. Caste role in distribution decisions	4.00	9	3.45	22	3.61	31
28. Economic role in distribution decisions	3.33	9	2.86	22	3.00	31
29. Selection of candidates	1.0	2	1.0	1	1.0	3
30. Loan distribution machinery	1.67	6	2.50	8	2.14	14

* The minus signs yielded in the factor scoring process do not always correspond with a low range. Hence, the variable scores may be read with the following in mind:

A minus score (and a lower score in general) indicates a higher value for the following factors: Average Landholding in Taluka. Agricultural Cooperative Activity. Agricultural Prosperity.

A minus score (and a lower score in general) indicates a lower value for the following factors: Urbanization. Communications Potential.

† Please see note (†) on pages 235–6, below, for coding classifications used for each variable in this cluster.

TABLE C (*continued*)

Variable No. and Title (within each cluster)	REBELS	Sample Size	LOYALISTS	Sample Size	REBELS and LOYALISTS	Sample Size
(*Behavior*)						
31. Simultaneous Office – No. of Spheres	3.08	12	2.42	31	2.60	43
32. Simultaneous Office – Cooperatives	2.67	12	1.67	31	1.95	43
33. Simultaneous Office – Party	2.08	12	1.64	31	1.77	43
34. Simultaneous Office – Government	1.92	12	1.84	31	1.86	43
35. No. of Spheres – Over Time	3.58	12	2.77	31	3.0	43
36 No of Offices – Cooperatives	3.75	12	1.81	31	2.35	43
37. No. of Offices – Party	2.92	12	1.90	31	2.19	43
38. No. of Offices – Government	2.25	12	2.00	31	2.07	43
39. Involved in Party Office – Village	1.83	12	2.93	31	2.63	43
40. Involved in Party Office – Taluka	14.33	12	8.74	31	10.30	43
41. Involved in Party Office – District	24.33	12	3.58	31	9.37	43
42. Involved in Cooperatives – Village	2.67	12	4.22	31	3.79	43
43. Involved in Cooperatives – Taluka	9.33	12	4.87	31	6.12	43
44. Involved in Cooperatives – District	27.67	12	6.16	31	12.16	43
45. Involved in Government – Taluka	54.33	12	50.55	31	51.60	43
46. Involved in Government – District	1.0	12	50.55	31	36.72	43
47. Involved in Government – Village	17.0	12	12.35	31	13.65	43

TABLE D. *Akola*

Group Means of Variables Used in Discriminant Analysis, According to Variable Cluster

Variable No. and Title (within each cluster)	REBELS	Sample Size	LOYALISTS	Sample Size	Total Sample: 44 Total Rebel Sample: 35 Total Loyalist Sample: 9 REBELS and LOYALISTS	Sample Size
(Environment)						
1. Distance – Panchayat Samiti (miles)	11.23	35	9.78	9	10.93	44
2. Distance – Zilla Parishad (miles)	43.71	35	26.78	9	40.25	44
3. Distance – Railway (miles)	13.40	35	7.78	9	12.25	44
4. Distance – Bus (miles)	7.83	35	5.37	8	7.37	43
5. Public electoral participation (votes cast as % of eligible voters in respondent's constituency)	57.63	25	55.84	9	57.16	34
6. Average landholding in taluka*	−1.40	35	−1.51	9	−1.42	44
7. Communications potential	0.17	35	0.32	9	0.20	44
8. Agricultural cooperative activity	0.03	35	0.07	9	−0.01	44
9. Urbanization	0.36	35	0.87	9	0.47	44

* The minus signs yielded in the factor scoring process do not always correspond with a low range. Hence, the variable scores may be read with the following in mind:

A minus score (and a lower score in general) indicates a higher value for the following factors: Average Landholding in Taluka.

Agricultural Cooperative Activity. Agricultural Prosperity. A minus score (and a lower score in general) indicates a lower value for the following factors: Urbanization. Communications Potential.

TABLE D (*continued*)

Variable No. and Title (within each cluster)	REBELS	Sample Size	LOYALISTS	Sample Size	REBELS and LOYALISTS	Sample Size
10. Agricultural prosperity	−1.26	35	−2.03	9	−1.42	44
11. Total valid votes polled by non-Congress candidates (%)	22.72	35	26.06	9	23.40	44
12. Total votes polled by non-Congress candidates (%)	40.49	35	45.28	9	41.47	44
13. % of cultivators serviced by village cooperatives in talukas	73.86	35	80.54	9	75.23	44
(*Economic Background*)						
14. Landholding size (acres)	140.97	34	162.44	9	145.46	43
15. Irrigated landholding size (acres)	3.64	33	3.0	8	3.51	41
16. Value of landholding (rupees)	108,107.00	34	170,062.00	8	119,908.00	42
17. Value of machinery (rupees – 'ooos)	4.73	34	9.22	9	5.67	43
18. Value of houses (rupees)	24,818.00	22	15,950.00	7	22,677.00	29
19. % of acres under cash crops	49.4	31	57.3	8	51.0	39
20. Number of acres under cash crops	66.5	31	69.4	8	67.1	39
21. Value of shares in coops. (rupees)	2355.57	33	829.55	9	2028.57	42
22. Value of loans from coops. (rupees)	4074.27	30	7071.43	7	4641.30	37
(*Attitudes*)*						
23. Predisposition to resign	2.06	31	1.87	8	2.02	39

230

24. Voting preference (majority v. unanimous)	1.70	30	2.0	8	1.76	38
25. Comments about Z.P. leadership	3.74	23	3.75	8	3.74	31
26. Evaluation of M.L.A.	4.57	30	5.28	7	4.70	37
27. Caste role in distribution decisions	3.73	34	2.75	8	3.55	42
28. Economic role in distribution decisions	3.20	34	2.62	8	3.09	42
29. Selection of candidates	1.21	29	1.11	9	1.18	38
30. Loan distribution machinery	1.48	31	2.0	9	1.60	40
(Behavior)						
31. Simultaneous Office – No. of Spheres	2.28	35	1.89	9	2.20	44
32. Simultaneous Office – Cooperative	1.83	35	1.75	8	1.81	43
33. Simultaneous Office – Party	1.37	35	1.44	9	1.39	44
34. Simultaneous Office – Government	1.94	35	1.78	9	1.91	44
35. No. of Spheres – Over Time	2.45	35	2.44	9	2.45	44
36. No. of Offices – Cooperatives	2.03	35	2.11	9	2.04	44
37. No. of Offices – Party	1.43	35	1.78	9	1.50	44
38. No. of Offices – Government	2.14	35	2.44	9	2.20	44
39. Involved in Party Office – Village	3.0	35	3.22	9	3.04	44
40. Involved in Party Office – Taluka	3.28	35	7.67	9	4.18	44
41. Involved in Party Office – District	4.43	35	5.44	9	4.64	44
42. Involved in Cooperatives – Village	2.14	35	3.22	9	2.36	44
43. Involved in Cooperatives – Taluka	5.57	35	3.22	9	5.09	44
44. Involved in Cooperatives – District	10.14	35	9.89	9	10.09	44
45. Involved in Government – Taluka	52.2	35	72.11	9	56.27	44
46. Involved in Government – District	44.88	35	1.0	9	35.91	44
47. Involved in Government – Village	13.80	35	18.78	9	14.82	44

* Please see note (†) on pages 235–6, below, for coding classifications used for each variable in this cluster.

TABLE E. *All Districts*

Group Means of Variables Used in Discriminant Analysis, According to Variable Cluster

Total Sample: 160
Total Rebel Sample: 73
Total Loyalist Sample: 87

Variable No. and Title (within each cluster)	REBELS	Sample Size	LOYALISTS	Sample Size	REBELS and LOYALISTS	Sample Size
(Environment)						
1. Distance – Panchayat Samiti (miles)	11.2	73	11.8	87	11.5	160
2. Distance – Zilla Parishad (miles)	47.0	73	48.4	87	47.8	160
3. Distance – Railway (miles)	33.7	73	32.6	87	33.1	160
4. Distance – Bus (miles)	6.9	73	4.8	86	5.8	159
5. Public electoral participation (votes cast as % of eligible voters in respondent's constituency)	47.2	45	38.4	61	42.1	106
6. Average landholding in taluka*	−0.55	73	−0.13	87	−0.32	160
7. Communications potential	0.03	73	−0.06	87	−0.02	160
8. Agricultural cooperative activity	−0.04	73	0.01	87	−0.01	160
9. Urbanization	0.22	73	0.02	87	0.11	160
10. Agricultural prosperity	−0.45	73	−0.09	87	−0.26	160
11. Total valid votes polled by non-Congress candidates (%)	15.2	73	12.4	87	13.7	160
12. Total votes polled by non-Congress candidates (%)	31.5	73	29.9	87	30.6	160
13. % cultivators serviced by village cooperatives in taluka	63.0	73	52.8	87	57.4	160

(*Economic Background*)

14. Landholding size (acres)	122.8	68	63.1	84	89.8	152
15. Irrigated landholding size (acres)	11.2	59	8.2	58	9.7	117
16. Value of landholding (rupees)	113,760.0	55	90,914.0	60	101,840.0	115
17. Value of machinery (rupees – '000s)	6.5	62	5.1	67	5.8	129
18. Value of houses (rupees)	22,902.0	43	20,599.0	62	21,542.0	105
19. % of acres under cash crops	43.1	58	30.2	71	36.0	129
20. Number of acres under cash crops	43.5	58	22.7	71	32.0	129
21. Value of shares in coops. (rupees)	2810.3	66	787.7	84	1677.7	150
22. Value of loans from coops. (rupees)	4386.8	51	2280.6	51	3333.7	102
(*Attitudes*)†						
23. Predisposition to resign	2.03	66	2.61	78	2.34	144
24. Voting preference (majority v. unanimous)	1.86	64	2.48	67	2.17	131
25. Comments about Z.P. leadership	3.67	58	3.87	75	3.78	133
26. Evaluation of M.L.A.	5.50	62	5.68	70	5.64	132
27. Caste role in distribution decisions	3.78	65	3.46	65	3.62	130
28. Economic role in distribution decisions	3.30	65	3.08	70	3.19	135
29. Selection of candidates	1.33	52	1.87	47	1.58	99
30. Loan distribution machinery	1.52	58	1.86	37	1.65	95

* The minus signs yielded in the factor scoring process do not always correspond with a low range. Hence, the variable scores may be read with the following in mind:

A minus score (and a lower score in general) indicates a higher value for the following factors: Average Landholding in Taluka. Agricultural Cooperative Activity. Agricultural Prosperity.

A minus score (and a lower score in general) indicates a lower value for the following factors: Urbanization. Communications Potential.

† Please see note (†) on pages 235–6 below, for coding classifications used for each variable in this cluster.

TABLE E (continued)

Variable No. and Title (within each cluster)	REBELS	Sample Size	LOYALISTS	Sample Size	REBELS and LOYALISTS	Sample Size
(Behavior)						
31. Simultaneous Office – No. of Spheres	2.70	73	2.49	87	2.59	160
32. Simultaneous Office – Cooperatives	2.29	73	1.91	86	2.08	159
33. Simultaneous Office – Party	1.67	73	1.69	87	1.68	160
34. Simultaneous Office – Government	2.04	73	1.86	87	1.94	160
35. No. of Spheres – Over Time	2.94	73	2.82	87	2.87	160
36. No. of Offices – Cooperatives	2.68	73	2.29	87	2.46	160
37. No. of Offices – Party	1.89	73	1.98	87	1.94	160
38. No. of Offices – Government	2.31	73	2.13	87	2.21	160
39. Involved in Party Office – Village	3.46	73	3.58	87	3.50	160
40. Involved in Party Office – Taluka	6.75	73	8.36	87	7.62	160
41. Involved in Party Office – District	9.77	73	6.52	87	8.0	160
42. Involved in Cooperatives – Village	3.74	73	4.56	87	4.19	160
43. Involved in Cooperatives – Taluka	7.85	73	5.88	87	6.79	159
44. Involved in Cooperatives – District	14.15	73	8.91	86	11.31	159
45. Involved in Government – Taluka	60.62	73	53.96	87	57.0	160
46. Involved in Government – District	43.08	72	65.73	87	55.4	160
47. Involved in Government – Village	15.03	73	14.24	87	14.6	160

Appendix 2

† The Group Means appearing here may be interpreted by reference to the coding classifications used for each variable, as indicated below:

Predisposition to resign
1. Would resign (unqualified)
2. Would resign (qualified)
3. Would not resign (qualified)
4. Would not resign (unqualified)

Voting preference (majority v. unanimous)
1. Majority voting preferred (unqualified)
2. Majority voting preferred (qualified)
3. Unanimous voting preferred (qualified)
4. Unanimous voting preferred (unqualified)

Comments about Z.P. leadership
1. Not favorable and pessimistic
2. Not favorable
3. Not favorable but hopeful
4. Favorable – with qualifications
5. Favorable – without qualifications

Evaluation of M.L.A. (vis-a-vis Z.P. officials)
1. M.L.A. more important than Chairman and President of Z.P.
2. M.L.A. more important than Chairman and President of Z.P. (qualified)
3. M.L.A. more important than Chairman, but on par with President (or qualifications regarding President) of Z.P.
4. M.L.A. more important than Chairman but less important than President of Z.P. (with or without qualifications)
5. M.L.A. on par with both
6. M.L.A. less important than President but on par with Chairman (or qualifications regarding Chairman)
7. M.L.A. less important than President and Chairman, with qualifications regarding both
8. M.L.A. less important than Z.W. President and Chairman (without qualifications)

Caste role in distribution decisions
1. Caste plays a dominant or important role in distribution decisions made by Z.P.
2. Caste plays a partial role, along with other factors, in distribution decisions made by Z.P.
3. Caste plays a minor role in distribution decisions made by Z.P.
4. Caste plays no role in distribution decisions made by Z.P.

Economic role in distribution decisions
1. Economic interests play a dominant or important role in distribution decisions made by Z.P.
2. Economic interests play a partial role, along with other interests, in distribution decisions made by Z.P.
3. Economic interests play a minor role in distribution decisions made by Z.P.
4. Economic interests play no role in distribution decisions made by Z.P.

Appendix 2

Selection of candidates
1. Improper
2. Impropriety implied but not expressed
3. Proper

Loan distribution machinery
1. Does not want Z.P. to take over from cooperatives their loan distribution machinery
2. Does want Z.P. to take over from cooperatives their loan distribution machinery (with qualifications)
3. Does want Z.P. to take over from cooperatives their loan distribution machinery (without qualifications)

DISTRICT-WISE AND ALL-DISTRICT TABLES SHOWING WITHIN-GROUP CORRELATIONS COMPUTED IN DISCRIMINANT ANALYSIS AND IDENTIFYING VARIABLES USED ACCORDING TO VARIABLE CLUSTER

TABLE I. *Environment*

Variables Used In Discriminant Analysis Listed According to Order of Appearance in Within-Groups Correlation Matrix

1. Distance from Panchayat Samiti
2. Distance from Zilla Parishad
3. Distance from Railway
4. Distance from Bus Station
5. Public Electoral Participation
6. Average Landholding in Taluka
7. Communications Potential

8. Agricultural Cooperative Activity
9. Urbanization
10. Agricultural Prosperity
11. Eligible Votes Polled by Non-Congress Candidates
12. Total Votes Polled by Non-Congress Candidates
13. % Cultivators Serviced by Village Cooperatives in Taluka

TABLE I.A *Ramagiri*

Within-Groups Correlation Matrix – *Environment*

Variable	1	2	3	4	5	6	7
1	1.00000						
2	0.01666	1.00000					
3	0.26201	0.33267	1.00000				
4	0.18917	0.19184	0.37211	1.00000			
5	0.29345	0.11396	0.39054	0.13058	1.00000		
6	−0.03895	0.20467	0.04127	−0.08769	−0.21881	1.00000	
7	−0.15529	0.38433	−0.25329	0.07127	−0.41528	0.36925	1.00000
8	0.23100	−0.44942	0.11809	−0.28362	0.05369	0.00058	−0.56133
9	−0.15810	−0.04166	−0.18850	−0.01533	−0.26548	−0.41373	0.32437
10	0.16906	−0.43017	−0.02952	0.00188	0.08080	0.01579	−0.33073
11	0.39307	0.14118	0.53999	0.18825	0.86702	−0.09226	−0.34278
12	0.35172	0.00470	0.47410	0.10012	0.78035	−0.06391	−0.40136
13	0.04342	0.05493	0.21864	0.40783	0.23216	−0.39272	0.21716

Variable	8	9	10	11	12	13
8	1.00000					
9	−0.43033	1.00000				
10	0.57958	−0.37579	1.00000			
11	0.15233	−0.40547	0.05777	1.00000		
12	0.29224	−0.48102	0.08140	0.95527	1.00000	
13	−0.62044	0.66272	−0.37174	0.13581	−0.01069	1.00000

TABLE I.B *Poona*

Within-Groups Correlation Matrix – *Environment*

Variable

Variable	1	2	3	4	5	6	7
1	1.00000						
2	0.39651	1.00000					
3	0.03251	0.55402	1.00000				
4	0.13578	0.02163	-0.09869	1.00000			
5	0.06956	-0.03890	0.07522	0.23212	1.00000		
6	-0.42434	-0.35644	0.31215	0.07375	0.14580	1.00000	
7	0.38141	0.28943	0.07374	-0.20776	0.03317	-0.44913	1.00000
8	-0.39101	-0.54424	0.01297	0.24545	0.13177	0.72100	-0.63040
9	-0.02269	-0.28953	-0.50621	0.29644	-0.02262	-0.41980	0.15469
10	0.22629	0.40745	0.28766	-0.36275	-0.13756	-0.21669	0.11395
11	0.18335	-0.09373	-0.13030	0.16841	0.80365	0.08827	0.04627
12	0.25058	-0.13118	-0.25537	0.13061	0.64821	-0.02622	0.04671
13	0.19970	0.34041	-0.12099	-0.12693	-0.00666	-0.26771	0.63797

Variable

Variable	8	9	10	11	12	13
8	1.00000					
9	0.07004	1.00000				
10	-0.45791	-0.51990	1.00000			
11	0.09419	0.02135	-0.19567	1.00000		
12	0.04197	0.05285	-0.14064	0.91404	1.00000	
13	-0.53199	-0.05120	0.26703	0.05313	0.02843	1.00000

TABLE I.C *Aurangabad*

Within-Groups Correlation Matrix – *Environment*

Variable	1	2	3	4	5	6	7
1	1.00000						
2	0.31976	1.00000					
3	−0.04181	0.52676	1.00000				
4	0.43793	0.60222	0.43066	1.00000			
5	0.06673	0.36269	0.22113	0.44090	1.00000		
6	0.10949	−0.05136	−0.01536	0.00745	0.00739	1.00000	
7	0.16558	0.42634	0.40007	0.46590	0.23773	−0.11547	1.00000
8	0.05739	−0.05242	−0.36729	−0.34200	−0.21194	−0.36579	−0.42452
9	−0.12993	−0.47267	−0.53911	−0.36182	−0.07283	0.11032	−0.49212
10	0.13005	−0.51340	−0.63704	−0.43532	−0.38857	0.13507	−0.56208
11	−0.05217	0.24626	0.28087	0.32290	0.83695	0.11831	0.20631
12	−0.04225	0.19034	0.12949	0.31880	0.92184	0.01006	0.19521
13	−0.08868	−0.00357	0.09118	0.13024	0.18069	0.17904	0.55466

Variable

Variable	8	9	10	11	12	13
8	1.00000					
9	0.05101	1.00000				
10	0.49938	0.65147	1.00000			
11	−0.28853	−0.18188	−0.45336	1.00000		
12	−0.19968	−0.11041	−0.41052	0.87832	1.00000	
13	−0.77898	0.10375	−0.39514	0.17737	0.19792	1.00000

TABLE I.D *Akola*

Within-Groups Correlation Matrix – *Environment*

Variable	1	2	3	4	5	6	7
1	1.00000						
2	0.00260	1.00000					
3	0.26906	0.35277	1.00000				
4	0.11348	-0.00783	0.40116	1.00000			
5	0.05979	-0.07571	-0.12943	0.05881	1.00000		
6	0.31896	0.11385	0.58701	0.21402	-0.03301	1.00000	
7	0.14988	-0.51447	-0.17522	-0.07111	0.12616	-0.17158	1.00000
8	0.05310	-0.49096	-0.31375	-0.11905	0.11092	-0.40783	0.96628
9	-0.02227	-0.52607	-0.49472	-0.28265	0.09198	-0.68096	0.43456
10	-0.18794	0.68039	0.07068	0.02368	-0.13507	-0.02056	-0.88965
11	0.01733	-0.05001	0.00700	0.09621	0.84703	0.08619	0.06372
12	0.08691	-0.01083	0.05325	0.15609	0.85956	0.08727	0.07500
13	0.07844	-0.64915	-0.43303	-0.27246	0.13296	-0.57440	0.64859

Variable	8	9	10	11	12	13
8	1.00000					
9	0.55084	1.00000				
10	-0.80264	-0.48627	1.00000			
11	0.02757	-0.02784	-0.08374	1.00000		
12	0.04444	-0.03491	-0.05622	0.93700	1.00000	
13	0.71660	0.94667	-0.64334	0.01494	0.01138	1.00000

TABLE I.E. *All Districts*

Within-Groups Correlation Matrix – *Environment*

Variable	1	2	3	4	5	6	7
1	1.00000						
2	0.07751	1.00000					
3	−0.03639	0.59922	1.00000				
4	0.24996	0.18386	0.10125	1.00000			
5	0.07074	−0.10786	−0.23533	0.14763	1.00000		
6	−0.04601	0.29996	0.65570	−0.16490	−0.31534	1.00000	
7	0.00214	0.30254	0.07207	−0.12781	0.08319	0.07480	1.00000
8	−0.15834	−0.06173	0.20323	−0.18403	0.04465	0.29181	−0.05293
9	−0.08808	−0.32284	−0.35215	−0.19681	0.14940	−0.22103	0.27228
10	−0.03292	0.26505	0.44307	−0.18998	−0.38515	0.71298	−0.16604
11	0.05777	−0.10651	−0.21904	0.17646	0.85238	−0.31838	0.04153
12	0.12095	−0.06809	−0.11167	0.15078	0.81262	−0.17088	0.00308
13	−0.05654	0.02117	−0.02064	0.02749	0.32901	−0.25453	0.44300

Variable	8	9	10	11	12	13
8	1.00000					
9	0.09434	1.00000				
10	0.10515	−0.27417	1.00000			
11	−0.05120	0.04909	−0.39112	1.00000		
12	0.04038	−0.00427	−0.22421	0.88162	1.00000	
13	−0.08108	0.42917	−0.47124	0.27008	0.21292	1.00000

TABLE II. *Behavior*

Variables Used In Discriminant Analysis Listed According To Order Of Appearance
In Within-Groups Correlation Matrix

1. Number of Spheres – Simultaneous
2. Simultaneous Office – Cooperatives
3. Simultaneous Office – Party
4. Simultaneous Office – Government
5. Number of Spheres – Over Time
6. Number of Offices – Cooperatives
7. Number of Offices – Party
8. Number of Offices – Government
9. Involved in Party Office – Village

10. Involved in Party Office – Taluka
11. Involved in Party Office – District
12. Involved in Cooperative Office – Village
13. Involved in Cooperative Office – Taluka
14. Involved in Cooperative Office – District
15. Involved in Government Office – Taluka
16. Involved in Government Office – District
17. Involved in Government Office – Village

243

TABLE II.A *Ratnagiri*

Within-Groups Correlation Matrix – *Behavior*

| | | Variable | | | | | | | |
Variable	1	2	3	4	5	6	7	8	9
1	1.00000								
2	0.42681	1.00000							
3	0.56123	0.06866	1.00000						
4	0.31015	-0.09250	0.38118	1.00000					
5	0.80112	0.36653	0.66128	0.44654	1.00000				
6	0.28412	0.87640	-0.05056	0.08143	0.31447	1.00000			
7	0.47912	0.10058	0.85138	0.24761	0.56739	0.00829	1.00000		
8	0.36218	0.21894	0.45794	0.75848	0.56464	0.26566	0.43283	1.00000	
9	0.20121	-0.29886	0.46670	0.07115	0.12078	-0.31627	0.39592	0.00924	1.00000
10	0.26770	-0.07135	0.74151	0.29913	0.41553	-0.13433	0.77591	0.32671	0.06435
11	0.56563	0.46191	0.54595	0.23989	0.52428	0.31509	0.49498	0.47467	-0.23004
12	-0.08190	0.09652	-0.30538	-0.18577	-0.12252	0.18552	-0.36158	-0.30218	-0.12366
13	0.02548	0.40220	0.16128	0.33899	0.26010	0.56595	0.11489	0.47078	-0.29329
14	0.22175	0.73634	-0.00067	0.16531	0.25769	0.84138	-0.03627	0.41298	-0.16034
15	0.11765	-0.27624	0.34579	0.49574	0.24183	-0.21517	0.27455	0.45753	0.14843
16	-0.06240	0.12075	-0.00560	-0.03756	0.04164	0.13875	0.00196	0.06714	-0.18051
17	0.09044	-0.19901	0.09147	0.53926	0.12315	-0.03522	0.03488	0.34797	0.34520

| | | Variable | | | | | | |
Variable	10	11	12	13	14	15	16	17
10	1.00000							
11	0.36931	1.00000						
12	-0.30409	-0.17765	1.00000					
13	0.30277	0.16209	0.09583	1.00000				
14	-0.17892	0.30468	0.05622	0.47521	1.00000			
15	0.34204	0.02338	-0.43683	0.07176	-0.02287	1.00000		
16	0.20626	0.12144	-0.28985	0.12193	0.20862	-0.25331	1.00000	
17	-0.02683	-0.16496	0.37029	0.12228	0.06685	0.06373	-0.31098	1.00000

TABLE II.B *Poona*

Within-Groups Correlation Matrix – *Behavior*

Variable	1	2	3	4	5	6	7	8	9
1	1.00000								
2	0.59600	1.00000							
3	0.29576	0.10170	1.00000						
4	0.66716	0.30541	-0.12513	1.00000					
5	0.91044	0.54012	0.32648	0.68191	1.00000				
6	0.58125	0.94445	0.13365	0.32190	0.52016	1.00000			
7	0.34592	0.08839	0.85841	-0.01898	0.36201	0.16532	1.00000		
8	0.70782	0.56550	0.03412	0.34143	0.75384	0.52387	0.05736	1.00000	
9	0.19377	-0.14354	0.61364	0.01488	0.17933	-0.13471	0.58281	-0.05394	1.00000
10	0.10215	0.02303	0.61010	-0.19101	0.12201	0.05901	0.65493	-0.17125	0.31637
11	0.48116	0.21591	0.45385	0.07497	0.44464	0.23247	0.53747	0.28696	-0.04384
12	0.36602	0.54999	-0.13730	0.22934	0.43965	0.50073	-0.01054	0.35832	-0.20885
13	0.67755	0.59020	0.02524	0.59999	0.56444	0.63953	0.16517	0.57166	0.03526
14	0.59813	0.70372	0.24667	0.32429	0.50549	0.62609	0.13072	0.47949	0.07663
15	0.38913	0.07797	-0.14105	0.66195	0.41782	0.09748	0.01414	0.55167	0.01108
16	0.39274	0.54354	0.21475	0.09479	0.38478	0.52702	0.09453	0.38791	-0.00454
17	0.37033	0.12890	-0.11739	0.69923	0.39455	0.14637	-0.02817	0.50558	0.06622

Variable

Variable	10	11	12	13	14	15	16	17
10	1.00000							
11	0.16536	1.00000						
12	-0.04196	0.22203	1.00000					
13	0.00226	0.22562	0.35971	1.00000				
14	0.04823	0.19407	0.10155	0.33655	1.00000			
15	-0.02188	0.13648	0.31955	0.32855	0.01052	1.00000		
16	-0.16128	0.18796	0.19399	0.24076	0.49295	-0.24001	1.00000	
17	0.02065	-0.09758	0.01733	0.29477	0.13762	0.27121	-0.18211	1.00000

TABLE II.C *Aurangabad*

Within-Groups Correlation Matrix – *Behavior*

Variable	1	2	3	4	5	6	7	8	9
1	1.00000								
2	0.39792	1.00000							
3	0.43552	0.06291	1.00000						
4	0.50841	0.21242	0.07108	1.00000					
5	0.73014	0.43406	0.67131	0.56278	1.00000				
6	0.34720	0.70289	0.25224	0.22594	0.53378	1.00000			
7	0.60854	0.21202	0.77198	0.01458	0.58748	0.33346	1.00000		
8	0.53936	0.14432	0.10330	0.87234	0.50350	0.15463	0.17166	1.00000	
9	0.19451	−0.04919	0.53708	0.11262	0.34962	0.02195	0.31634	0.12815	1.00000
10	0.32551	−0.22993	0.71240	0.04859	0.44671	0.01255	0.62815	0.16663	0.26476
11	0.40670	0.37195	0.20675	−0.01129	0.27044	0.18639	0.53800	0.18106	0.00563
12	−0.09101	0.16378	0.17522	0.06977	0.24782	0.15285	0.00589	0.03007	0.12882
13	0.21409	0.09398	0.20810	0.12738	0.34322	0.48622	0.14411	0.04782	0.21285
14	0.28655	0.45800	−0.02216	0.34356	0.30020	0.51330	0.16533	0.28425	−0.07410
15	0.15473	−0.07522	−0.20968	0.59027	0.04405	0.02352	−0.14321	0.64584	−0.09615
16	0.20570	0.09576	0.13687	0.23204	0.28588	0.04599	0.18731	0.21338	−0.14703
17	0.17662	−0.07414	0.16173	0.50776	0.38647	0.10700	0.02429	0.52659	0.31103

Variable	10	11	12	13	14	15	16	17
10	1.00000							
11	−0.06365	1.00000						
12	0.19524	−0.12771	1.00000					
13	0.15246	−0.21396	0.02857	1.00000				
14	−0.23968	0.38243	−0.22534	−0.01557	1.00000			
15	−0.09644	−0.09852	−0.07564	−0.04548	0.14069	1.00000		
16	0.16095	0.22390	0.00675	−0.12666	0.15013	−0.03057	1.00000	
17	0.17317	−0.17399	0.26556	0.38095	−0.18011	0.12195	−0.01233	1.00000

TABLE II.D *Akola*

Within-Groups Correlation Matrix – *Behavior*

Variable

Variable	1	2	3	4	5	6	7	8	9
1	1.00000								
2	0.29724	1.00000							
3	0.65340	−0.04453	1.00000						
4	0.56588	0.05545	0.22282	1.00000					
5	0.74338	0.35698	0.54350	0.55399	1.00000				
6	0.49185	0.84049	0.20902	0.10330	0.52970	1.00000			
7	0.48743	−0.00556	0.75964	0.28085	0.66950	0.20171	1.00000		
8	0.55654	−0.10038	0.27392	0.84804	0.52180	0.08352	0.32093	1.00000	
9	0.13148	0.18610	0.30695	0.06497	0.36944	0.19716	0.59159	−0.04666	1.00000
10	0.21470	−0.12285	0.51323	0.25353	0.47605	0.05353	0.71805	0.36406	0.08469
11	0.51902	−0.10373	0.42132	0.15063	0.38898	0.11858	0.32723	0.30418	−0.16129
12	0.21658	0.02574	0.16777	−0.02998	0.33453	0.23807	0.44558	0.09548	0.12509
13	0.46500	0.69061	0.13894	0.13001	0.42505	0.77400	0.14383	0.02193	0.16570
14	0.56465	0.57103	0.43122	0.14012	0.58920	0.70777	0.46012	0.09926	0.39748
15	0.41528	−0.10047	0.18480	0.69139	0.41144	−0.07205	0.26774	0.72454	0.01020
16	0.20373	0.32385	−0.01605	0.02060	0.22695	0.47859	−0.03672	0.04858	0.09029
17	0.31878	−0.04069	0.11264	0.69139	0.32369	0.00143	0.26822	0.63814	0.12490

Variable

Variable	10	11	12	13	14	15	16	17
10	1.00000							
11	0.07217	1.00000						
12	0.35293	0.33347	1.00000					
13	−0.03958	0.04012	0.31060	1.00000				
14	0.21683	0.20615	0.10217	0.39929	1.00000			
15	0.22590	0.36136	0.03926	0.02823	−0.03434	1.00000		
16	−0.08793	−0.08147	−0.09168	0.29866	0.28549	−0.22232	1.00000	
17	0.22590	0.03936	0.17514	−0.08725	0.07604	0.34101	−0.22232	1.00000

247

TABLE II.E *All Districts*

Within-Groups Correlation Matrix – *Behavior*

Variable

Variable	1	2	3	4	5	6	7	8	9
1	1.00000								
2	0.47191	1.00000							
3	0.51424	0.10698	1.00000						
4	0.52370	0.13356	0.12307	1.00000					
5	0.81176	0.45848	0.56532	0.54213	1.00000				
6	0.49041	0.87218	0.19869	0.18647	0.50408	1.00000			
7	0.50121	0.14280	0.82518	0.11124	0.56132	0.23193	1.00000		
8	0.53349	0.20423	0.19595	0.82943	0.55832	0.27233	0.21059	1.00000	
9	0.20271	−0.03538	0.50189	0.09190	0.25994	−0.03149	0.44759	0.02317	1.00000
10	0.26954	−0.03002	0.67281	0.08958	0.39945	0.07314	0.71527	0.15860	0.20714
11	0.51286	0.25122	0.45119	0.09741	0.44728	0.27297	0.55107	0.28517	−0.07563
12	0.19122	0.27627	0.05602	0.08905	0.27908	0.32442	0.04851	0.09531	0.03823
13	0.40470	0.50228	0.15741	0.30502	0.43198	0.61414	0.16962	0.26875	0.04933
14	0.44784	0.61879	0.21005	0.22126	0.45407	0.65289	0.22805	0.29300	0.05983
15	0.26698	−0.07239	0.00582	0.60727	0.27025	−0.02181	0.05299	0.61849	0.01495
16	0.21852	0.31939	0.11591	0.09775	0.23014	0.35545	0.07413	0.18631	−0.01226
17	0.24675	−0.01787	0.07722	0.61037	0.30735	0.07733	0.08573	0.52231	0.20463

Variable

Variable	10	11	12	13	14	15	16	17
10	1.00000							
11	0.21107	1.00000						
12	0.08166	0.08341	1.00000					
13	0.12151	0.09488	0.22848	1.00000				
14	0.02628	0.32109	0.01102	0.31200	1.00000			
15	0.08011	0.08623	−0.00388	0.10198	0.02265	1.00000		
16	0.00989	0.11667	0.01913	0.14896	0.27709	−0.17839	1.00000	
17	0.12279	−0.06625	0.20176	0.17910	0.04261	0.20932	−0.17207	1.00000

TABLE III. *Economic Background*

Variables Used In Discriminant Analysis Listed According To Order Of Appearance
In Within-Groups Correlation Matrix*

1. Size of Landholding
2. Size of Irrigated Landholding
3. Value of Landholding
4. Value of Machinery Owned
5. Value of Houses Owned

6. % of Acres Under Cash Crops
7. Number of Acres Under Cash Crops
8. Value of Shares in Cooperatives
9. Value of Loans from Cooperatives

In the districts of Ratnagiri and Aurangabad, there is a slight variation in the sequence of variables owing to the fact that some of them were not included in the discriminant analysis. The appropriate changes are indicated at the bottom of Tables III.A and III.C for Ratnagiri and Aurangabad, respectively.

TABLE III.A *Ratnagiri*

Within-Groups Correlation Matrix – *Economic Background**

Variable

Variable	1	2	3	4	5	6	7
1	1.00000						
2	0.15271	1.00000					
3	0.38337	0.00405	1.00000				
4	0.25216	−0.01293	0.29296	1.00000			
5	0.55895	0.03563	0.25883	0.66535	1.00000		
6	0.17334	−0.09677	−0.02675	−0.05835	0.04793	1.00000	
7	0.02910	0.01105	0.23613	−0.09165	−0.11791	0.08509	1.00000

* Variables 3 and 5 (see Table III, above) were not included in the analysis for Ratnagiri. Hence, the sequence of variable numbers corresponds not with the titles on Table III, above, but with the following titles: 1, Size of Landholding; 2, Size of Irrigated Landholding; 3, Size of Machinery Owned; 4, % of Acres Under Cash Crops; 5, Number of Acres Under Cash Crops; 6; Value of Shares in Cooperatives; 7, Value of Loans from Co-operatives.

TABLE III.B *Poona*

Within-Groups Correlation Matrix – *Economic Background*

Variable	1	2	3	4	5	6	7	8	9
1	1.00000								
2	0.14385	1.00000							
3	0.58366	0.19419	1.00000						
4	0.34037	0.71111	0.32615	1.00000					
5	−0.17366	−0.09530	0.04771	−0.09287	1.00000				
6	−0.14535	0.29327	0.10486	0.06262	−0.14071	1.00000			
7	0.11543	0.66198	0.53356	0.48667	0.00736	0.52536	1.00000		
8	−0.27751	0.19002	0.11147	0.21871	0.39158	0.23784	0.39466	1.00000	
9	0.46406	0.25271	0.73422	0.31275	−0.00094	0.08018	0.48454	0.28874	1.00000

TABLE III.C *Aurangabad*

Within-Groups Correlation Matrix – *Economic Background**

Variable	1	2	3	4	5	6	7	8
1	1.00000							
2	0.25398	1.00000						
3	0.69324	0.02145	1.00000					
4	0.58655	0.51723	0.64431	1.00000				
5	0.11080	−0.14724	0.32152	0.12119	1.00000			
6	0.37764	0.25151	0.49147	0.50086	−0.03827	1.00000		
7	0.75495	0.11491	0.90814	0.65221	0.25031	0.71113	1.00000	
8	0.20339	0.44714	0.02403	0.49628	0.11031	0.27230	0.13739	1.00000

* Variable 9 (see Table III, above) was not included in the discriminant analysis for Aurangabad. Otherwise, the sequence is unchanged.

TABLE III.D *Akola*

Within-Groups Correlation Matrix – *Economic Background*

Variable	1	2	3	4	5	6	7	8	9
1	1.00000								
2	0.34858	1.00000							
3	0.83318	0.39755	1.00000						
4	0.56372	0.31498	0.56835	1.00000					
5	0.37817	−0.01556	0.37892	0.37610	1.00000				
6	0.19448	0.07470	0.01919	0.32564	0.30082	1.00000			
7	0.82250	0.20378	0.53018	0.61348	0.54060	0.56667	1.00000		
8	−0.01274	−0.12492	−0.03797	0.05206	−0.05213	0.01492	−0.00903	1.00000	
9	0.25038	−0.03998	0.32565	0.68270	0.27703	0.27161	0.33936	0.12547	1.00000

TABLE III.E *All Districts*

Within-Groups Correlation Matrix – *Economic Background*

Variable	1	2	3	4	5	6	7	8	9
1	1.00000								
2	0.25295	1.00000							
3	0.67825	0.21685	1.00000						
4	0.50998	0.63729	0.51777	1.00000					
5	0.10676	0.00422	0.28584	0.12845	1.00000				
6	0.11743	0.01698	0.18260	0.16542	0.04068	1.00000			
7	0.54753	0.03907	0.54554	0.39704	0.25867	0.59805	1.00000		
8	−0.00134	0.28180	0.11098	0.28175	0.15862	0.03539	0.04719	1.00000	
9	0.42735	0.28482	0.45112	0.52863	0.07884	0.12703	0.28648	0.28293	1.00000

TABLE IV. *Attitudes*

Variables Used In Discriminant Analysis Listed According To Order Of Appearance In Within-Groups Correlation Matrix

1. Predisposition To Resign
2. Voting Preference (majority v. unanimous)
3. Comments About Z.P. Leadership
4. Evaluation of M.L.A.

5. Caste Role In Distribution Decisions
6. Economic Role In Distribution Decisions
7. Selection of Candidates
8. Loan Distribution Machinery

TABLE IV.A *Ratnagiri*

Within-Groups Correlation Matrix – *Attitudes*

Variable	1	2	3	4	5	6	7	8
1	1.00000							
2	0.05916	1.00000						
3	0.40927	0.08793	1.00000					
4	0.06587	0.34726	−0.25658	1.00000				
5	0.13117	0.60033	−0.02861	0.32863	1.00000			
6	0.20260	0.62282	0.18984	0.40561	0.81970	1.00000		
7	0.43566	0.07850	0.23829	−0.08562	0.07230	0.25226	1.00000	
8	0.17638	−0.00189	−0.03881	0.19176	0.15429	0.16304	0.23010	1.00000

TABLE IV.B *Poona*

Within Groups Correlation Matrix – *Attitudes*

Variable	1	2	3	4	5	6	7	8
1	1.00000							
2	0.05813	1.00000						
3	0.43599	0.26663	1.00000					
4	−0.24038	0.09820	0.12817	1.00000				
5	−0.32983	0.19312	−0.11679	0.46540	1.00000			
6	0.20486	0.23849	0.19076	0.16784	0.39317	1.00000		
7	0.43940	−0.07252	0.19565	−0.56121	−0.45164	0.12253	1.00000	
8	−0.05461	−0.18996	−0.03522	0.06792	−0.00407	−0.00335	0.02590	1.00000

TABLE IV.C *Aurangabad*

Within-Groups Correlation Matrix – *Attitudes*

Variable	1	2	3	4	5	6	7	8
1	1.00000							
2	0.02946	1.00000						
3	0.10239	0.21387	1.00000					
4	0.01297	0.18449	0.36256	1.00000				
5	−0.01803	0.08732	0.03174	0.39168	1.00000			
6	−0.12640	0.13346	0.08406	0.29575	0.78411	1.00000		
7	−0.15541	0.12383	0.10002	0.15673	−0.02907	−0.01936	1.00000	
8	−0.02771	0.12377	0.03057	0.21253	0.12542	0.00514	−0.03942	1.0000

CIP

TABLE IV.D *Akola*

Within-Groups Correlation Matrix – *Attitudes*

Variable	1	2	3	4	5	6	7	8
1	1.00000							
2	0.17290	1.00000						
3	−0.13424	−0.19110	1.00000					
4	0.15485	0.04597	0.11554	1.00000				
5	0.14131	0.12536	−0.05041	0.02066	1.00000			
6	0.12044	0.44558	−0.17222	−0.12636	0.69992	1.00000		
7	−0.10833	0.11190	0.12299	−0.03268	−0.01844	0.02408	1.00000	
8	−0.00251	0.24344	−0.25451	0.17505	0.29010	0.16628	−0.04501	1.00000

TABLE IV.E *All Districts*

Within-Groups Correlation Matrix – Attitudes

Variable	1	2	3	4	5	6	7	8
					Variable			
1	1.00000							
2	0.09239	1.00000						
3	0.17310	0.10031	1.00000					
4	0.05077	0.15437	0.15565	1.00000				
5	−0.08402	0.22128	−0.04491	0.27544	1.00000			
6	0.06914	0.27475	0.05683	0.13973	0.65974	1.00000		
7	0.12607	0.10021	0.12773	−0.24472	−0.06546	0.19179	1.00000	
8	−0.02128	0.04986	−0.05701	0.10689	0.15292	0.08035	0.10327	1.00000

259

9-2

TABLE V.A.1

Variables Used In Discriminant Analysis Listed According To Order of Appearance
In Within-Groups Correlation Matrix

Combined Variables – Ratnagiri

1. Value of Machinery Owned
2. Number of Acres Under Cash Crops
3. Distance – Railway
4. Simultaneous Office – Cooperatives
5. Number of Offices – Party
6. Predisposition To Resign
7. Voting Preference (majority v. unanimous)

8. Caste Role in Distribution Decisions
9. Public Electoral Participation
10. Communications Potential
11. Agricultural Prosperity
12. Involved in Party Office – Village
13. Involved in Cooperative Office – District
14. % of Cultivators Serviced by Cooperatives In Taluka

TABLE V.A.2 *Ratnagiri*

Within-Groups Correlation Matrix – Combined Variables

Variable	1	2	3	4	5	6	7
1	1.00000						
2	0.25883	1.00000					
3	-0.03091	0.42935	1.00000				
4	-0.02187	0.17560	-0.20589	1.00000			
5	-0.31063	-0.19220	0.05118	0.10058	1.00000		
6	-0.18923	0.20127	0.41536	-0.08639	-0.03608	1.00000	
7	0.23451	0.28170	0.17512	0.00317	0.13902	0.09916	1.00000
8	0.22105	0.19588	0.17356	0.01362	0.19589	0.13117	0.60033
9	-0.04710	0.29771	0.39054	-0.12250	0.10259	0.15980	-0.01497
10	-0.48872	0.00429	-0.25329	0.00241	-0.18495	-0.24638	0.30289
11	-0.29613	-0.08190	-0.02952	0.17377	0.30275	-0.06548	0.22084
12	-0.18202	-0.10387	0.10540	-0.29886	0.39592	-0.32629	0.16863
13	0.06847	0.34899	-0.09042	0.73634	-0.03627	-0.20283	0.24756
14	0.46130	0.59397	0.21864	0.21941	-0.14786	-0.00655	0.00737

Variable

Variable	8	9	10	11	12	13	14
8	1.00000						
9	-0.08309	1.00000					
10	0.09040	-0.41528	1.00000				
11	0.15074	0.08080	-0.33073	1.00000			
12	0.03409	0.06756	-0.06152	0.24277	1.00000		
13	-0.00255	-0.12516	0.13572	0.15781	-0.16034	1.00000	
14	0.01430	0.23216	0.21716	-0.37174	-0.09077	0.29137	1.00000

TABLE V.B.1

Variables Used In Discriminant Analysis Listed According To Order of Appearance
In Within-Groups Correlation Matrix

Combined Variables – Poona

1. Landholding Size
2. Irrigated Landholding Size
3. Value of Shares Owned In Cooperatives
4. Distance – Railway
5. Simultaneous Office – Government
6. Number of Spheres – Over Time
7. Evaluation of M.L.A.
8. Average Landholding in Taluka

9. Communications Potential
10. Urbanization
11. Involved in Party – Taluka
12. Involved in Cooperatives – Village
13. Involved in Cooperatives – Taluka
14. Involved in Government – Village
15. % of Cultivators Serviced by Cooperatives in
Taluka

TABLE V.B. 2 *Poona*

Within-Groups Correlation Matrix – Combined Variables

Variable	1	2	3	4	5	6	7	8
1	1.00000							
2	0.14385	1.00000						
3	−0.27751	0.19002	1.00000					
4	−0.13626	−0.04492	−0.06267	1.00000				
5	0.13903	0.01873	0.22795	0.05175	1.00000			
6	0.29825	0.00987	0.08538	0.03202	0.68191	1.00000		
7	−0.03379	0.06329	−0.03463	0.24994	0.15187	0.00864	1.00000	
8	0.12783	−0.28363	−0.33123	0.31215	0.15446	0.17834	0.13757	1.00000
9	−0.14093	0.36087	0.17398	0.07374	−0.05352	−0.07125	0.37248	−0.44913
10	0.04091	0.01036	0.09370	−0.50621	0.02117	0.02847	−0.07154	−0.41980
11	0.06013	−0.21217	−0.03504	0.10264	−0.19101	0.12201	0.02071	0.02865
12	0.18671	0.02539	−0.13018	0.15119	0.22934	0.43965	−0.02402	0.07163
13	0.26887	0.24955	−0.3504	0.05162	0.59999	0.56444	0.23687	0.04174
14	0.04374	−0.01414	−0.01810	0.08002	0.69923	0.39455	0.19982	0.17024
15	−0.08515	0.42669	0.09769	−0.12099	0.07058	0.04924	0.28900	−0.26771

Variable	9	10	11	12	13	14	15
9	1.00000						
10	0.15469	1.00000					
11	−0.15209	−0.15872	1.00000				
12	0.11736	−0.13562	−0.04196	1.00000			
13	−0.04522	−0.10700	0.00226	0.35971	1.00000		
14	−0.04932	−0.00195	0.02065	0.01733	0.29477	1.00000	
15	0.63797	−0.05120	−0.16839	−0.07432	0.11010	−0.01477	1.00000

TABLE V.C.1

Variables Used In Discriminant Analysis Listed According To Order of Appearance In Within-Groups Correlation Matrix

Combined Variables – Aurangabad

1. Value of Shares Owned in Cooperatives
2. Distance from Panchayat Samiti Headquarters
3. Voting Preference (majority v. unanimous)
4. Comments About Z.P. Leadership
5. Selection of Candidates
6. Average Landholding in Taluka

7. Communications Potential
8. Involved in Party – Taluka
9. Involved in Party – District
10. Involved in Cooperatives – District
11. Involved in Government – Village
12. % of Cultivators Serviced by Cooperatives in Taluka

TABLE V.C. 2 *Aurangabad*

Within-Groups Correlation Matrix – *Combined Variables*

Variable	1	2	3	4	5	6
1	1.00000					
2	−0.01501	1.00000				
3	−0.10314	0.07275	1.00000			
4	0.18990	0.30816	0.21387	1.00000		
5	0.15785	0.06573	0.15602	0.14069	1.00000	
6	0.12383	0.10949	0.21051	0.12007	0.00739	1.00000
7	0.23989	0.16558	−0.03284	0.17815	0.23773	−0.11547
8	−0.07925	0.09566	0.22444	0.04724	0.27541	0.06469
9	−0.11174	−0.26575	0.26360	−0.15326	−0.00456	0.14984
10	−0.10848	−0.25179	−0.02072	0.21125	−0.25854	0.13881
11	0.22272	−0.13973	−0.06339	−0.05457	0.11027	0.13759
12	0.28234	−0.03868	0.02738	0.17626	0.18069	0.17904

Variable	7	8	9	10	11	12
7	1.00000					
8	−0.04105	1.00000				
9	−0.03960	−0.06365	1.00000			
10	−0.18296	−0.23968	0.38243	1.00000		
11	−0.04523	0.17317	−0.17399	−0.18011	1.00000	
12	0.55466	0.03086	0.26365	0.23360	0.06137	1.00000

TABLE V.D. 1

Variables Used In Discriminant Analysis Listed According To Order of Appearance
In Within-Groups Correlation Matrix

Combined Variables – Akola

1. Irrigated Landholding
2. Value of Machinery Owned
3. Value of Houses Owned
4. Distance from Zilla Parishad Headquarters
5. Distance from Railway Station
6. Distance from Bus Station
7. Simultaneous Office – Government

8. Number of Offices – Cooperatives
9. Caste Role in Distribution Decisions
10. Loan Distribution Machinery
11. Involved in Party – Taluka
12. Involved in Government – Taluka
13. Involved in Government – Village

TABLE V.D. 2 *Akola*

Within-Groups Correlation Matrix – *Combined Variables*

Variables

Variable	1	2	3	4	5	6	7
1	1.00000						
2	0.31498	1.00000					
3	−0.01556	0.37610	1.00000				
4	0.17555	−0.35007	−0.38892	1.00000			
5	−0.09404	−0.02918	−0.20348	−0.00783	1.00000		
6	−0.19512	0.18984	0.27333	−0.25714	−0.09970	1.00000	
7	−0.10065	−0.05502	0.29669	−0.18206	−0.14364	0.56588	1.00000
8	−0.02633	0.12873	0.16574	−0.27511	−0.27449	0.49185	0.10330
9	0.21705	−0.04853	0.14441	0.10387	0.01961	0.02740	0.09573
10	0.09653	−0.00947	0.04778	−0.03082	−0.34517	−0.23566	−0.08038
11	0.18856	−0.13260	−0.09762	0.05627	−0.21938	0.21470	0.25355
12	0.06872	0.15762	0.22593	−0.01299	−0.05871	0.41528	0.69139
13	−0.01143	−0.31145	−0.08391	−0.04913	0.07650	0.31878	0.69139

Variable

Variable	8	9	10	11	12	13
8	1.00000					
9	−0.00106	1.00000				
10	−0.04263	0.29010	1.00000			
11	0.05353	−0.30226	−0.01781	1.00000		
12	−0.07205	0.22429	−0.06990	0.22590	1.00000	
13	0.00143	0.08893	0.03018	0.22590	0.34101	1.00000

267

TABLE V.E. 1

Variables Used In Discriminant Analysis Listed According To Order of Appearance
In Within-Groups Correlation Matrix

Combined Variables – All Districts

1. Size of Landholding
2. Value of Machinery Owned
3. % of Acres Under Cash Crops
4. Value of Shares Owned in Cooperatives
5. Distance from Railway Station
6. Simultaneous Office – Government
7. Number of Offices – Party

8. Caste Role in Distribution Decisions
9. Public Electoral Participation
10. Average Landholding in Taluka
11. Involved in Party – District
12. Involved in Government – District
13. Eligible Votes Polled by Non-Congress Candidates
14. % Cultivators Serviced by Cooperatives in Taluka

TABLE V.E. 2 All Districts

Within-Groups Correlation Matrix – Combined Variables

Variable	1	2	3	4	5	6	7
1	1.00000						
2	0.50998	1.00000					
3	0.11743	0.16542	1.00000				
4	-0.00134	0.28175	0.03539	1.00000			
5	-0.28553	-0.26464	-0.02064	-0.16364	1.00000		
6	0.17098	0.20960	0.02312	0.09904	0.02384	1.00000	
7	0.09732	-0.05418	-0.20196	0.05203	-0.00469	0.11124	1.00000
8	0.08262	0.02147	0.16357	-0.09664	0.16438	0.06506	-0.08499
9	0.16097	0.09259	0.24717	0.05932	-0.23533	-0.26314	-0.11869
10	-0.21641	-0.11827	-0.33796	-0.05548	0.65570	0.15501	0.17010
11	0.11492	0.05475	-0.09001	0.05797	-0.00330	0.09741	0.55107
12	0.14950	0.06598	0.02737	-0.06329	-0.05683	0.09775	0.07413
13	0.10642	0.06578	0.23540	0.05070	-0.21904	-0.31226	-0.07229
14	0.11330	0.05094	0.31614	-0.02572	-0.02064	0.06922	-0.15372

Variable	8	9	10	11	12	13	14
8	1.00000						
9	0.02620	1.00000					
10	-0.02556	-0.31534	1.00000				
11	-0.14825	-0.12329	0.13899	1.00000			
12	0.00444	-0.04362	0.10340	0.11667	1.00000		
13	0.02502	0.85238	-0.31838	-0.13522	-0.09724	1.00000	
14	0.08577	0.32901	-0.25453	-0.05701	0.01996	0.27008	1.00000

NOTES

1 For studies or discussions of political factions in India, see the following: Paul R. Brass, *Factional Politics in an Indian State: The Congress Party in Uttar Pradesh* (hereinafter, 'Brass, *Factional Politics*') (Berkeley: University of California Press, 1965). Myron Weiner and Rajni Kothari, editors, *Indian Voting Behaviour – Studies of the 1962 General Elections* (hereinafter, 'Weiner & Kothari, *Voting Behaviour*') (Calcutta: Firma K. L. Mukhopadhayay, 1965). *Party Building in a New Nation – The Indian National Congress* (hereinafter, 'Weiner, *Party Building*') (Chicago: The University of Chicago Press, 1967). Myron Weiner, editor, *State Politics In India* (hereinafter, 'Weiner, *State Politics*') (Princeton: Princeton University Press, 1968). Oscar Lewis, *Group Dynamics in a North Indian Village – A Study of Factions* (hereinafter, 'Lewis, *Group Dynamics*') (Delhi: Planning Commission, Programme Evaluation Organisation, 1954).

2 V. O. Key, Jr., *Politics, Parties and Pressure Groups* (New York: Thomas Y. Crowell Company, 1959), p. 320.

3 See, Stanley A. Kochanek, *The Congress Party of India – The Dynamics of One-Party Democracy* (hereinafter, 'Kochanek, *Congress Party*') (Princeton: Princeton University Press, 1968), Chapter XVI; and Norman D. Palmer, 'India's Fourth General Elections', *Asian Survey*, Volume VII, Number 5, May 1967, pp. 275–91.

4 Ministry of Community Development and Cooperation (Department of Community Development), Government of India, *Panchayati Raj At A Glance* (New Delhi: Government of India Press, 1964), pp. 5–6.

5 See, Committee On Plan Projects, *Report of the Team for the Study of Community Projects and National Extension Services* (Delhi: Government of India Press, 1957) (three volumes).

6 See, Law and Judiciary Department, Government of Maharashtra, *The Maharashtra Zilla Parishads and Panchayat Samitis Act, 1961, Maharashtra Act No. V of 1962* (as modified up to the 1st January 1965) (hereinafter, '*Z.P. Act*') (Bombay: Government Central Press, 1965), Chapter VI, Sections 100–1.

7 See, Finance Department, Government of Maharashtra, *Statements Showing Annual Accounts of Zilla Parishads For The Year 1962–63*. (For subsequent years, see similar statements which are issued annually.)

8 *Census of India 1961, Maharashtra* (hereinafter, '*Census of India 1961*'), Volume X, Part II–A, Union Table A–I, pp. 49–74.